★ ★ ★ ★ ★

Ten Stars

★ ★ ★ ★ ★

✱ ✱ ✱ ✱ ✱

TEN STARS

The African American Journey of Gary Cooper

Marine General, Diplomat, Businessman, and Politician

✱ ✱ ✱ ✱ ✱

KENDAL WEAVER

NEWSOUTH BOOKS
Montgomery

NewSouth Books
105 S. Court Street
Montgomery, AL 36104

Publisher's Cataloging-in-Publication data

Weaver, Kendal
Ten stars : the African American journey of Gary Cooper—Marine general,
diplomat, businessman, and politician / Kendal Weaver
p. cm.

ISBN 978-1-58838-324-2 (hardcover)
ISBN 978-1-60306-414-9 (ebook)

1. Cooper, Gary. 2. African American—Biography.
I. Title.

2016954618

Design by Randall Williams

Printed in the United States of America
by Edwards Brothers Malloy

For my parents,
O. C. and Laura

Contents

Preface

E dgar Huff. Hashmark Johnson. Those were the first two names Gary Cooper mentioned to me when we began a series of interviews and conversations—a late-in-life education, for me—in 2011. I had never heard of Huff, or Johnson, but soon learned they were two black men, both from hardscrabble beginnings in Alabama, who became honored legends in the United States Marine Corps and heroes of Gary Cooper.

He had other heroes, too, some with names I knew: Father Theodore Hesburgh. Astronaut Neil Armstrong. Air Force General Benjamin O. Davis Jr. and the Tuskegee Airmen. These were men, like Huff and Johnson, who Gary would meet personally, even enjoy as friends, in a long, varied, path-setting career.

It was a career that first took shape in Mobile, Alabama, in a neighborhood known as "Down the Bay." Until he told me about it, I had never heard of Down the Bay—and it was just a short drive from my own home when I was a correspondent in Mobile for the Associated Press in the late 1970s. But by then, the Down the Bay community in which Gary and his African American friends grew up, in the harsh era of Jim Crow, had been forever altered, cut off and lost to new urban avenues reaching to interstates.

I had first met Gary in the mid-1970s when he arrived at the Alabama Capitol among the first African Americans elected from Mobile to the state Legislature since Reconstruction. Tall, with a stylish Afro, he was a man of galvanizing charm and good cheer. He was hard to overlook.

I didn't. As the years went by I heard about Gary Cooper setting new high-water marks of personal achievement—Marine General, Assistant Secretary of the Air Force, U.S. Ambassador. I started kicking around the idea of a book about him. When I called, he was agreeable; it turned out he had been kicking around the idea himself for a number of years.

He and Beverly, his wife, already had a favored title: "Ten Stars." He had to explain to me that, along with the two stars attached to his rank of Major General in the Marine Corps, there were non-military rank stars attached to his civilian post with the Air Force and his diplomatic status as Ambassador to Jamaica—both were presidential appointments requiring Senate confirmation, and their trappings of office included flags with four stars each. Altogether there were ten stars on the Gary Cooper resume, pretty rare in American life no matter how you counted them.

This account of one man's life came together inside the rich and fascinating biographical stitching of the broader Gary Cooper family and its era. From slavery and Jim Crow this era extended through the civil rights movement into the modern racial world, a conflicted society still wracked by divisions. Gary's ancestors, parents, siblings and children—all were contributors to the vindicating accomplishments of their times. For me, Gary's ten stars also referred to the many, many stars in the wider Cooper galaxy.

Not too many years back, the renowned Harvard naturalist and Pulitzer Prize-winning author Edward O. Wilson returned to Mobile. His project was to collaborate with photographer Alex Harris on a book of words and pictures about Wilson's childhood hometown, the coastal region around it, and its history and people, including an "epic cycle of tragedy and rebirth." It is understandable that one of the Mobilians they sought out and photographed was General Gary Cooper.

Cooper, in many ways, embodies what Wilson called the rebirth of a city and region. Harris photographed him standing on the porch of the Cooper family funeral home with his beloved mastiff, Huff—named in honor of his early Marine hero. Regal in a navy blue blazer and a striped bow tie, Cooper beams at the camera, warm and welcoming.

His life story—the biography, the oral history here—is not without its sense of loss and pain, but at every turn the kid who rose from Down the Bay wanted to make a better place, a better life, warm and welcoming, for all.

A Note on the Content and Formatting

This book is partly oral history. Unattributed passages typeset in italics reflect Gary's thoughts and recollections in his own words, as recorded during my many interviews with him. The text also quotes extensively from several dozen interviews with Gary's family members, friends, and former colleagues, both military and civilian. Other content is based on material drawn from Gary's personal documents: letters, articles, and comments in newspapers, magazines, and books, along with a transcript of his 1993 "WWII Commemoration Interview" that covers mostly his Marine Corps experiences and is included in the italicized text.

While this is not a scholarly biography, I have referenced with endnotes the interviews, publications, documents, and other sources cited in the book. Significant background material in the text, but not cited in the endnotes, is from my work as a political reporter, correspondent, and state editor for the Associated Press in Alabama over nearly forty years.

★ ★ ★ ★ ★

Ten Stars

★ ★ ★ ★ ★

Prologue

Da Nang, 1966

For Gary Cooper, a young black Marine captain newly arrived in Vietnam, the decision was almost unthinkable. He would have to "Request Mast."

To request mast, to ask for a hearing before the commanding general, was the last thing on his mind when he stepped off the plane at Da Nang that morning.[1] Requesting mast was a process full of risk. It could ruffle feathers of superiors in the chain of command. At one extreme, it could invite retaliation and put a career in jeopardy.[2]

In the spring of 1966, this was particularly true for a black officer, and Cooper was one of only a small number of African American officers in the entire U.S. Marine Corps. In fact, he was the Corps' only black infantry captain in all of Vietnam.[3]

But Cooper was tall and well-spoken, he conveyed a sense of presence along with an easy camaraderie, and he was certain about his mission as a Marine officer: he was supposed to be assigned command of a rifle company in Vietnam. The post, Cooper knew, was an essential steppingstone for any Marine officer with higher aspirations. Also, no African American Marine officer had ever been tapped to lead a rifle company in combat.

He would be the first.

Instead, in the swelter of Da Nang, he had been told to report as a supply officer to an anti-tank battalion. Cooper objected. He explained that he had been trained to lead a rifle company, but he got nowhere. His insistence was rattling the patience of a major handing out assignments. He had no choice but to request mast.

Soon he was sitting outside the commanding general's office of the First

3

Marine Division, waiting to make his case, waiting for a turning point in his life. Hours would pass—the noon meal was missed as he held his place—but his sense of conviction grew. Commanding a rifle company in combat was a dream he could not surrender.[4]

It was a big dream, but big dreams were an enduring characteristic of his family, the Coopers of Mobile. They might have been little-known outside the black community in the bustling Alabama port city, where they had gained a substantial financial foothold. But as the 1960s unfolded, the extended Cooper family would begin to claim a much larger role in the life of their country. In time, across generations, they would become one of America's most emblematic success stories.

Gary already had become the first African American Marine officer to command a detachment aboard a Navy ship, and bigger milestones were in his sights—over the decades they would extend into politics, business, government and diplomatic service, as well as the military. Two of his siblings, Jay and Peggy, would carry the Coopers' mostly quiet but persistent fight against Jim Crow to new venues in New York and Washington, while on the way to making history themselves in law, politics, education, and the arts.

Brother Billy helped save the family insurance company, sister Dominic majored in dance, and the youngest, Mario, became a national player in the Democratic Party and the public health fight against HIV. Later generations went to America's best schools—including Yale, Harvard, Stanford Law, and Wharton—and carried on the family tradition of success and service. Gary, a devout Catholic, would see his family become the first in which three generations of African Americans graduated from the University of Notre Dame.[5]

By the end of the 1960s, the Coopers' founding matriarch, Pearl Madison, would be pictured in an *Ebony* magazine article celebrating "giants of black capitalism."[6] And Gary's mother, Gladys Cooper, would be described lovingly and fittingly by a family friend as "the Rose Kennedy of Alabama blacks."[7]

For Gary and his family, the decade also would end in tragedy with the death of his father, Algernon Johnson Cooper, known as "A. J.," a highly respected businessman and civic leader. The death would be transforming for the Coopers in many ways, not least for Gary, whose career path would be forever changed.

But in May 1966, on a steaming hot day in Vietnam, the future that Gary had envisioned as a Marine officer was hanging in the balance.

The general's chief of staff approached. Gary leapt to attention.

It was time to see the general.[8]

1

An All-American Family Tree

W ith no maternity clinic or hospital delivering black babies in Mobile, the Alabama port city where his parents had settled after their marriage, Jerome Gary Cooper was born in his mother's childhood home, a white frame house in Lafayette, Louisiana, on October 2, 1936.[9]

For the delivery, his mother was under the experienced care of two highly regarded black midwives. One was Gary's great-grandmother, Julie Mouton, a descendant of slaves and one of the first black women to live openly with a white man in the community. The other was his grandmother, Agnes Mouton, the daughter of Julie and, like her, a woman undiminished by the social strictures of segregation.

Through Julie and Agnes, on his mother's side, Gary Cooper's family tree extends its Deep South ancestral roots back to Africa and the slave era, but also into the often cruel, disquieting American melting pot of that time and place.[10] Within this mix, Gary's African or slave ancestors were connected to the community's ruling white class of Acadians, including the eleventh governor of Louisiana, Alexandre Mouton.[11]

Mouton was a wealthy plantation owner of French Catholic fore-bears whose expansive property at Vermilion Bayou covered land that is now Lafayette. Mouton (pronounced MOO-tahn) owned more than one hundred slaves, served as a U.S. senator as well as governor, and, in 1861, was elected president of the state convention that voted to secede Louisiana from the Union.[12]

According to Cooper family lore, one of the governor's sons, Alfred Mouton, was a part of Gary Cooper's family history.

The story that I remember when I would go to Lafayette, there was a monument of a Confederate general in the square. I can remember as a little boy them taking me down and seeing this. They would tell me that was the guy who had these twins from Africa. One apparently was my grandmother Agnes's mother. I had seen pictures of them: two big, black women, strong-looking women. Evidently they were the ones who had the children who formed the Mouton part of the family, and evidently they were slaves of General Mouton.

Alfred Mouton was born in 1829 to Alexandre Mouton's first wife, Zelia. If there was a call to military service in this family's blood, Alfred carried it. He graduated from the U.S. military academy at West Point before returning home, where he retained his Southern allegiance and rose to become a Confederate general in the Civil War. Killed by Union troops at Mansfield, Louisiana, in 1864, his legend was revered in the Acadian community over ensuing decades, and a statue of him, presumably the one Gary viewed, still stands in Lafayette.[13]

The twins were Julia and Julie—the Julie who in old age helped midwife Gary's birth. A faded, yellowing photograph shows the dark-skinned twin sisters standing side by side in sunlight, both wearing white, long-sleeved blouses and dark dresses that reach down near the ground. Julie thrived better than most in the post-Civil War period, thanks in large part to another son of the governor, Paul Mouton.[14]

This Mouton—Paul Joseph Julien Mouton—was born in 1848 to Alexandre Mouton's second wife, Emma. Paul was the half-brother of Alfred Mouton but nearly twenty years younger. Paul was either blind when born or became blind as a young boy, but he fell in love with Julie. She is listed in family records as Marie Julienne Andrus, who had three children—the first in 1878—before living with Paul.[15]

"The Beautiful Brass Bed"

Paul's dedication to Julie was great enough that they lived together in the charming home on Oak Avenue where Gary was born and that would remain in Julie's family for generations. Paul and Julie had two children—Gary's grandmother, Marie Agnes, in 1888, and her brother,

Gilbert, in 1891, according to the family's records. Their home had been a source of pride from the start; it had made Julie the first black in Lafayette to live in a house with electricity and indoor plumbing.[16]

Through her relationship with Paul, Julie was able to navigate both the white Acadian culture and the black or Creole world of Lafayette with relative impunity. When in failing health Paul moved back into the columned Mouton family mansion, Julie was allowed to visit (although not through the front door). By family accounts, Paul's grave in Lafayette was eventually flanked on one side by his white wife and on the other by Julie, who essentially, though perhaps not legally, was his black wife.[17]

For years after Gary was born, the faces of Julie and Paul still looked out from portraits in the living room of the Oak Avenue home.

"From the time I was three years old, I knew that the large oval por-traits over the front door in the living room were my great-grandparents, Paul and Julie Mouton," said Gary's first cousin, Judi Stephenson. "They were the original owners of this family home. The front door opened onto 'white' Oak Avenue—a very, very lovely street, a wide street with big oaks, obviously. No other blacks were on that street, but the back door led into a long backyard that ended on a very lovely Creole neighborhood. Everyone seemed related."

"The dining room in that house was originally a cabin," said Judi's sister, Marilyn Funderburk, who also remembered the home well. "Everything was added on around it."

Like Gary, his cousins Judi and Marilyn had been born in what Judi called "the beautiful brass bed" in the front bedroom of the Mouton home on Oak Avenue. So had Gary's mother, the light-brown-skinned beauty Gladys Catherine Mouton, and all of her sisters—Judi and Marilyn's mother, Helen, as well as Geraldine and Martina Marvel Mouton.

"They were known as the four beautiful Mouton sisters and all gradu-ated from college, with the two youngest, Geraldine and Marvel, receiving master's degrees in French and English," Judi said.

"A lot of whites living on Oak Avenue referred to my grandmother, Agnes, as 'Cousin Agnes,' and they did it with a French accent—'Couzee Agnee'—that's how they talked. They knew they were all related. That's just the way it was," said Judi. "Because her father was Paul Mouton, my grandmother was able to keep the house she had lived in as a kid."

Judi said there was never any question that Grandmother Agnes was the child of the former governor's son, Paul Mouton. "My grandmother, 'Mama Agnes,' as we called her, she had blue eyes," Judi said. "She was definitely a child of that relationship."

She said her mother in later years told vivid stories of the childbirths of Gary, Marilyn, and Judi in the fine brass bed.

"Julie stood at the front of this bed," Judi said. "My mother's name was Helen, and Julie called her 'EH-len'—French for Helen. 'EH-len, push! Push!'"

The four sisters were the daughters of the self-educated Agnes and Clarence Mouton, a local man who was part Indian and no close relative of Agnes—"Everybody and their brother was named Mouton in Lafayette," Judi said.

All four sisters were Catholics and considered Creole. For them and for Gary and the extended Cooper family, there is little to match the extreme racial divide of Julie and Paul Mouton's backgrounds—one the descendant of a slave, the other the son of a governor who owned slaves on a huge sugar plantation. Their children had a foot in two worlds.

"They were strong in their beliefs about being black but yet they very much identified with their mixed-race heritage," said Judi. "They wanted us to know that."

Family recollections differ, but in all accounts Governor Alexandre Mouton looms in the Cooper family ancestry in Lafayette, as does one or more of his sons.

Gary's daughter, Shawn Cooper: "In Lafayette now, Moutons are everywhere. There are white ones and black ones, and I just say that governor was very generous with his sperm."

OSCEOLA

It was at Hampton Institute, the historically black college that is now Hampton University in Virginia, where Gary's mother, Gladys Mouton, met his father, A. J. Cooper of Mobile.[18] Gladys's sisters had matriculated elsewhere—Helen at Prairie View in Texas, Geraldine and Marvel at Xavier in New Orleans.[19] But Gladys chose Hampton, founded in 1868 on grounds near the Chesapeake Bay and the site of the Emancipation Oak, a tree under which freed slaves had been taught.[20]

A. J.'s lineage gave Gary and the Coopers another notable ancestral link.

On A. J.'s mother's side, there were the Johnsons of Mobile, Ben and Louisa, a very light-skinned black couple who also valued education and self-reliance. In time, they would prosper. One of their daughters, Alice, attended the historically black Fisk University in Nashville, where she met and married a man with an intriguing name—Osceola Osceola Cooper—and later gave birth to their son, Algernon Johnson Cooper, Gary's father, known as "A. J."[21]

According to family lore, O. O. Cooper, born in Kentucky around 1880, was a descendant of the fierce Indian warrior Osceola, who fought the federal campaign to remove the Seminoles from their lands in Florida. By this account, O. O. Cooper's mother, born Adelade Choat of Tennessee, is presumed to be a descendant of Osceola and one of his two wives, either Che-cho-ter, meaning "Morning Dew," or a second woman whose name isn't clear.[22]

Osceola Osceola Cooper's father, John Cooper, was a barrel-maker from England. His mother was Adelade Choat. They married in Paducah, Kentucky. I once had a piece of paper in Daddy's handwriting telling the date of their marriage in Paducah. Daddy said Adelade was a direct descendant from Osceola, the Seminole Indian chief. Why else would you name a child "Osceola Osceola"?

Documents to confirm the connection have not been found—"I've been peeling back that onion, but none such luck yet," said Shawn—and the ancestry of Osceola, Che-cho-ter, and the other wife is in some historical dispute as well. In one version, Osceola was born Billy Powell, of mixed Indian and white blood, in east Alabama, but took the name Osceola and described himself as a pure-blood Indian after moving to Florida.[23] Some say at least one of his wives was black; others disagree.[24]

Whatever the truth on that score, Cooper family oral history says that O. O. Cooper was a descendant of Chief Osceola, and that O. O.'s father

John was the son of an Irish woman and a Cooper (as barrel-makers were known in England and early America).

By this telling, Gary's paternal grandfather, O. O. Cooper, was parts black, English, Native American, and Irish. But Census records designate the race of his mother, Adelade Choat Cooper, simply as "black." In America, under the pernicious "one drop rule," O. O. Cooper's blood ties meant that he would live his life as a black, as would his son, A. J., and all of A. J.'s children.[25]

A Home on Delaware Street

A. J. was born in 1908 in Mobile, in the family home of his mother, the former Alice Johnson. It was a fine home on a corner of Delaware and Warren streets in what was known as the Down the Bay neighborhood. But Alice and Osceola Cooper took the child with them as they moved north, to Chicago, where Osceola had a job with the U.S. Post Office.[26]

This did not sit well with the close-knit Johnsons in Mobile.

My daddy's mother's sister, Pearl Johnson, and her family didn't like Osceola Cooper. They particularly didn't like him because he took Alice and moved to Chicago after they got married. My daddy was born in Mobile at the Johnson house, but Osceola took Alice and the baby and they moved north. Then when my daddy was around eight years old, Alice caught pneumonia and died. My daddy, a young boy, was brought back to Mobile. The word is that maybe my daddy's Aunt Pearl—Pearl Johnson—maybe she even kidnapped my daddy, took him from Osceola in Chicago. They were so mad that he had taken their sister up to Chicago. So they raised my father in Mobile.

Aunt Pearl raised my daddy as though she was his mother and they taught him not to like Osceola. They said that Osceola was responsible for Alice's death in that cold horrible place called Chicago. They barely ever spoke, my daddy and Osceola. They were not close at all.

A. J. was raised in the Delaware Street house by Pearl Johnson along with Pearl's mother, who was known as "Miss Lou." Pearl attended State Street A.M.E Zion Church and married William Madison, who had come to Mobile from Pensacola, Florida. But she would remain childless except for the nephew she raised, A. J. Cooper.

A tall, commanding woman throughout her life, Pearl Johnson Madison clearly was the central figure in A. J.'s youth. She put emphasis on a solid education. He was class treasurer when he graduated in 1926 from Emerson Normal Industrial Institute, a school for blacks that produced notable graduates while being funded totally with private out-of-state donations through the American Missionary Association.[27]

Resources were meager even for Mobile's black schools like Dunbar High which received some public support: "There was no library," said Walter Hugh Samples, who attended Dunbar in the early 1930s, "no cafeteria, no biology or chemistry labs, no gymnasium, no athletic field or tennis court; no physical education classes and no free textbooks."[28]

A. J., whose graduating class would be the last before Emerson became a county public school,[29] set his sights on Hampton Institute.

At Hampton, he would also set his sights on that Creole beauty from south Louisiana, Gladys Mouton. Graduating with a bachelor of science degree in accounting, he married Gladys and remained at Hampton as a cashier for the school until 1935, when the couple moved to Mobile.[30] A job as auditor for the Benevolent Christian Burial Association—Aunt Pearl's expanding business—awaited him.

That enterprise would help define Gary Cooper's family for a new generation and more.

BIRTH OF A LANDMARK BUSINESS

By 1935, the Great Depression was taking its toll on much of American life, but Pearl Johnson—known to the family as "Shug," short for "Sugar"[31]—had retained financial well-being despite the general economic collapse. She and the man she would marry, W. H. Madison, had joined in the formation of a burial insurance company, a formidable industry in the African American world.

The Benevolent Christian Burial Association, like other burial associations, was born out of necessity. According to the company's historical account, when two A.M.E Zion ministers died penniless in Pensacola, Florida, in 1922, it took financial help from others to bury them. At the

urging of residents, a burial association was formed by another A.M.E
Zion minister, Dr. G. W. Johnson—no relation to Pearl—and local undertakers, the Goldstuckers. Churches and ministers helped spread the
word to potential customers, with joining fees as low as a quarter and
initial premiums ranging from five to twenty cents.[32]

Branching into south Alabama with business in Brewton, Flomaton,
and Evergreen, the burial association opened a Mobile office in 1924 and
incorporated in Alabama in 1926—the year A. J. graduated from Emerson,
Gary said. With its home office now in Mobile, the business-savvy Pearl
Johnson was secretary and W. H. Madison came over from Pensacola to
be manager. In the next couple of decades, its name would be changed to
the Christian Benevolent Burial Association, it would become an insurance company, and it would change from a mutual to a stock company.
W. H. Madison would become president.[33]

*Evidently the idea and the formation of the company was done in
Pensacola. I guess after a while the Pensacola partners dropped out and
they reorganized in Alabama. The Goldstuckers remained in Florida
and the Reverend G. W. Johnson died. He died in Shug's house. When
he got ill, they took care of him, and I'm sure he gave them the stock.
That's how Mr. Madison and his wife, Pearl Johnson, ended up being
the major shareholders.*

In 1928 the company added a funeral home, an attractive white
wooden two-story building on North Hamilton Street in a quiet, shady
part of downtown, but close enough to the bustling black business district
and black churches.[34] By then, Christian Benevolent was one of a small
number of burial insurance firms owned by African Americans in the
South and in Northern cities. These firms found a ready, almost exclusive
market for their services in the early part of the twentieth century. Black
undertakers and burial policy salesmen, like black hairdressers and bar-
bers, took care of black people; there was at times even a hostile view of
black clients by white insurers.[35]

"In the South, the conduct of white agents in Negro homes has not
been commendable," wrote Merah S. Stuart, the historian of the National
Negro Insurance Association, in 1940. "Their haughtiness, discourtesies

and not infrequent abuses of the privacy of the home were resented but
to a great extent tolerated until the organization and entry of Negro
companies into this field."[36]

As the historical marker now standing outside the Christian Benevolent
Funeral Home notes: "Mrs. Pearl Johnson Madison was one of the first
African-American women to own a business in the state of Alabama in
1928." Her business, Christian Benevolent Funeral Home and Insurance
Company, was one of only a few in the Mobile area to provide funeral
services to the African American community at that time.

After lives of indignities and economic hardship, many poor blacks
viewed the trappings of a proper burial as worth the cost.

"Burial insurance is usually the first to be taken out and the last to be
relinquished when times grow hard. It is considered more important by
the very poor than sickness or accident insurance," the anthropologist
Hortense Powderbaker wrote in her 1969 book, *After Freedom: A Cultural
Study in the Deep South.*[37]

While critics viewed the burial insurance business as a form of ex-
ploitation of poor, uneducated people, the black funeral and insurance
companies helped fuel the economies of black neighborhoods and were
among the biggest supporters of church and civic projects and charities.[38]
This was true of Pearl and W. H. Madison, later Gladys and A. J. Cooper,
and eventually their son, Gary Cooper.

*I think this is a tribute to black business. My great-aunt Pearl, who
was like my grandmother, and her husband, my great-uncle, lent S. D.
Bishop his first funds to buy a building to start what became Bishop
State Community College. From the funeral home and the insurance
company they ran, they were able to lend the money to start that school.*

Many black insurance company owners became very rich. In Birmingham, A. G. Gaston would become a multimillionaire and one of
the nation's wealthiest African Americans by turning a burial insurance
company into a wide-ranging empire geared to a black clientele.[39] In Mobile, the Christian Benevolent Burial Association under Pearl Madison
did not branch out beyond its core business, but it was highly profitable,
and it helped the Madisons, and subsequently A. J. and Gladys Cooper,

become well-known figures in the port city's black establishment.

NEXT DOOR TO PEARL

When Gladys and A. J. brought the newborn Jerome Gary Cooper back to Mobile from his birth in Lafayette, home was in a duplex on Cuba Street. The family physician was Dr. Escous Blackwell Goode, an Emerson Institute graduate who had earned degrees at Talladega College and Meharry Medical School.[40]

Cuba Street was on the north side of town, right off Davis Avenue. It was on Davis Avenue that Dr. E. B. Goode had his office on the second floor. He was the family doctor, and I was circumcised by Dr. Goode. They told me I was so big and bouncing around, he had to go out on the street and hire two winos to hold me down.

Davis Avenue was the heart of the black community.

"In my mind's eye," says Gary's childhood friend, Joaquin Holloway Jr., "I can see the Pike theater, Jim's Barbecue and Ella's Barbecue, and the drugstore, the tailor shop, the pool halls. This was where the people frequented because they felt comfortable in this part of town. Some people lived here, around Davis Avenue, others lived in a part of town called Campground, and others in a community called the Bottom. There was a whole thriving, bustling community in this part of Mobile, which was called Across Town. Dr. E. B. Goode was the one who actually gave me my first spanking: he delivered me at the house. He was my mom and dad's doctor."

Dr. Goode, prominent in social, civic, and civil rights projects, delivered some five thousand babies while practicing nearly sixty years, beginning when Davis Avenue was just a muddy street.[41]

Joaquin: "I happened to be present when Dr. Goode took his last breath. He was present when I took my first breath and I was present when he took his last breath. We had gone to a funeral together. At the bottom of the stairs, he collapsed. He had an aneurysm."

The second of four Cooper sons, William Madison Cooper, known as Billy, came along four years after Gary, again with Dr. Goode on hand.[42]

Billy was born on the Fourth of July. The doctor walked out of the bedroom and announced: "We have a new little firecracker for the Fourth of July!"

However, by the time of Billy's birth, A. J. and Gladys had moved from the Cuba Street duplex to a sumptuous two-story home they had built, with a large fireplace and a sunken living room, at 603 Delaware Street, next door to Aunt Pearl's house.

"It had a really nice gazebo in the back yard," said Joaquin. "It was the first I'd ever seen, an elevated gazebo built around a tree. It was a very imposing structure. The first time Gary and I were in regular contact with each other, we both were in the Cub Scouts."

The Cub Scout troop met at my house. My mother was the den mother.

Gary's new neighborhood, known as Down the Bay, included nice homes, with bay windows, broad porches and upstairs bedrooms, but scattered among them were shanties with wooden privies out back.

The majority of homes were like shotgun homes and the people were very poor.

"Generally people who lived in Down the Bay may have been thought of as slightly upper crust," said Joaquin. "But it was a mix. There were always pockets of people who had less."

In an interview videotaped for a Mobile Tricentennial project, Gary recalled:

Kids used to like to pick on me because I was the little rich kid in the neighborhood, My parents had a car and everyone else lived in shotgun houses. We had—I guess it seemed like a huge house compared to those back then—so kids would always like to tease me and I was always quick to fight.

During those days it was pretty unusual to live in a household where both your parents were college graduates—and your grandparents. Most people around us were very, very poor. Not that they knew they were poor, not poor in the sense of their being famished or doing without things, but not the luxuries.[43]

Down the Bay, which generally was south of Government Street and east of Broad Street, was named for its location away from Mobile's busy waterfront, where the Mobile Bay ship channel fed maritime commerce.

"If you look at a map of the bay, you could see that it was not Up the Bay but Down the Bay," said Joaquin. "Davis Avenue was a compact, self-sufficient community, with doctors, grocers, tailors, while Down the Bay was more residential than commercial.

"I don't remember many commercial things other than maybe Sam Joy Cleaners, Naman's grocery store, or maybe a barbershop, a drugstore, and the Harlem Theater. That was the black theater. Everything was segregated. There was a little place called Pope's Luncheonette, some other little clubs down in that area, but nothing in terms of businesses like on Davis Avenue."

In Down the Bay, you had most of your commercial activity on Texas Street. That's where you had the barbershops, the hardware store, pharmacies, and grocery stores.

For Gary, the neighborhood was full of kids who played football in the fall, kids who enjoyed knocking each other into the ditches on the sides of the dirt streets, kids who would join him on a long walk to catch crawfish in the "Big Ditch" in woods beyond the end of Dearborn Street.

Pearl's house, a fine house on the corner of Delaware Street and Warren, had been there for years. As a little boy, I can remember Pearl's mother—when I look at the year she died, I only was three or four years old—they called her "Miss Lou." I can remember her sitting on that back porch. She was a very fair-skinned, white-looking lady, very old when I saw her.

I remember her. But her husband, Ben, I never met. My brother Billy had a portrait of him. What a distinguished looking gentleman! You couldn't tell he was black. Maybe slightly brown, with a mustache. My understanding, maybe Shug told me, was that he was a freedman. He had been a slave but later got a job working for the railroad, maybe the L&N. That was Ben Johnson.

He had done well. To have that property on Delaware Street, back in those days, even to buy property, you had to be unusual. But that house had been there a long time, in the Johnson family. Evidently they owned the property next to them, and that's where Daddy built my family's house.

I think when we originally moved into it, it was all wood. But later they got it refurbished and it became brick. I think maybe they were really overspending money. I can remember Mother going to New York and picking out furniture, really spending money.

Mother was known to be a very fashionable dresser, a good-looking woman who wore sharp clothes. She used to make trips to New York to buy clothes.

A HOUSE ACROSS THE BAY

While perhaps less interested in fashion, Pearl Johnson Madison had an eye for value. It was part of her business acumen. Exactly where her aptitude for finance came from is uncertain. There is little recollection of her ever mentioning going to college.[44] But she stressed education, displayed a keen intellect, and had about her a sixth sense for propriety and achievement.

"She was a very stern, financially astute, and sophisticated person," said Gary's son, Patrick Cooper, who knew Shug when he was growing up. "She had a sort of living presence over the family. If anybody had created any wealth in the family, it was her. Every year she would buy a new Cadillac. She'd keep it for one year and then buy a new Cadillac."

One of her more astute acquisitions was bayfront property on the Eastern Shore of Mobile Bay, a tranquil stretch of tree-shaded bay homes with long wooden piers stretching out into the softly lapping brown bay waters.

"That tells you a lot," said Matt Metcalfe, a venerable white business executive and civic leader in Mobile who became one of Gary's close friends, "because over the bay was the place for all the rich white people. But it gives you some idea of the Madisons and their status."

The bay property at Fairhope apparently was purchased in the 1940s, around the time A. J.'s sprawling new home was built on Delaware Street in Down the Bay. Little known or little remembered by the well-to-do whites who turned the Eastern Shore into a serene, scenic, and increasingly expensive sanctuary, blacks had owned some of the property there before it became highly sought-after.

"What's interesting is, blacks owned property back then on the Eastern Shore," said James Harrell, one of Gary's friends who visited this bayfront house often. "This was some of the last property that blacks owned on the bay. A lot of people didn't discover the beach until later, didn't think it was worth anything until later in life. This old schoolteacher they bought it from, it had belonged to her for a long time."

I can remember being younger than a teenager over there. I would go over on the weekend with Shug and Uncle Willie. They used to have to promise my Mama that they would take me to Mass on Sunday. They went to an A.M.E. Zion church; they weren't Catholic like my family, so they'd take me to Mass. I'd be wearing knickers and they'd take me up to Daphne and drop me off at the Catholic church, then come back to pick me up.

As the Cooper family grew eventually to six children, the expanded bay house, with red peppermint-like stripes running up and down its outside walls, became a kids' paradise for swimming, boating, water sports, and games.

Over the years, the bay house fronting the water became far more valuable than the family homes in Down the Bay, where the Madisons remained as their burial insurance business flourished.

Shug bought that bayfront property with no connection to my parents at all. When she died, she left in her will that we didn't get that property. We had to buy it from her estate. We did.

"GIANTS OF BLACK CAPITALISM"

"Pearl was a nice lady," said Joaquin Holloway Jr. "You had a little fear when you met her because she was very imposing, a big woman. Bigger than her husband. She was, I guess, pretty firm, rigid in terms of her ideas."

Her size seemed to indicate that Gary and his three brothers—all were tall men—got their height from the Johnson side of the family. But Gary isn't so sure. Maybe it came from both sides.

"In Lafayette, on my mother's side, we had an Uncle Dick. There's a picture of him with a horse by a barn, and he was like six-foot-seven."

Even among light-skinned Coopers, Johnsons, and Madisons—Aunt

Pearl's husband, W. H. Madison, "looked just like he was white," Gary said—there was one other feature about Pearl that was memorable.

"She had piercing blue eyes," said Patrick, "which was highly unusual."

There has been speculation in the family that perhaps Shug was the child of a white man, but on one point there is no doubt: she was "the stern matriarch of my family," as Gary's sister Peggy and others described her,[45] and the proximity to Shug on Delaware Street was a distinct advantage for Gary and his siblings, who looked upon her with great fondness throughout her life.

"She was funny," said Gary's other sister, Dominic. "One time my sister had a party and Shug could see in our yard. She called my mother and said, 'There's not even room for the Holy Ghost between those children dancing!'

"But she was the classic matriarch. She may have been stern, and she was six feet tall and all that, but still, when we went over to the bay, she'd be right in the water with the kids, playing with the kids. It's not like she was a hands-off person. It's not like she was a lovey-dovey person, either. She was there. She was present."

Her husband became president of Christian Benevolent Insurance in 1942 when Dr. G. W. Johnson stepped down due to ill health. W. H. Madison held the post for twenty years, while company assets increased more than a dozen-fold. With her husband's death in 1963, Pearl Madison became president and chairman of the board.[46]

"The white business community knew her and respected her because she held herself with such dignity," said Metcalfe. "She was tall like Gary, very erect, gray hair, soft-spoken, courteous, great manners. She was an aristocrat. Regardless of the color, she was an aristocrat."

Nor was Pearl Madison's business judgment lost on the wider world of black entrepreneurs. It is no surprise that in May 1969 she was among those whose photographs ran in an *Ebony* magazine piece titled "Giants of Black Capitalism." Its subhead: "Forty-six black insurance companies have combined assets approaching $½ billion, insurance in force totaling $2 billion."[47]

The article featured photographs of thirty-six black insurance company owners or executives from across America; Pearl Madison was one of only three women among them. A. G. Gaston of Birmingham was also among those pictured, along with Alex L. Herman, president of Unity Burial and Life Insurance Company in Mobile, whose daughter Alexis would be close to the Cooper children and a key figure in Cooper family prominence years later.

While Pearl Madison and others were saluted for their financial success, the *Ebony* article cited the stigma of race as creating obstacles for blacks in the insurance profession.

"Out of every dollar black people spend on life insurance," it said, "only eight cents goes to black insurance companies. If by some miracle all of these dollars were earmarked instead for the nation's forty-six black-owned companies, these firms would control more than twenty percent of the total market rather than their present piddling share of less than one-fourth of one percent."

"They are plagued by that widespread folk psychology which says they are automatically second-class because they are black, even though there is mounting evidence that their insurance is competitive with the rest of the industry," the article said. "Finally, they have not successfully countered the raiding of their trained personnel by the larger companies which, until recently, were not only reluctant to hire black salesmen, but also discouraged sales to black insurance prospects."[48]

Largely because of Pearl Madison, and A. J. and Gladys Cooper, there would be nothing "automatically second-class" about the family's next generation, beginning with Gary Cooper.

2

Confronting Jim Crow

T he privileges of wealth may have made the Cooper family the envy
of many other blacks, but they too were stung by the indignities
of the Jim Crow system and blocked by segregation's barriers the
same as other African Americans.

Those were some interesting days in Alabama. It was really, really
segregated. If you were an African American, it didn't matter whether
you were light-skinned like me or black as the ace of spades. You were
totally segregated.

You've heard about riding in the back of the bus. That was the least of
your problems. We couldn't even walk in Bienville Square [the historic,
tree-lined park in the heart of downtown Mobile], let alone sit down.
We couldn't walk there.[49]

In 1937, the year after Gary was born, the names of A. J. Cooper and
Pearl and W. H. Madison appear on the membership list of the NAACP's
Mobile branch, supporting the work of the local indefatigable civil rights
champion, John LeFlore.[50] They played key support roles but were not
activists like LeFlore, preferring instead to use their financial means and
position in society to help the black community. But they had many frustrations with the racial divide, as it undermined all manner of black life.

These frustrations had a long history. Mobile had been the state's largest slave trade center before the Civil War,[51] near the time when Gary's
great-grandfather, Ben Johnson, and Ben's future wife, Lou, grew up. Even
into the 1940s and 1950s, when Gary began to experience segregation
as a youth and grade-school student, there had been episodes of racial
violence in the port city. During World War II, as blacks poured into

Mobile seeking defense jobs, racial friction was frequent, including a violent attack on blacks by whites enraged over the first integrated crew at a Pinto Island shipbuilding firm.[52] In another incident, a black soldier was shot to death in a confrontation with a white bus driver.[53]

You'd almost get a little angry thinking of how it was in Mobile. I was pretty lucky, because in my household our parents taught us that white folk were crazy, they had serious problems treating us like this. I can't speak for all my sisters and brothers, but thanks to our parents, we didn't have any inferiority complex.[54]

The movies were all segregated. When I'd go to the Saenger Theater downtown, you'd have to crawl up and go in the balcony. Every once in a while we'd get to acting a little crazy and we'd drop little things down from the balcony.

No, we did not like those days in Mobile.

Unfortunately, the Catholic church did not help much at all. We had a parade celebrating the Feast Day of Christ the King. Boy, this was quite a parade. All the Catholics took part. Guess where the black Catholics would march? The back of the parade.

If we go to Mass at the Cathedral, guess where we had to sit? The last two rows.[55]

As it was across the South, the school system in Mobile was strictly segregated, including the Catholic school system. Gary, like all five of his siblings, would begin his formal education attending all-black Catholic schools, starting with Saint Peter Claver for elementary grades. With the Catholic church a focus for the family, the Cooper children's introduction to segregation came early.

In a 2012 television interview, Jay Cooper echoed Gary:

The experience of going to a Catholic school and learning that the school was segregated, I think it came from doing something like marching in the Christ the King Day parade, where all of the white schools marched in the front of the parade and the black schools had to march in the back of the parade, and me asking my father why that was, and his having to explain that to me. And I think that was the first real understanding I began to have.[56]

Family ties to the Catholic church, which began in the Oak Avenue home of the devout Grandmother Agnes Mouton in Lafayette, left a lasting mark. For some, Catholicism seemed paired with racial discrimination.

"The little church in Lafayette that was not a block away from my grandmother's house, they went there to daily Mass," said Gary's cousin, Judi Stephenson, "but they had to sit in the back three rows of the church. All the whites sat in the regular church but they left these three rows."

"THERE'S ALWAYS ROOM AT THE TOP"

Gary's father was increasingly concerned over the dual school system run by the Diocese.

"The desire by [A. J.] Cooper and other blacks to integrate the Catholic schools in Mobile was heightened in the fall 1949 academic year when St. Peter Claver Elementary Catholic school opened without the Sisters of the Holy Ghost who usually taught classes there," Shawn Bivens wrote. "With their departure, the Diocese hired recent high-school graduate lay teachers."[57]

Joined by Dr. John Finley Sr. and the Reverend Vincent Warren, A. J. Cooper questioned Bishop Thomas J. Toolen about segregation throughout the school system in the Diocese, particularly since Gary was to start high school the next year.

Bivens continued: "Cooper asked that Gary be allowed to transfer to Most Pure Heart of Mary, a black Catholic school where the Sisters had more teaching experience, even though it was not accredited. This was approved, but Bishop Toolen refused to consider allowing Gary or other blacks to go to McGill High School that year or next."[58]

Even five years later, when A. J. Cooper tried again, the bishop held firm to the dual system. The U.S. Supreme Court had struck down the "separate but equal" doctrine in its *Brown v. Board* ruling in May 1954, but Toolen would not relent: McGill High must remain all-white.[59]

Despite segregation, Gary felt his schooling in the black Catholic system was solid.

We had Catholic nuns and they were very, very serious about you getting good grades. And the discipline—listen, if you acted up in school, your mama knew about it in a minute.

When you think about these nuns, they don't have the distraction of their families and other things to do. They just did a good job.

The other thing that helped me and could well have been a key is having parents who were college graduates. I can remember as a little kid Mama having me in the Book of the Month Club and me having to read the book and report to her at the end of the month what was in the book. How few kids anywhere had to do that for their parents?

One of Gary's most influential and memorable teachers at Most Pure Heart of Mary High School was a Dominican nun named Sister Eulogia.

I have mentioned many times what sort of influence those nuns had on me. They were Dominicans. They called them OP—the Order of Preachers.

Sister Eulogia. She had a red scar down the side of her face. She wouldn't put up with any bull. She'd pop you.

She was from Sinsinawa, Wisconsin—a geometry and math teacher. Almost several times a week, before she would dismiss the class, she would say, "You know, things around here aren't quite like they should be, riding in the back of the bus and all. But I want you always to re-member that if you make yourself the very best, it doesn't matter where you are from, what you look like, how much money your daddy has got, there's always room at the top."

It was a phrase I never forgot: "There's always room at the top." I would remember it years later, as a Marine officer, when I was in my stateroom aboard ship and I was thinking, what is it I should do next?

"There's always room at the top." A number of us still remember that.

SPORTS MEMORIES

By his own admission, Gary was not a good athlete, but he was a first-string tackle on the Heart of Mary High School football squad and prizes the memory. Basketball was another story:

I was horrible. Couldn't shoot, couldn't jump.

At times segregation did not make for level playing fields even when two black teams were playing each other. Gary humorously tells a story from the early 1950s of a ludicrous white man who threatened the young black football players. But it was the kind of truly frightening act that blacks had to anticipate and contend with, even on fields of play.

Heart of Mary played football games across the line in Moss Point and Waynesboro, Mississippi. One night we played a team in Waynesboro. We got off the bus and changed clothes in the workshop. They didn't have any other place to put on gear and uniforms, no field house or locker room.

We go out on the field and this white guy comes up to us with a shotgun. He says, "Y'all niggers come around here." We said, "Yes, sir." He said, "Let me tell you something. You see this chair and this shotgun? I'm going to be sittin' in this chair behind that goal. And that team over there, those are my niggers from Waynesboro and I don't want to see you cross that goal. Do you understand me?" We said, "Yes, sir."

So we played this game and we'd get down near the goal line and the quarterback would say, "Two twenty-two on two!" And the halfback would say, "I'm not running that ball!"

So we didn't score. And when we changed sides, then that white guy, he'd take that chair and gun and walk to the other end.

Gary's lifelong friend, Harold Jackson, was a member of the Most Pure Heart of Mary team and vividly recalls the game and the threatening white man. "He parked in the end zone. He had his shotgun and he told us, 'Don't go over the goal line.'"[60]

There was no appeal to law officers in that era in places like rural Waynesboro. While Gary and even Jackson can laugh at the memory now—the white man's threat was frightening. "It wasn't funny at the time," Jackson said.

The Most Pure Heart of Mary team was furious.

"After the game was over—we did lose—we had to dress in an industrial class, where they had all kinds of tools," said Jackson. "When we finished dressing, there were people outside who were threatening us. They told us they would kill us."[61]

We were so mad, we did bad things. We tore up the workshop. The police escorted us out of town.

CROSSING BROAD

Even black youths from families of considerable accomplishment, like Gary and his friend Joaquin Holloway Jr., weren't spared the slights and humiliations of the racial code of the era. Joaquin recalls how his mother's father, Dr. H. Roger Williams, balked at hanging a "Colored" sign outside his drugstore and doctor's office in 1901.

"The drugstore at 607 Dauphin Street was in the downstairs portion of a two-story building," Joaquin said, "and his office was on the second floor. His drugstore was called 'Live and Let Live.'

"He was one of the first African Americans to have a drugstore and office in that area. There were a number of black people who had their businesses there, and back in the early 1900s it's my understanding that, if you were not white, they wanted you to put 'Colored' on your sign.

"Well, my grandfather, who was very dark-skinned, was somewhat militant for that age, and he refused to put the word 'Colored' on there. Instead, he stuck his photograph in the window. So if anybody had any doubts about his racial background, then the photograph should let them know."

His father, Joaquin Holloway Sr., who had worked for years in the public school system, decided to take a government job at Brookley Field rather than become a principal, because the school position would not pay as much.

"My dad was kind of a quiet man," said Joaquin, "I owe him a lot of gratitude and a lot of respect. At Brookley Field, one of his bosses, who was white, asked him if he could read and write, which was really an insult. My daddy had graduated cum laude with a degree in physics and chemistry from Talladega College. This person who was his boss may not have even finished high school."

"In Down the Bay," Joaquin said, "I used to actually have to walk past Russell Elementary School, a white school, to get to Emerson, the black school I attended. Russell was just around the corner from where I lived.

My dad's mother was rather fair and had a good relationship with Russell's principal, who was a white woman. But I couldn't go there because it was a white school."

After graduating from historically black Talladega College in 1957, Joaquin went to Indiana University for his master's degree. "I probably would have gone to the University of Alabama, but, again, things were segregated back then. I had to go out of state."

Gary and Joaquin's neighborhood, however, was comfortable. Down the street from Gary's boyhood home, Leander and Delena Hall lived in a house at the corner of Delaware and Dearborn, where Mrs. Hall taught piano lessons. The Halls ran a small insurance company and sent their daughters to college, but most memorable for the young Gary, when he took piano lessons, were the black baseball players who would board at the Halls' home during the summer.[62]

As Gary recalls it, some of these players would become famous with the Brooklyn Dodgers, whose farm team during the mid-1940s was the Mobile Bears. This was the era when Jackie Robinson broke major league baseball's racial barrier and was joined on the Dodgers by black stars like Roy Campanella and Don Newcomb.

There was always more than one staying at the Hall house. I think it was Campanella one year. Jackie Robinson. The pitcher Don Newcomb. I would go down and sit on the front steps. They were on the front porch. Maybe we would toss a ball out on the grass, something like that. That's where they had to live because they weren't allowed to stay in a hotel. They were staying at Mrs. Delena Hall's house, a private residence.

A demarcation line for blacks in the Down the Bay neighborhood was Broad Street.

The big deal at Christmas was to cross Broad Street and you didn't have to worry about the white folks bothering you. Probably the reason was because right across Broad Street, for a couple of blocks, was an area called Texas Hill, and on Texas Hill they had some black folks living there. So you cross Broad Street—and there were a lot of you on Christmas Day—you would cross Broad Street and skate. People would skate up with their new skates. That was the big deal on Christmas Day. Crossing Broad.

Growing up, Gary would visit his mother's family in Lafayette and on occasion experience one of the hated, hellish chores of earlier days: picking cotton. However, at least for him, conditions were much different.

I can remember picking cotton. I had a cousin there in Lafayette, a guy, and if you wanted to be with kids your age, you had to get up at four-thirty and be on a corner to get on the back of a truck that would take you to a place called Breaux Bridge.

You'd get with them and you'd go pick cotton all day. You'd get a long bag with a strap. I thought it was fun. I'd throw cotton bolls at girls. The girls would be leaning over and we'd be throwing bolls at their behinds. Then we'd pour water on the cotton in the bag before weighing to make it heavy. We'd pour water—sometimes you'd pee in it, to make it heavier. People would do that!

This was no arduous task in the cotton fields like those of old.

No. It was fun. I went there to be with my cousins. It was fun. We'd brag about it. What I remember was the white guy, dressed like a cowboy. He'd say in French: "Pick that damn cotton faster!"

At the Mouton home in Lafayette, when adults didn't want youngsters like Gary to know what they were saying, they would converse in a French or Creole patois that kept their discussions a mystery.[63]

Gary's cousin, Judi Stephenson, grew up in Detroit, Michigan, but also would make trips to Lafayette, then Mobile, with her family during summers. Invariably it was an eye-opener for her. Even going to get ice cream had its challenges.

"My sister Marilyn is three years older than me," Judi said, "and Marilyn, you would never know she's black to look at her. We, as kids, liked to go to this ice cream shop that was not too far. We knew that blacks—whatever they called us at the time, Negroes, whatever—were not allowed to go in the front door. So Gary and I would stand in the bushes off to the side and send Marilyn to the front door to get our ice cream."

Visiting Gary on summer trips was a treat in itself.

"Gary always had quite a presence, a great, fun personality, and grew quite tall. He knew everyone and loved to take us on walks around the neighborhood to meet his friends. We, in turn, adored him.

"His family owned a vacation home property 'over the Bay' and we had quite a few fun picnics and sleepovers at this property. Gary is one of six kids, so there was always lots of noise and fun with the kids. I remember his dad, Uncle A. J., being quite a disciplinarian, and we all kind of avoided him."

Marilyn: "One of my best memories of visiting the Coopers was our saying the family Rosary every evening led by Gary's dad. We would all kneel around twin beds in their guest room and recite the prayers. Peggy, in particular, was so funny saying 'Momma of God' instead of 'Mother of God.'

"For some reason Judi and I would get hysterical and have to leave the room."

Judi: "As we got into our teen years, Marilyn and I were so excited to have Gary take us to some of the backcountry dances. Gary always knew where we could sample some spiked punch. These were fun times, especially for two Catholic schoolgirls, experiencing life in segregated Mobile, Alabama.

"On occasion, we got into trouble with our moms when we returned home later than curfew."

A Visit Pays Dividends

A. J. Cooper was not only a devoted husband and father but an astute businessman eager to share financial knowledge:

> Talk about an experience that I'm sure few children either black or white had, when I was a little boy my daddy would take me to the bank vault to clip coupons off bonds. I can remember going to the bank and doing that when I was a little kid.

In the community, A. J. was a leader among black civic and social groups and helped raise funds for a maternity hospital for black women. When Gladys Cooper had traveled to her home in south Louisiana in 1936 to deliver her first child, it was not solely because her mother and grandmother were skilled midwives. She was still new to Mobile and did not feel there was adequate medical care there for pregnant women of color.[64]

At that time, licensed black physicians could not work in Mobile's white-run hospitals, and pregnant black women, if they were admitted, often felt neglected. Even at Providence Hospital, run by the Catholic church, only a few black patients would be admitted, but their family members were not allowed inside the building. "During a patient's stay," Shawn Bivens reported, "families of color stood across the street from the hospital and waved at the family member who stood at the window of the hospital room and waved back."[65]

They couldn't get in Providence Hospital, they couldn't get in Mobile Infirmary. So when you had a child, you either had to go home to your mama or you had to find a midwife or doctor to come to your home. That was as recent as the '40s and '50s.

Against this backdrop, A. J. Cooper joined Father Vincent Warren and other Mobile Catholics in raising funds to build Mobile's first maternity hospital for black women. Warren, traveling to Baltimore and Washington, enlisted the support of Archbishop Fulton J. Sheen, who at the time was a highly popular national radio personality with "The Catholic Hour" program.[66] Sheen made a nationwide appeal for funds to build the hospital in Mobile. He also made a trip to the Cooper home in Down the Bay, accompanied by former Congresswoman Clare Booth Luce, a celebrated writer who was the wife of *Time* magazine publisher Henry Luce.

It was a visit that would pay many dividends.

They arrived in a limousine with a police escort. Police lights flashing on this dirt street, right where we lived. This was 1948, I think, and I was maybe eleven or twelve years old. They came to offer support to my father, who was leading a fundraiser to build the hospital that would accept black women. The archbishop heard that this group was trying to raise money so that our women could have babies in hospitals.

The hospital became a reality with the construction of St. Martin dePorres Hospital on Washington Avenue and Virginia Street. This was not far from my home in Down the Bay. As a young altar boy, I served Mass in the hospital chapel many times.

Mobile's first maternity hospital for black women opened in 1950, the only hospital in the city to allow African American physicians to treat its patients and to provide care exclusively for people of color. It was aptly named the Blessed Martin dePorres Maternity Hospital in honor of a Peruvian—the son of a Spanish nobleman and a freed slave—who died in 1639, was canonized by the pope in 1962 and considered the patron saint of social justice.[67]

Along with meeting A. J. Cooper about funding the maternity clinic, Archbishop Sheen also spoke about another possibility—where young Gary would go to college.

While visiting with my family the Archbishop told me about a university named Notre Dame. I don't think I had ever heard of it or knew anything about it. But he told me that if I decided that I wanted to go to Notre Dame, he would write a letter for me and help me get a scholarship. So Notre Dame became my college of choice.

About five years later, on October 5, 1953, Archbishop Sheen wrote to thank Gary for his "kind and warmhearted letter, which brought to mind the happy occasions when I visited with your wonderful family in Mobile.... You have my hearty approval to use my name on your application blank to Notre Dame University. I shall be delighted to recommend you."[68]

"I still have that letter in my files—and I did receive an academic scholarship."

Years later a Marine general speaking at Camp Pendleton mentioned the black officers in the Corps.

He mentioned my name—Gary Cooper—and then described me as a Marine officer "who went to Notre Dame on a basketball scholarship."

I called him up and said, 'General, let me make sure you understand this: It was an academic scholarship. Not basketball. All of us can't jump!'

In retrospect, Cooper felt he probably did not miss out on anything academically by not getting to attend white schools in Mobile. "If I missed anything it was the ability to understand and know different people, but I was lucky enough to go to Notre Dame to pick that up, because at Notre Dame I got to live with people from all over the country, all over the world."

Along with an academic scholarship, Gary also received tuition support from the state—a rare benefit for blacks under Alabama's segregated system of higher education.

I don't know how I found out about it, but if you had a major that was offered in a white college or university and not in a black university, they would pay the difference in your tuition if you went out of state. So for three-and-a-half years, I got the damn difference between what it cost to go to Notre Dame and major in finance and what it would have cost at Auburn or Alabama. Amazing.

Gary also received a small amount of financial support from his proud grandfather, O. O. Cooper, who had retired from the Post Office and moved from Chicago to Los Angeles before Gary arrived at Notre Dame.[69] In a July 1953 letter to his son A. J. in Mobile, O. O. Cooper explained the attraction of the City of Angels:

It is the most beautiful city which I ever visited. It is simply lovely. Colored people live all over it, there is no place which is exclusively white.

I am glad that I made up my mind to live here. This place has cool nights in summer—short winters and no snow. This city seems to be run exceptionally well. There is plenty of work here and colored people seem to be doing alright.[70]

Gary's cousins in Detroit were happy he chose Notre Dame because it was close enough for visits during college breaks.

"Sometimes, we stayed up until 2 a.m. exchanging stories and sneaking vodka from my parents' liquor cabinet," Judi said. "Gary always filled the bottle with water before returning it to the cabinet!"

THE JIM CROW CAR

As fall approached in 1954, with his mother and father at the old L&N station at the foot of Government Street to see him off, Gary boarded the "Hummingbird," a train headed for Chicago, on his way to the University of Notre Dame. Out of Mobile, as elsewhere across the South, Gary climbed aboard the segregated train's all-black car, known as "the Jim Crow car."

The Jim Crow car did not always provide black passengers a guarantee of food service, so many brought aboard bags of fried chicken and other snacks to eat. The trains became known as "the Chicken Bone Special" as blacks rode out of the South during the Great Migration.[71] As Gary recalled, there was a purple curtain separating blacks and whites in the dining car; it would be pulled back when the train had left the South.

The train would stop for the Mason-Dixon line. When you crossed that line, you could sit anywhere. But you only went to the dinning car if you had saved your money. Otherwise you had your fried chicken that your mama had fixed.

The disadvantage of the Jim Crow car was that the trains were coal-fired and soot was a problem where blacks were seated. But also you had the black porters and they were all very nice. And in the dining car the black waiters would make sure you had great food.

On my first trip to Notre Dame, Carol Russell, the daughter of a dentist, was going to Chicago, too. I sure felt I was big-time. I may even have had cigarettes hidden in my socks.

BANNED BY THE BISHOP

Gary's departure for Notre Dame came just months after the U.S. Supreme Court's *Brown v. Board* ruling. Against this backdrop, A. J. Cooper enrolled his second-oldest son, Billy, in McGill, the white Catholic high school in the Mobile diocese.

He may have tried to get Billy in McGill because some of the nuns teaching in the black schools had left, or their presence in classrooms had been reduced. What would happen sometimes at the Catholic schools is the nuns would not leave but they would reduce the number from seven to two and you would have lay teachers, who were dedicated, too, make up the difference. I'm not sure if Daddy tried to enroll Billy in McGill because he was concerned about the quality, or whether he was saying, "Hey, I'm going to do this and see if it works."

When I grew up as a kid, my family was very religious. We ate dinner together and we said the family Rosary. We'd actually get around the bed and kneel down, every night of the week. I was an altar boy. My daddy went to church many times during the week. He raised money for the maternity clinic and many church functions. Of course, Mother coming from a religious family was a reason we were so devout.

All this went along well until my dad decided, when my brother Billy graduated from Saint Peter Claver, that he was going to enroll him in McGill. Billy has light skin, hair is a little blond. Everything is fine, Billy was enrolled, Billy was welcome. After about the second, third or fourth week, they looked at Billy's record and saw he came from this black elementary school.

They put Billy out. The archbishop issued an order, that because of what Daddy had attempted to do, none of his children could go to any Catholic school, black or white, in the diocese. Daddy had to send Billy to Detroit, to live with an aunt, to go to high school. That was the end of Daddy and Catholicism. He went downhill at a rapid pace after that. I think how sad that was.

Not a one of my brothers and sisters went to high school in Mobile. For two reasons. One was my daddy was pissed off. The other one was by that time he had left my mother and moved in with another woman. You can imagine in a very small community like that, where everybody knew you—you know how parents can pit one parent against another— that was one of the reasons he sent the children out of state to schools.

While his private and spiritual life had unraveled after Billy was removed from McGill, A. J. Cooper remained key to the operations of the family business and a figure of influence in the black community. He was tapped in 1956 to serve on a biracial committee formed by the politically progressive white mayor, Joe Langan, as an arm of the Alabama Council on Human Relations.[72]

A story in the *Mobile Press-Register* that year reported that A. J. Cooper would be one of the division chairmen of the United Fund campaign, and it listed some of his accomplishments:

> A prominent Catholic layman, Cooper is a member of St. Peter Claver Catholic Church, a forth Degree Knight of Peter Claver and has served that national Catholic organization for many years as its internal auditor. He holds many offices in religious and civic organizations. . . .

He is serving now his second term as president of the Utopia Club, Incorporated, which organization has just completed a new clubhouse on Mon Luis Island. He is also a member and has served for many years as auditor of the Colored Carnival Association.

Cooper has recently been nominated as Omega's Mobile Man of the Year for 1956, which honor will be conferred during National Achievement Week in November.[73]

Like others in the family, Gary's brother Jay never forgot how their father had enrolled Billy in the white Catholic high school—and how the bishop had kicked Billy out and banned him from attending any Catholic school in the Alabama diocese.

"That was so outrageous," Jay said. "The memory of that stuck with me, and my father's courage in doing it."[74]

For Gary, the tribulations of the Cooper household in Mobile in the mid- and late-1950s would be left behind—both mentally and geographically—as he found a challenging new world at the University of Notre Dame, a community far removed from the racial segregation of down-home Alabama.

3

Leaving Home

I n Chicago, Gary left the Hummingbird and went to the South Shore
station for the commuter to South Bend. Stepping off that train, he
headed for the university—and a new world.

NOTRE DAME

*When I walked onto the campus of Notre Dame, it was a revelation.
I still clearly remember seeing the Golden Dome for the first time.*

*That literally was my first time not living in the segregated South.
I thought I had died and gone to heaven. There were no "colored" or
"white" signs on the drinking fountains or bathroom doors. Notre
Dame was a wonderful experience. People were friendly. The famous
young president of Notre Dame was the 37-year-old Father Theodore
Hesburgh.*

*When I went in as a freshman, we had a class of 1,500 and only
three of us were African Americans. One was my roommate, Mervin
"Corky" Parker. He wore thick glasses and studied organic chemistry.
He became a chemist and worked with Gillette almost his whole career.*

*The other was Aubrey Lewis, a star halfback on the football team
and a star hurdler. He was the first black captain of an athletic team
at Notre Dame, with the track squad. Later he was one of the first two
blacks to go through the FBI's training academy.*

*Father Hesburgh would come by our rooms at night to see how we
were doing. He knew that we were in a strange situation. At first, after
he left, we would look at each other and say, "Well, why would he stick
his head in OUR door?" But we were the only black students and he*

was just checking to see if we were OK. He was always kind, gracious, someone we respected.

While the atmosphere on campus was friendly, Hesburgh, who had just become president two years earlier, wanted to make sure race relations were good.

"I wanted them treated the best," Hesburgh recalled. "I was certainly pushing that because I got on the U.S. Civil Rights Commission and we were right in the middle of integration."[75]

Hesburgh became a member of the newly formed commission in 1957. An early case involved Circuit Judge George Wallace, who would become widely known as the segregationist governor of Alabama and would repeatedly make noises as a presidential candidate. The commission's case was before Federal District Judge Frank M. Johnson Jr. of Montgomery, a prominent jurist to whom Hesburgh later would present an honorary degree.[76]

"So I wanted Notre Dame to be one of the best-integrated places around there was," Hesburgh said. "And Gary was a big help. Having a guy like Gary Cooper made it easy to integrate. Everybody liked him. Everybody wanted to be around him."

Notre Dame's first black student, Frazier Leon Thompson, had arrived in 1944 as part of the Navy's officer training program during World War II. Hesburgh arrived in July 1945 to teach a course in moral theology.[77]

"During the war, which was just winding up, we had a black guy who came here by mistake—the Navy made a mistake thinking he was white," Hesburgh said. "We had three thousand officer trainees here and only one is black. So I said, 'When the war is over, come on back and finish up your college at Notre Dame.' Which he did. He graduated, in 1947, and he was the first black graduate, and I was proud of that.

"But in those early days, when we finally managed to get a handful of blacks here, among them was Gary. He was so outstanding. He didn't have to take a back seat to anybody on campus. He helped me a great deal in bringing a good number of blacks on campus."

"You go from zero to spending more time getting black students than white students," he said. "I found having a guy like Gary helped us amazingly in that endeavor because bringing black students in was quite a feat. It was happening all over America. But here it came off very easily and very well, simply because we had a guy like Gary Cooper who was a quintessential black student who was not just as good but better than many of the white students."

Social life for blacks was minimal, at least when it came to finding a date.[78]

There were damn near no black women, and I was scared to look at white women. At Saint Mary's, Notre Dame's sister college, there were a few black girls. I mean three or four, and they were very nice.

Pat LaCour was one. She was at Saint Mary's, and there were Sunday afternoon mixers in the LaFortune Student Center. I had stopped going there, but a classmate, Bob Moretti—he was an Italian from Detroit, he later became Speaker of the California State Assembly—he came over and told me, "There's a pretty black girl over there. Go get her!" In the whole student center, she was the only black girl.

Pat LaCour. A most beautiful girl. We dated. She lives in Atlanta now, and I've seen her since. I told her, "Girl, you don't know, but when I saw you in the student center I ran over there!" She said, "Boy, you don't know how happy I was!"

Once on campus, Gary learned about the Navy ROTC program, the first step toward his service in the U.S. Marine Corps.

At the time, I didn't know the ROTC existed, but I see these guys wearing these blue uniforms, and I inquired. It was a program in which your first two years, you took naval courses. But if you chose the Marine Corps, your junior and senior years you put the Marine Corps emblem on and you took Marine courses. They had a Marine major there, so when I saw these guys with the blue uniform on and these Marine emblems, I signed up. I became what you call a contract student, as opposed to a scholarship student. The kids who knew about it applied while they were still in high school and they got a full scholarship.

Also, as a contract student, I was commissioned as a reserve officer in the Marine Corps. That would make a difference later on. When I wanted to be a regular officer, I had to apply for it.

He had dreamed of being a Marine since he had gone as a boy to the movies one day in Mobile and seen John Wayne star as Sergeant Stryker, a tough Marine in *Sands of Iwo Jima.*

> *My entry to the Marine Corps was sort of stimulated by growing up in a racist Southern town. Near where I lived was a theater called Harlem, and on Sunday, the Harlem had double features—that meant they played the same movie twice! The movie I saw was the* Sands of Iwo Jima, *starring John Wayne. I remembered Sergeant Stryker. I thought, "Anybody as tough as Sergeant Stryker, I want to join that outfit." So I can honestly say that Sergeant Stryker had landed one more recruit, because at that time I had never seen any black Marine officers.*

Sergeant Stryker eventually may have landed a second recruit. That would be Alden Lawson Jr.

> *Alden was truly a character. I met him in Chicago, maybe I was a sophomore in college. Corky and I used to hitchhike to Chicago. We didn't have anywhere to stay, so sometimes we would buy a ticket to the all-night theater and sleep through the movie.*
>
> *On one of these trips I went to a party and I met this little kid, Alden Lawson. I must have been 18 and Alden 16. He asked me where was I staying. I said, "Man, I'm staying at the damn theater. I got a ticket." He said, "Naw, come home with me." He took me home that night and introduced me to his parents and we got to be great friends.*
>
> *He chose the Marines because I had.*

After his freshman year, Gary returned to Mobile for the summer of 1955 and needed to take a course in trigonometry. The only college in the area that would allow black students was the Jesuit school, Spring Hill College.[79] It was the first Catholic college in the Southeast and it had just opened its doors to blacks in the past year when Gary took his course that summer.[80]

Being from a business-minded family, Gary majored in finance. This put him in courses such as Principles of Economics, Accounting, Business Finance and Life Insurance, all in his sophomore year. He did well, scoring in the above average or superior achievement levels by his final semesters.[81]

Although he was a lanky six-foot-six, Gary by his own admission had little jumping ability. He recalls with amusement that he tried out for the Notre Dame basketball team, but the coach said he needed to learn three things: to shoot, to pass and to dribble. "That means you need to learn how to play basketball," said Corky.

Gary gave it up.

I played basketball just briefly. I played on the intramural football team for a while, I think my freshman year. They had an honor society. How I got in it, I don't know. I surely didn't have any world-class grades to put me in an honor society. But it was called the Blue Circle Honor Society, and they played intramural football, they would volunteer to usher at the theater, stuff like that. Youngsters there now have never heard of it, but it was pretty hot stuff when I was a student. Maybe I did just well enough to get in it, and they wanted to diversify even back in those days. It sounds like something Father Hesburgh would be wanting to do.

A Summer to Remember

It was Father Hesburgh, or "Father Ted," who steered Gary to a job at the U.S. Steel plant in Chicago the summer after his sophomore year. It was a summer that would change his life.

I got a call that I should report to Father Hesburgh's office. You can imagine, it was my sophomore year, I was scared to death. So I go up to the president's office. He asked me if I had a job for the summer. I said, "No."—not even in Mobile did I have a job. That's when he told me that, if I knew somebody I could stay with in Chicago, he could get me a job at the steel mill. Was I interested? Absolutely!

That's how I ended up at U.S. Steel in Chicago.

"I was looking out especially for them," Hesburgh said. "I wanted our early black students to be very successful, and I wanted to get them good jobs. So that's why I did it."

The job I got—I was a stamper. They don't have stampers any more. I actually stood on a platform where the white-hot steel came by, and I had a sledge hammer with a number on it. When the steel came by and paused, I hit it, put an identifying number on it.

At the end of the day, you were tired. You didn't want anybody to know you were tired because they still had women working there. The women were called to work when the men all went off during World War II. Some of these women stayed on; they wouldn't give their jobs up when the men came back. These women could sling those sledge hammers like young men, and you'd be afraid to show these women you were tired and they were doing the same work!

I lost so much weight my mama cried when she saw me.

That summer in Chicago, Gary lived at first in the home of family friends from Mobile, the Bells. The mother was known to Gary as Aunt Margaret, although she was not a relative.

She was married to a dark-skinned man who was a Pullman porter. She was light skinned. She would ride a circuitous route to get to downtown Chicago to work as a teller in a bank, where they thought she was white her whole life.

She had two children, who were college kids at the time. Her son Spencer and her daughter Pat. Pat was afflicted with polio and had a limp. But she is just a super person. For a number of weeks, Pat used to get up like at 3:30 in the morning to fix me breakfast so I could go to the steel mill. What a great lady.

Gary later moved into a rooming house, but he and Spencer remained close.

Spencer told me he wanted me to meet this lady, Charlesetta Ferrill. I think he brought her by or she came to the apartment. Boy, she was a breathtaking beauty. She was going to Marquette, the Jesuit school in Milwaukee.

I was hit like a thunderbolt.

"It's just ninety miles from Chicago to Notre Dame," Charlesetta recalled. "I would catch the South Shore down or he would come up. The train was known as the 'Vomit Comet.' He was in his junior year and we fell in looove.

"We had many, many funny times. When we'd get together, that's where we had something in common, the humor. We used to say to one another, 'We're just jokes.' It's good to have that in college. It keeps you from remembering anything regressive!"

Like Gary, Charlesetta was born in Louisiana—New Orleans, where there were relatives—and she was raised a devout Catholic, attending all-black parochial schools in Chicago. Also like Gary, she had a beautiful mother, Otis Huckabee, who was born in Louisiana of apparently mixed heritage.[82]

"She was supposedly—none of us know this for sure, this is bits and pieces I picked up—she had a Jewish mother who had her illegitimately with an Italian father," Charlesetta said. "And Italians were looked upon like niggers, so her mother's Jewish family didn't want to keep the child. They graced Nane, a black woman, and her sister with the child, Otis. They just gave her the child and some funds. There's no birth certificate so we don't know anything other than the word of mouth. But Nane—it's Creole for 'godmother'—brought her to Chicago's South Side and raised her."

"Because she was a dark Italian, a dark Jewish chick," said Shawn, "she was basically raised as a black woman, and supposedly gorgeous. I only knew her when she was a fat granny, but she supposedly was beautiful when young, and that's who she was when she hooked up with Charlie Ferrill. So her grandchildren are part Italian and part Jewish. And you look at my brother Patrick and he looks so Jewish it's unbelievable."

Like Gary's dad, Charlesetta's father was a member of the black elite.

"My mother was quite a beautiful woman," Charlesetta said, "and my father was quite a well-off man. He was a 'policy' man. That's the numbers. There was a fellow who wanted to interview me about my father. Talking about the 'policy kings' of Chicago. My girlfriend's father was a policy king, too, and we talked about this. We decided not to do the interview."

The book she referred to was Nathan Thompson's *Kings: The True Story of Chicago's Policy Kings and Numbers Racketeers*. Published in 1994, it includes snapshots of her father, Charlie Ferrill, who in the 1930s and early 1940s ran one or more "wheels" on the South Side, an area of Chicago known as Bronzeville, and tried to keep his distance from the police and from Al Capone's Italian mob. Ferrill's legitimate enterprise was a real estate firm he ran with Leon Motts, and by Thompson's account he was a patriot and philanthropist as well as part of a coterie of wealthy black men who lived a swanky nightlife.[83] Thompson wrote:

> Born Charles Clyde Ferrill in Savannah, Georgia on Christmas Day 1892, Ferrill was a respected war veteran of the Eighth Regiment Armory and tied to old political factions as [black city council member Oscar] DePriest's collector in the 2nd Ward. . . .[84] Through the years, the Policy Kings were big supporters of race advancement. There were always food drives, clothing drives and much more. [Johnny] Wooley, Motts, Henry Young and Charlie Ferrill backed groups like the Wabash YMCA and the Chicago Defender Charities and were among the first financial backers of the first ever Bronzeville Parade, Bud Billiken Picnic and later the Bud Billiken Parade.[85]

The Eighth Regiment Armory in Chicago, now a historic landmark, was built for the "Fighting Eighth," a regiment of African American soldiers.[86] DePriest was Chicago's first black councilman and helped with the political arm of policy.[87]

"Of course the biggest social event going on in Chicago is what they call the Bud Billiken Parade," said Gary's friend, James Harrell. "It's like a Mardi Gras parade, and Charlesetta was a queen of the Bud Billiken Parade. It was about money and prestige, and she came from a privileged background."

Years later, Charlesetta laughed about being a Bud Billiken Parade queen. "I was just a plump ten-year-old," she said. But there were privileges in her youth, including being sent to a boarding school in Canada to learn French, after her father saw the benefits of being bilingual when traveling in Europe.[88]

She disagreed with Thompson about where her father was born.

"My first airplane trip was to Savannah, Georgia, with him. That was supposed to be his birthplace, but he wasn't born there. He was born in Macon. But he had friends there in Savannah in the mortuary and funeral home business. So we stayed with them. He wanted me to know he came from poor circumstances. He didn't want me to be a spendthrift, which I sure as hell was going to be if I ever got hold of it."

Charlesetta's parents did not get married or live together—her mother married another man and became Otis Brown—but they both doted on Charlesetta. She lived about ten years with one parent and ten with the other.[89]

"My father and mother had a going thing—'She's my child.' 'No, she's my child,'" Charlesetta recalled. "They were childish, but I remember that very well. My father wanted me to be with him. His saying was, 'Daddy and I stick together.'

"My mother, he just kind of ran roughshod over her."

Charlesetta was a beautiful, sharp girl. When I met her, I think she was with her father. Her home was on 60th and St. Lawrence streets, either a duplex or a house. There were huge rooms. These were nice homes, brick homes.

Her mother was very light skinned. I didn't get to know either of them very well, but they were always very nice.

For Charlesetta in her youth, there was overseas travel, most memorably to Rome. "We went on several European trips but mainly it was to go to Rome for the Holy Year," she said. "That was 1950. We were Catholic, so we went for the whole year of the Pope's blessing."

While her father was wealthy, he was not ostentatious.

"He was very conservative," she said. "He would just winter in different places, but he never had a summer home or anything like that. He owned apartments and we lived in one of his apartments. He was partners with Leon Motts, a realtor in Chicago at the time. They had a real estate office they worked out of on 51st Street and Michigan on the South Side."

While other black policy kings had run-ins with the Italian mob as it increasingly eyed the Bronzeville business, Ferrill apparently avoided any serious conflicts before he left the rackets.

"He was quite a get-along, jolly, hail-fellow, well-met man," said Charlesetta. "So he had few disagreements."

The weekend of Gary's graduation from Notre Dame, he and Charlesetta, with a child on the way, were married at Saint Anselm's church on the South Side. His childhood friend, Harold Jackson, was his best man,

and the Cooper family contingent from Mobile was on hand—young
Dominic, his sister, was excited to get a part in the wedding—as was his
proud grandfather, Osceola Osceola Cooper.[90]

A little guy, with a bald head, he rode a Greyhound bus from Los
Angeles to Notre Dame for my graduation. He was wrinkled, he had
wet on himself, but he was there.

While he and my father were not close at all, he and I got along.
When he died—I think I was with the Marines in Hawaii when he went
into a nursing home in Los Angeles. As best I can remember, when he
died he left me an apartment building in Chicago. It was on the South
Side. I don't remember getting much money for it. I remember it was
a two-story brick building, but nothing of great value.

The one missing figure at the wedding was Charlesetta's father, Charlie
Ferrill, who was ill with cancer.

"My father didn't like Gary," Charlesetta said, "so he feigned that he had
to stay in the hospital, but he did have cancer. But Gary's family came up
from Mobile for the wedding. That was pretty much the first time I had
met them. My dad was strict. He wouldn't allow me to go down there to
Mobile. So when they came up for the wedding, I met them—all of the
family except the youngest, Gary's brother, Mario."

A QUARTET OF MILESTONES

Along with graduation, marriage, and looming fatherhood, Gary
counted another milestone in 1958: he was commissioned a second lieutenant in the Marine Corps. This was a first. No African American had
ever gotten commissioned from the University of Notre Dame, certainly
not in the Navy ROTC.

So after the weekend of graduation and exchanging vows, he and
Charlsetta headed first for Mobile. Gary had talked about buying a station
wagon before graduation—*"because we would be traveling in the South*
and there was no motel for us to stay in, so we would sleep in the car"—but
their first purchase was a small sedan.

"We bought a Vauxhall," said Charlesetta. "It was an English small
car. It was crap, it wasn't worth two cents. We were driving in it once

from Washington back to Quantico and everything went off except the brakes. It was red. We got it in South Bend. We drove it from Chicago to Mobile. After we got rid of the Vauxhall, we got a blue station wagon. It wasn't that big, either. It was funny because you'd see Gary and he looked like a circus clown getting out of those cars. He was so tall and the cars were so small."

In Mobile, Charlesetta was introduced to the port city—and to Gary's youngest sibling, Mario. "He was the last child, you know, and when I was down there he was running around biting people. He was a character."

Then it was on to Quantico, Virginia, and Gary's first year of Marine officer training. And they didn't have to sleep in the car. When overnighting in Atlanta, they stayed in the Waluhaje Hotel. Opened in 1951 for a black clientele by developer Walter Aikens, it was a comfortable five-story hotel with apartments and a jazz nightclub.[91]

Just to show you how times have changed, it was one of the few places black people could stay when you were passing through Atlanta.

For Gary, the next stop after Atlanta was the Basic School, where his full-time Marine service would begin and a page of racial history in the U.S. Marine Corps would start to be turned.

4

A Black Marine Officer

When Gary Cooper was five years old, the Commandant of the Marine Corps, Major General Thomas Holcomb, made a withering declaration: "If it were a question of having a Marine Corps of 5,000 whites or 250,000 Negroes, I would rather have the whites."[92]

The last of the military services to desegregate, the Marine Corps viewed itself as a small, elite force. Given the prevailing racial climate during the Jim Crow era, the Corps remained all-white until World War II. But new manpower needs were pressing at a time when blacks were increasingly vocal about equal treatment and opportunities. At the insistence of President Roosevelt—who issued Presidential Executive Order 8802 to make it official—the door opened. On May 25, 1942, the commandant reluctantly called for the recruitment of "colored male citizens."[93]

So the word went out around the country that black youngsters could be Marines, and they came from all over. One guy was from Gadsden, Alabama, and his name was Edgar Huff. The other was Gilbert "Hash-mark" Johnson, from Mount Hebron in west Alabama.

Montford Pointers

Two of Gary Cooper's heroes, Huff and Johnson married sisters from Anniston and became legends in careers that began at the training camp known as Montford Point.[94] Unwilling to assign the new black recruits to a training center with whites, the Marines established a separate boot camp for blacks at Montford Point, which was adjacent to Camp Lejeune in North Carolina. Several hundred blacks had enlisted by the fall of 1942. Among those arriving in the early wave was Huff.

And he tells me that he hitchhiked from Anniston, Alabama, with a quarter in his pocket to become a Marine, there at Montford Point.

He said about the fourth night there the DI came in around midnight and he had a swagger stick. He ran it around a garbage can and that made a lot of noise. He got all of them up and said, "Niggers, come up here. Let me tell you something. You know, we've been fighting battles for 150 years, and we didn't need you then, and we don't need you now. I've talked to the sentry on the gate, and all you got to do is pack and walk home and nobody will charge you with nothing. You don't have to stay. But if you stay, it's going to be hell."

So he left. Huff was about the tallest of the guys, and they gathered around him and said, "Huff, what do you think? What should we do? Should we leave?"

And Huff said, "Well, look, man. I came down here with a quarter in my pocket, and yesterday I got two new pair of boots, six new pair of drawers and an overcoat, so I ain't going nowhere."

Indeed, they stayed. And Huff became the first black sergeant major and the first black man to spend thirty years in the Marine Corps.

Huff and Johnson were the first black drill instructors in the Corps and were the only two black Marines with the rank of sergeant major during World War II. In time Johnson became Battalion Sergeant Major of the Montford Point Recruit Depot. After his death in 1972, the Montford Point training center was renamed Camp Gilbert H. Johnson in his honor.[95]

They called him "Hashmark" because of the three diagonal service stripes, or "hashmarks," that he wore when he joined the Marines. The reason he had those three stripes is that he had been a Buffalo Soldier with the Army out west and then joined the Navy. When he switched to the Marines after it was opened to blacks, he was a private with three hashmarks, and in the town of Jacksonville, North Carolina, next to Camp Lejeune, the law officers knew that couldn't be right. So they kept arresting him for impersonating a Marine. Finally the general had to give him a letter authorizing him to wear the stripes, and that's how he got the nickname, "Hashmark" Johnson.

I met him—maybe at his home, I'm not sure where—but one thing about him was unforgettable: His eloquent voice. He spoke like a Harvard lawyer, just as clear and proper.

Black recruits at Montford Point initially were trained only by whites, but by mid-1943 most instructors were black. While discrimination was ending at the camp, it remained a fixture in the segregated South beyond the camp's walls. Being from Alabama, Huff and Johnson were familiar with segregation's rules, but others were not.[96]

"This was my first time in the Deep South," Montford Pointer Joseph Carpenter recalled for the Fleet Reserve Association publication, *FRA-today*. "We'd heard of all the lynching and read about the Ku Klux Klan and all that, so I wasn't too anxious to go out on the town on liberty."[97]

Racial discrimination also remained within the Corps generally as blacks kept being discouraged when they sought promotions, positions of leadership and roles in combat. But Montford Pointers, as they became known, set a standard and created a legacy of achievement that paved the way for generations of African American Marines, including Gary Cooper.

"The experience of our Montford Point Marines is one that I respect," said Major General Ronald Bailey, who came after them and rose to be the first African American commanding general of the 1st Marine Division, ". . . because they are the ones who, just like me, they volunteered. Can you imagine volunteering to go fight for your nation when you are called names and are denied the basic opportunities and rights that everyone else [had] that you served with? Yet they did and they endured."[98]

It was not until July 26, 1948, that racial discrimination in the military was officially abolished. President Truman's edict—Executive Order 9981—helped end segregation in the military services, including the Marines, but the larger society remained unchanged.[99]

"When you went off base," said Lieutenant General Frank E. Petersen, the first black Marine general, "it was a totally different environment in that the Truman edict had cleaned up most of the segregation in the military establishment, but once you went off base then you were subjected of course to the local rules of segregation. As an example, we would ride the bus into town from base. We could sit anywhere we wanted on the bus when we were on base. As soon as we went outside the gate, we had to get up and move to the back of the bus. It was the same in reverse coming back on board the base. Very crazy situation."[100]

Cooper did not know about Montford Point when he was commissioned at Notre Dame. It was not until later, when he was a captain preparing to be the first African American to command a Marine rifle company in combat, that the courage of Montford Pointers hit home.

If they could do it then, I told myself, I could do it now.

QUANTICO

When Gary arrived at the Basic School for officer training in the summer of 1958, he already had memories of the place—memories of enduring racially biased tests of his willpower—that he would never forget.

He had undergone ROTC training at the Marine Corps base at Quantico, Virginia, during the summer after his junior year at Notre Dame. This training was a fixture of the Navy ROTC program, giving future Marine officers a taste of the rigors of the military regimen. As a rare black among the cadets, there were tests he alone faced.

It was the summer of 1957 and, as he later recalled, the train from Washington, D.C., to Quantico was segregated.

I can remember pulling up at the train station, and I was the only one who got off the back car. There was a bunch of young white kids in the front that said, "Hey, boy, you're coming with us." And I ran.

That's probably the best line I ever got in, in my life, because guess what they were giving away? They were teaching you how to be a leader.[101]

At Quantico, Gary was assigned to barracks by the river, and a white staff sergeant, in particular, put Gary in his crosshairs. Among his tricks: He would get Gary out of the rack in the middle of the night, while everybody else was sleeping, and take him down to the basement to do pushups.

The sergeant would say, "Give me ten more, nigger. Give me ten more."

I would do the ten.

"Now ten more, nigger. Ten more."

When I finally could not or would not do ten more, the sergeant

looked at me and snarled, "Hit me. Hit me. Aren't you mad at me?
Swing at me, goddam it!"

To this day Gary does not know exactly where he got the fortitude to
resist punching the man out. All he knew was that if he so much as lifted
a hand, his career would be over.[102]

There was more.

One morning I was the Student Company Commander and we were
out in the field. The white DI didn't like something I did, and he said,
"Come over here, Cooper, you shithead." And he took me over and he
took a sapling—this sapling must have been ten feet high—and he bent
it and put it under my arm. "Cooper," he said, "hold this tree until I
tell you to stop."

So they went somewhere and ate chow, and I'm still holding this tree.
Hell, it got to be 14-hundred hours, 15-hundred, 18-hundred. It started
getting dark. I'm still holding this tree.

The company goes back in the barracks, and I guess they had a
muster and found out Cooper was gone. So about 20-hundred that
night, out come these jeeps and these lights. People are searching for
me. "Cooper, Cooper, where are you?" Then the battalion commander
drove up.

"Cooper," he said, "why in the hell are you here? What in the hell
are you doing?"

"Sir, I'm holding this tree!"

"Why are you holding this tree?"

"Sir, the staff sergeant told me to hold it until he told me to stop!"

The battalion commander, unamused and making plans to chew out
the staff sergeant, told Gary he could go. That test was over.

But the young Marine ROTC cadet had learned a lesson: *I knew that*
they didn't need much of an excuse to send my ass home.

A year later, in the summer of 1958, when Gary arrived at Quantico
for the thirty-two-week officer training program at the Basic School, he
would find no similar acts of racial bias, at least not on the Marine Corps
base, where blacks were scarce anyway. Away from the base, however,
segregation remained a way of life.

The thirty-two weeks was much fairer. In fact, when I think of those thirty-two weeks, I don't remember anything in the Marine Corps that I found not to be fair. Now of course your wife couldn't go to the laundromat, you couldn't go to lunch in town. But that's the bigger society. The base, I remember it being pretty fair.

"The segregation was thick. It really was," Charlesetta said of the off-base community at Quantico. "In the apartment complex in town, there was one black officer across the street. It was just him and his wife. We would go into town to do washing and I put my clothes in and she put her clothes in. The lady who ran the place came up and said, 'What are you doing?' We said we're washing our clothes. She said, 'Don't you know no black son of a bitch can come in here?' I said, 'Well, we're officers' wives.' She said, 'I don't care if you're the general's wife. Get out of here! Take your clothes and get out of here!'

"We were mortified, but we got out of there."

For Cooper, the overriding mission of the thirty-two weeks was to be an infantry officer—the John Wayne kind of Marine—and it began to fall into place.

I was particularly thrilled, and one reason I worked hard—a lot of us worked hard—was because I wanted to be an infantry officer. During those days, very few minorities got assigned infantry. It was very unusual for them to put a black officer in infantry. They would send you to supply school, they would send you to motor transport, they would send you to communications, but not somewhere where you could command other Marines.

The tall, self-assured Cooper, already showing the leadership skills that would mark his life's work, won his infantry assignment, known as his MOS, or Military Occupational Specialty.

To my joy, I was assigned an 0302 MOS, an infantry unit leader, which really thrilled me, because I loved shooting, even though I didn't grow up owning guns or doing a lot of camping. I guess I liked what I saw Sergeant Stryker do.

Also, I was convinced if I could not become an infantry officer, the Marine Corps was not going to be for me for very long.

But now he was one, and the opportunity to command Marines was distinctly a possibility.

If you look at it from the student's point of view, you might say it's the luck of the draw that you get picked for Infantry. But maybe from the view of the people—the seniors who make the decision—it's earned. They observe you giving orders in the field and excelling in similar drills and they base their decision on real accomplishments.

He also was assigned to the Marine base at Kaneohe on the Hawaiian island of Oahu.

Kaneohe was the first duty station I was sent to after going through the thirty-two weeks at the Basic School. There was a day where they said they were going to tell you where your first duty assignment was going to be and they posted it on the door at a place on the base. You had to go and look to find out. Some of my buddies saw where they were going and I said, "Where am I going?" They said, "Go see your damn self!" Because they were pissed. They were going to Camp Lejeune and Camp Pendleton, and guess where I was going—Oahu, Hawaii!

What they didn't tell us in those days, what I found out later, was that they tried to send the black officers to these bases like Kaneohe on Oahu to avoid the segregation problems at Camp Lejeune and other places.

Getting the infantry assignment meant that Cooper, a black Marine officer, would be leading an infantry unit, a platoon, as its commander. But to make history, he would need to lead a rifle company in combat. It was a thought the twenty-two-year-old Cooper didn't dwell on at the time—his overriding desire, then and later, was simply to be a top Marine officer outstanding in his assignments. But while racial milestones were scarcely on his mind, as he left Quantico in March 1959 for his first posting, his race remained a significant factor in his military future.

KANEOHE

Second Lieutenant Gary Cooper's paperwork preceded his arrival at Marine Base Kaneohe. It went to the headquarters of E 2-4. That was Echo Company, an infantry company with the 2nd Battalion, 4th Marine Division.

We liked that because 2-4 was a very famous unit in the Marine Corps. They had been in a lot of battles. They were well-known for being a good fighting unit. They call them the "Magnificent Bastards." At E 2-4, 1st Lieutenant Bill Bates was the executive officer.

"The day Gary Cooper checked in as a brand spanking new lieutenant right out of the Basic School, I was executive officer of E 2-4," Bates said. "I was the first officer to meet him when he came in the door. Me and the first sergeant sat side-by-side. Gary was brought in by a clerk. He appeared to be a really big Caucasian with a good sun tan.

"I took Gary in to meet the company commander, a fellow named Nick Hart, who retired as a colonel and is probably one of my best friends in the world. I still didn't have an impression of Gary yet, it hadn't hit me yet.

"I took him in to meet Nick, and when I took him in the first sergeant was standing there, a big Pole, I should say he's a slob actually, a big, tall, black-haired guy, a gentleman of the first order, and he's got a smile on his face. He handed me the record, Gary's record book, and pointed to 'Race.' And of course it said 'Black.' I was flabbergasted. First black officer I ever met."

Gary's paperwork actually used a phrase from that era—"Negroid"[103]— and it's not surprising Bates had not met a black Marine officer: They were few and far between, even at Kaneohe, which was home to a Marine air base. Then-Captain Frank Emmanuel Petersen, who had made history as the first black Marine aviator, arrived at Kaneohe in 1958, the year before Gary.

Black officers at the time were a rarity in the Corps. So you can understand how absolutely happy I was, after being posted to Hawaii, to find out about Frank Petersen—until my arrival he was the only black Marine officer on the whole island. And to find out he was the first black fighter pilot the Marine Corps had ever had was another thrill.

I'd never known a pilot before and here was Frank. We'd go to the officers' club together, and we'd both be asked for our identification cards. And when we'd go to the post exchange, whether we were together or not, we always had the feeling we were being followed. And we were—but we didn't mind. You see, we'd turn around suddenly when we got that

feeling and we'd catch some rather embarrassed black enlisted Marines
following us around—amazed at what they were seeing—real, live black
Marine officers on deck. They couldn't believe it. They simply couldn't
believe it. They had to get close, to see whether or not we were real.[104]

"We socialized together quite a bit," Petersen said, "because quite
frankly with so few black officers we all tended to work together, and
subsequently by the time I left, there was a group of about six or seven
of us including the man who would become the first African American
admiral, Sam Gravely."[105]

There was little or no talk among them about making history.

"We didn't think of ourselves that way as opposed to just trying to
get the job done," said Petersen. "No one had visions of 'I'm going on to
become an admiral, I'm going on to become a general.' That was never
part of our discussion. We were just satisfied with what we were doing."[106]

You know in those days I didn't think of becoming the first black. I
was thinking about becoming a captain.

Cooper and Petersen had their families with them for frequent get-
togethers. And the men would enjoy nights out at the bars—maybe out
longer than their wives back at home with the children found agreeable.

We talked a lot because we were the only black officers probably in
the entire Pacific, and lived not far from each other. So we would go
out on Liberty together, and stayed in trouble with our wives, but had
great fun. We would go over to Waikiki on liberty and come back late.
He would be driving and say, "I'm not stopping at your house. I'm just
slowing down and you jump out of the car. I don't want your wife to
get me."

He was so funny, and we have a lot of laughs about those days now.
One day at Kaneohe was no laughing matter. It was one of those mild
Hawaiian days with heavenly blue skies that normally would transport
the spirit into bliss. But this was just the opposite.[107]

We got a report of a mid-air collision and the pilots were missing.
Frank was a jet pilot. He's one of the few people we know who ejected
twice in combat—once in Korea and once in Vietnam. Now at Kaneohe
Bay there were three planes flying and there was a mid-air collision.

Nobody knew who was involved, but Frank had been flying.

I remember the word going around. I was at home. We lived in housing on the base then and you knew most of the people. But even in knowing most of the people, the infantrymen kind of stayed by themselves and the aviators did too. But since I knew him, they called me and we all went around to his house. We were with his wife, Ellie. Everybody was waiting. Nobody had heard anything and it was pretty somber.

But lo and behold, down the street comes Captain Petersen! Had a parachute on his back. Everybody was thrilled. We were very sad the other guys didn't make it, but thrilled that he was not the one who had the mid-air collision.

As Petersen noted in his autobiography: "Helluva way to have your friendship validated."

It would be a lasting friendship between Petersen and Cooper, long after Kaneohe when they went mostly their separate ways. But Kaneohe was especially memorable.

There was the indignity of being treated differently than whites, even on base, where they alone were asked for ID cards at the officers' club.

*I remember the first time we went in the officers' club at Kaneohe Bay and they came up and asked for our ID card. So we gave them the ID card. We were mad as hell, and we left. This was like on Friday, and [Petersen] said, "Cooper, let me tell you what we're going to do tomorrow night. Let's go wait until that son of a b**** is really crowded." When the staff sergeant came, we said, "You ask everybody in here for their ID card, then you come back and ask us. If you don't want to do it, call the MPs." That was the end of that.*[108]

Off base, there was little of the segregationist mindset in Honolulu as there had been in the town outside the base at Quantico where Charlesetta's eyes were opened to the racism.

"I wasn't so naive that I didn't know it to exist," she said. "But I was light-skinned. Many times I was mistaken to be Caucasian rather than African American. So it didn't affect us too terribly much.

"That was the difference between Pete Petersen and Ellie and Gary and me. Ellie was fair but Pete was very dark. When they came to Hawaii they didn't seem to have the ease of renting like we did."

"Hawaii was fairly open," said Petersen. "There was no off-base discrimination so to speak because, let's face it, Hawaii was a nation populated by people of many colors."

"But there wasn't sufficient housing on the base to accommodate all the families," he said, "so what we would do is go off base and rent civilian dwellings until such time that base housing became available. In one of those, I was turned down on several occasions by off-base realtors who quite frankly did not want to rent to minorities, or blacks I should say specifically.

"Base officials weren't really aware of the problem. But as soon as I voiced my concern, they jumped in and gave assistance to help me get off-base housing."[109]

While Petersen did have trouble finding a real estate agent willing to rent to a black man—Petersen said President Barack Obama's father, in Hawaii at the time, even got involved as an advocate for less restrictive housing—the Coopers had no similar problem. Their first home was even on the beach at Kailua, a short drive to Kaneohe. It was better than the base housing that came later.

The beach house had windows with no panes, just wooden shutters. It was beautiful.

"Kailua was fun," said Charlesetta. "The military housing we had later was at Kaneohe. This was a house on the beach at Kailua—it belonged to a Mississippi doctor, he rented to us—and it was very nice." She laughed: "We got more visitors there!"

They included Bates, who was with Echo Company several more months before rotating out.

"There were not any racial boundaries over there in Hawaii. Families would meet for cookouts, dinner parties, picnics, the whole nine yards," he said.

It was during Gary's tour on Kaneohe that his two daughters, Joli and Shawn, were born on Oahu. With little Patrick in tow, Charlesetta had her hands full.

Her father, Charlie Ferrill, also visited, but he was looking old and ill with cancer, no longer the shrewd and smooth king of policy and real estate on Chicago's South Side. He died in 1961.[110]

I would walk with him around the block. He would get tired and stop and sit on the curb and talk to me. That's when he would tell me the stories about Al Capone and the Jones brothers who had a run-in with Capone.

The Jones brothers, as vividly recounted by Nathan Thompson in his book on Chicago's policy kings, were legendary African American vice chiefs out of Mississippi—Edward, George and Mack Jones—who took charge of the policy market in Bronzeville, became famously rich and married eye-catching women. But the world they once controlled—with Gary's father-in-law, Charlie Ferrill, in a supportive role—was in time undermined by a Capone successor, Sam Giancana. By then, Ferrill had left the racket to others.[111]

"Dad visited in Hawaii," said Charlesetta." He was very sick, but he came before he died. His big desire was to see the hula girls with the Arthur Godfrey show. He gave me a prime compliment. We were going to Mass one Sunday and he said, 'You know, Charlesetta, I wanted to see the hula girls to see how pretty they were. But you're the most beautiful of all. That was because I was getting up each morning and fixing him breakfast and giving him hot baths, alcohol baths, because he was in a lot of pain."

While Gary had only fond memories of his father-in-law—and no recollection of a business offer Charlie Ferrill supposedly made—Charlesetta in later years felt that her dad had never really warmed up to her husband and his desire to be a Marine officer.

"He offered to buy into an insurance company in New Orleans so that we—or specifically I, wouldn't need to live in Mobile, which he knew was a small town comparatively," she said. "And Gary raised hell. He said, 'My family has an insurance company.'

"I was in business administration and I thought we were going together into the insurance business with his family. But when he said he wanted to be a general, I knew that his heart was set with the Marines.

"So it was okay with me."

A VIEW FROM A HILL

While socializing with the families of friends made Gary's Kaneohe tour enjoyable, he was excelling as a platoon leader and making the assignment memorable.

When I was in Kaneohe, we would go to sea. They would put the Marine battalion on a ship and we would cruise around in case they needed you to land somewhere. They would plan an operational problem and we would land in Taiwan and play like we're going into battle. So there were training exercises in Taiwan while we were stationed in Kaneohe.

Once when I was in Taiwan, we went out on shore patrol—we were like military policemen—and I go in this bar and I see some guy under the table, stretched out, with a uniform on. I pull him over—he was a classmate from Notre Dame!

It was an experience. You'd go in the hills of Taiwan and the natives would have on loin cloths and carrying bows and arrows.

On one of these trips, I saw Chiang Kai-shek, the leader of Taiwan. He had been a leader of the Chinese Nationalist Party on the mainland China before the Communist takeover. I was marching in front of him. There was Chiang Kai-shek.

At Kaneohe, we had a major by the name of Kurt C. Lee, a Chinese officer, the only one in the whole Marine Corps. He was immaculate. I mean, he looked like he had just stepped out of a pressing machine all the time. When we went to Taiwan, when I was a young lieutenant, people would be lined up all outside the base. The colonel would ask Kurt Lee to go out to greet them because they had heard there was a Chinese U.S. Marine officer. And there he was.

He was impressive.

Lee's record gave Gary and other minorities plenty of reason to admire him—a Korean War hero, he was the first Asian American officer in the Marine Corps.

"His legacy will always be that he broke down barriers," Freeman Lee, past commander of VFW Chung Mei Post 8358, told the *Sacramento Bee* in a Lee obituary. "He had to go up against prejudices and racism, and he was able to overcome that."[112]

At Kaneohe, Cooper's abilities to lead a Marine platoon and drive up morale at all levels were evident.

"While there were black Marines obviously in the company," said Bates, "I would say the majority of his platoon were white. I'm almost positive that his platoon sergeant and most of his sergeants were white at that point. I don't remember a black sergeant.

"He didn't have any problems, and I wasn't aware of any of them having problems. If they did, they probably got over it quickly."

In the fall of 1959 Cooper's leadership skills were seen by the right person, General Frederick L. Wieseman.

Kaneohe is where I got command of my first unit, a platoon, in the Marine Corps. And of course that was where, out in the field one day, General Wieseman saw me.

I was out with my platoon and we were maneuvering as if fighting the enemy. I didn't know it but General Wieseman was watching, and about a week or two later I get a call from my colonel. He said, "Get up here, lieutenant. The general wants to see you."

I didn't have a clue why the general wanted to see me. I'm scared to death—a goddam general and here I am a second lieutenant! But I went up, and the general had something to tell me.

"Lieutenant Cooper," he said, "you didn't know it but I was on a hill and I observed you run the infantry in the attack exercise with your platoon, and I was impressed. And I find out that you are a reserve officer and only obligated to serve two years. I want to encourage you to apply for a regular commission, because I was impressed with your action. The reason I want you to apply, one day we're going to need more colored officers. I will write a recommendation personally for you."

Gratified and excited, Cooper applied for a regular commission. Wieseman's endorsement was ringing:

I have personally observed this young officer's performance as a platoon leader during field training exercises. He is a dynamic individual endowed with a fine physique and has acquired an unusual degree of professional knowledge. He employs these assets most effectively in leading his men.

Lieutenant COOPER is a negro whose fine character, conduct, intelligence, good sense and good fellowship are such that no residual bias on the part of his superiors or subordinates is manifest. Men of his qualifications do more to effect the desired ultimate integration of the races in the Armed Forces than all the other means combined. His contribution to that end will be a substantial dividend which the Marine Corps will gain by commissioning him a regular officer in addition to the great worth and potential for growth he possesses as a routine candidate.[113]

Cooper became a 1st Lieutenant in December 1959, and within two years he was on the USMC's radar as an African American officer who had taken a huge stride in the right direction. Back home, protests against racial segregation were spreading, including beatings and firebombings of Freedom Riders in his home state of Alabama. He was ending his tour in Hawaii in June 1962 as the segregationist rhetoric rose with George Wallace's successful bid for governor of Alabama. Cooper was staging a different sort of protest on behalf of black Americans, but resistance remained. Even in his prized Marine Corps.

No 8th & I

After Hawaii, I wanted to go to 8th and I, the oldest post in the Corps. I knew that at 8th and I, the historic Marine Barracks in Washington, only the sharpest Marines were assigned, and I knew that no sharper Marine walked than Cooper. So I applied to go to 8th and I, and felt certain that I was going to get those orders.

Known as 8th and I for its street location in Washington, D.C., the Marine Barracks was one of the most coveted posts in the USMC. I even heard that orders had arrived at Kaneohe for a lieutenant to be stationed at 8th and I.

I assumed they were for me, so I go up to check on these orders. But they weren't for Cooper. They were for another lieutenant. Instead they sent me to the Marine Corps Supply Center in Barstow, California. I was heartbroken.

Years later he would learn one possible reason he didn't get that plum assignment: They had a written memo saying that no black officers would be assigned to the Marine Barracks at 8th and I. No blacks.

A trailblazing Marine officer out of Guam, Brigadier General Ben Blaz—a graduate of Notre Dame like Cooper, but several years older— told him about the rule. Blaz, who became a brigadier general in 1977, was the first non-white Marine to reach that rank and the first person from Guam to become a flag officer in any branch of the U.S. military service.[114] He had a keen eye for the injustices of the system, and later represented Guam in Congress.

So instead of the East Coast posting at 8th and I that he wanted, Cooper and his family took a detour to a remote California base. Barstow was on an isolated track of the famous highway Route 66 on its run between Los Angeles and Las Vegas. It was a stopover in the desert. This was decidedly not a step toward leading a rifle company in combat, although the first stirrings of an expanding U.S. involvement in Vietnam's conflict had begun. Combat was a possibility.

Nobody wanted to go to Barstow. The rumor was you had been passed over, meaning you had been up for promotion a few times and didn't make it, or on your way out. Barstow was a supply center, and that's the last damn place an infantry man wants to go. But I had worked to become a real professional then and I told myself, "You know what I'm going to do? I'm going to be the best Marine that I can be."

Barstow was almost a disaster, though. Cooper, as assistant provost marshal for the base, followed protocol too closely when a certain general appeared.

The general was Herman Nickerson, and he somehow was rubbed the wrong way when he was driven past the Marine sentry, a short black kid whose snappy movements waving cars through the gate at Barstow usually drew raves.

People would come through the gate just to see him. He was so sharp, this kid was so good on the gate waving cars through that they used

to call him "Mr. Machine" because of his arm movements. All of my
Marines were immaculate.

But Nickerson's aide, a major, told Cooper the sentry's shirt was tai-
lored too tight.

"I'm going to come down and inspect your men on Saturday. Have
them ready at 10:00 o'clock," he said.

"Major, I take orders from my commanding officer, not from the
general's aide, so I suggest you call my commanding officer."

The major hung up. He was a former enlisted man and a little older
and pretty stern. The next day he called back, saying the general told
him to inspect my men on Saturday as previously planned.

I balked again: "Well, Major, I respectfully would like to remind you
that I take orders from my commanding officer, and I would appreciate
it if you called him."

It was one rebuff too many. By Monday, Cooper had been relieved of
his duties as assistant provost marshal. He was now the special services
officer, overseeing bowling allies, horse stables and the swimming pool. A
huge comedown. To his amazement, however, he got a good fitness report.

While the new assignment was anathema to an infantry officer, it
turned out to be an enjoyable—and survivable—career twist for a man
with a wife and three young children. He also would make captain at
Barstow in February 1963, and it was here that he expressed officially for
the first time his concern about the lack of black officers in the Corps.
In a letter, Cooper suggested the Marines recruit from the historically
black colleges.

We were all concerned about there being so few African American
officers. I was so concerned that I wrote a letter, making some recom-
mendations on how to get more officers. But even then I had enough
sense to know I didn't need to go around the chain of command. So I
gave it to my boss, my commanding officer, and it went up to our gen-
eral—this is General Nickerson. He was supposed to make comments
and forward it.

Instead, he called me in and starts to chew me out: "Look, the com-
mandant doesn't need any advice from you, a captain. What makes

you think the commandant of the Marine Corps needs your advice on recruiting?"

I didn't say too much, and he finally forwarded it because I wouldn't withdraw it and he had to forward it. But I never received a response.

Still, Cooper's push for more diversity persisted. In 1968, when he was assigned to Marine Corps Headquarters, it was Nickerson who had diversity on his plate.

This guy was now a three-star in charge of manpower at Marine Corps Headquarters, and he called me over to get my counsel on how to recruit minority officers. I said, "General, that's interesting. Do you remember that I was the one who sent you a letter about that at Barstow?"

Once again, Cooper had rubbed Nickerson the wrong way: He threw me out! He didn't want to be reminded.

He was that kind of guy. I might add, it wasn't just with me. He had that kind of personality.

But overall Barstow was a good tour, a time when Gary could be close to his young family.

"I do remember when he took me up to the shooting range," said his son, Patrick. "He had me run the obstacle course with him. This was when I was a kid, in Barstow, out in the desert."

We had a nice house there on base. Behind our house, maybe about three hundred meters, there was a base stable. I didn't know beans about riding horses. But I started going to the stables, I learned how to ride horses, and I got qualified where I could take trail riders out—officers' wives, little kids from town. We would go on picnics. We would go out the night before and put beer in places in the woods. We'd take people out on trails. That was an awful lot of fun.

But happy hour was another matter. We would get there about six o'clock, and man, about 7:30 or 8 o'clock I would feel myself getting drunk as a skunk. And I know, first of all, I can't be there staggering in front of these folks. So I would maybe get a ride home, sometimes I'd leave Charlesetta there.

And years later, after Vietnam, I'm at Marine Headquarters in Washington and I meet this black master sergeant.

He says, "You don't remember me, do you?"'

"No, I sure don't."

"Let me tell you something. You should. Because I used to be the bar tender at the club at Barstow, and every time I would give the white folk one drink, I'd give you two."

I could've beat him in the damn head! He thought he was being nice to me!

Having fun on trail rides and at happy hour was not the endgame for Cooper, however. Even at Barstow, he set high standards for himself.

"He was the most squared-away Marine I had ever seen to that point," said Joe Wilson, a young Marine at the time who would become a general and one of Gary's good friends. "I had only been a Marine on active duty since July of 1962. But when I met him at Barstow, he was impressive. Very distinguished, so neat and professional. It just made a great impression on me."

Cooper's next assignment also would portend great changes in his life and career.

MAKING WAVES

Finishing at Barstow, he got orders to report to the USS *Chicago*, a guided missile cruiser that was docked at Hunter's Point at San Francisco.

That's a choice assignment. Marines dream about it, going to sea. The term "Marine" means "soldier of the sea." So to command a Marine detachment on a cruiser, only the sharpest could go.

Arriving in San Francisco, Cooper was given orders to delay for one week before going aboard the *Chicago*. That was puzzling. Why the delay?

There was a problem, it seems. Cooper didn't know it at the time, but the Marines had a rule—possibly even a written order, he thinks—that blacks were not to command a detachment aboard a ship. A glance at Cooper's photo had not set off alarms. But, as an officer who was at head-quarters at the time told him later, a red flag went up when they looked at his file and it said "Negro" in the box for race.

The Marine Corps had never sent a Negro officer aboard a Navy ship, so they had to check with the Navy to get permission, and after the delay, the Navy gave permission. And on that day I became the first black officer to command a Marine detachment aboard a ship.

Only the major ships had Marine detachments—battle ships, cruisers and aircraft carriers. This was a guided missile cruiser, so one of our missions was the security of the nuclear weapons. We would stand guard, check the hatches every half hour, twenty-four hours a day.

And the Chicago *was a new ship, it was still in the shipyard when I got the assignment. Nobody had seen a ship with elevators! Also, when the captain wanted to speak to you, on the old ships he'd say, "Now hear this, now hear this," on the microphone. But on the* Chicago, *he could say, "Now see this. Now see this." We had television sets.*

There were about forty Marines in the detachment, and all but a handful were white. Cooper also knew the value of an experienced first sergeant, and he didn't have one when he arrived on the USS *Chicago*.

When I was the platoon leader at Kaneohe, my company gunny, who is like the senior staff NCO, he was a Montford Point Marine, and I was ready to do something foolish. I was about to throw my clothes in with the wash of the other men, the enlisted men, and the gunny called me aside and said, "Lieutenant, don't do that, and I'll tell you why. You don't let enlisted men wash an officer's clothes. You're not supposed to do that."

I wasn't thinking, but he reminded me I was about to do something that wasn't right. The gunny was really crucial.

Adding a gunnery sergeant to the Marines aboard the *Chicago*—a Montford Pointer, no less—was a memorable occasion for Cooper.

One day one of my black Marines was on duty, he was on watch duty, and he called down, "Captain Cooper, please come up here right away. I want to show you something." So I came up right away and I looked down toward the end of the pier, and walking toward the ship was a black Marine with his first-sergeant stripes on, coming to be our first sergeant.

His name was Jim McCargo, and he was a Montford Pointer. He was almost like a grandfather to us. He helped keep us out of trouble— "Captain, you've got to sign this, you've got to get this in." It was a great example of how these guys from Montford Point helped those of us who were officers and we sort of walked on their shoulders.

It's a case of those old guys looking out for you, keeping you from making stupid mistakes.

Now, the captain of this ship was a guy named John Dacey. He was maybe five-foot-two, wore glasses, didn't look like a big physical military man, never raised his voice. We did have a microphone on the ship, it was called a 1MC. He'd get on it: "Men of the Chicago, *this is your captain speaking. I'd like everyone to know how thrilled we are to have our Marines aboard. We welcome them so much. They're so important." One day he would say, "I'm here today to thank the men in the Engineering Department." Never raised his voice.*

He was a captain while he was on the ship, but he got selected to become an admiral. What a great guy he was. He was the one who took to me and allowed me to do training to serve as Officer of the Deck Underway, the first black Marine ever to serve in that position.

This was most unusual, to become qualified as Officer of the Deck Underway. What that means is you go through very strenuous training and when everybody is asleep at night you can be the senior person on the ship. You're the Officer of the Deck Underway. It was a big deal. If you mentioned to sailors that you were the OD Underway, that gets their attention.

It was while serving as Officer of the Deck Underway that Cooper was confronted by a young white Navy ensign who was trying to decide if he should call this black man "Sir."

I had been on watch from midnight to oh-four hundred. What happened, before you go to hit the rack, you go down to the wardroom to drink some coffee. That's when this young officer came in and spoke to me.

"You're Captain Cooper, right?"

"Yes."

"I'm from Mississippi, and I haven't decided whether I'm going to call you 'Sir' or not."

"That's no problem. What time is it now?"

"It's zero-four-forty five."

"You've got till zero-seven hundred in the morning when you see me to make your mind up. You understand me?"

"Yes . . ."—there was a long pause—". . . sir."

"Good!"

The white officer had come around. It just took him a few minutes.

Cooper was assigned to the USS *Chicago* for two years beginning in 1964. In 1965 the path-setting black Navy officer, Samuel Gravely, would take command of the USS *Taussig*, eventually putting both Cooper and Gravely at sea around the same time. Gravely, who would become the first black to reach flag rank in the Navy, already had been the first African American to command a U.S. fighting ship, the USS *Falgout*, in 1962. Now he was at the helm of a bigger warship.[115]

Cooper, who had met Gravely at Kaneohe, was aware of the Navy officer's posting on the *Taussig*.

I was on the USS Chicago, *where I served as Officer of the Deck Underway, and I sent Admiral Gravely—he was a commander then—a flag message passing along my respects. From the USS* Taussig *he sent back his regards.*

It was a brief exchange of correspondence at sea, but historic nonetheless.

For Gary, now in his late twenties, there was a growing sense that he was on top of his game, projecting an air of authority.

"You don't know it, but those young sailors are scared to death of you," his friend and fellow officer, Bruce Forester, told him. As a Marine officer, Cooper would at times wear a boat cloak—a striking cloak of dark blue, scarlet on the inside, laid over the shoulder and down the side. "You walk around with that swagger stick, they'd run when they saw you," Forester said.[116]

Hunter's Point, at San Francisco, was our shipyard, but when they finished up completing the ship we went down the coast to our port, at San Diego. There was a boxing club there, the Archie Moore boxing club. This was the club of the famous professional boxer Archie Moore. On weekends, I would go there. I would wear the boat cloak. I'd have the swagger stick.

I didn't know it at the time, but a young man there was impressed by the sharpness of my pressed uniform, the boat cloak and all, the demeanor of a Marine officer. He knew he wanted to be like that. And years later, this young man—Daniel Freeman—he knocked on my door in Mobile and introduced himself. He said he just wanted to tell me that he had become a pilot in the United States Marine Corps. He was a young second lieutenant going through flight school in Pensacola. It had all started for him at the boxing club.[117]

The training ring in San Diego may have been a memorable venue for Cooper, but boxing was not his strong suit.

Now, while I would visit the Archie Moore boxing club, I'm not a boxer, not a trained boxer. I always stayed in good shape, though, and when I had a platoon at my first duty station, back at Kaneohe—we're young lieutenants, maybe twenty-two years old—the troops were having a boxing battle. One lieutenant was named Kelly and one was somebody from New York. A call goes out, "We want to see the lieutenants box."

Kelly says, "I'll box you, Cooper."

So I get in the ring—man, the troops are cheering, I make it through one round, he's beating the shit out of me. Boy, this guy hit me so goddam hard, I saw stars. But I didn't want to get knocked out in front of the troops. I grabbed him and when that round was over, it luckily was the last round.

Nobody ever got me in a boxing ring again. I told them, "Next time I'll have my goddam pistol."

A NOTE TO MYSELF

Early in his USS *Chicago* assignment Cooper was feeling assured enough of his Marine career that he could set a goal, even write it down—like a bet with himself.

We were out at sea one night—it's June of 1964—and I was thinking about my career and what I wanted to do. I had only seen one or two generals in my life, and these were little white guys who didn't look that impressive to me. I thought: What makes these folks so sharp that they can get to be general and I can't?

So I sat down in my cabin, I wrote a note to myself, I sealed it, and I put down on the back, "Do not open for 20 years." I put it in my scrapbook and kept it on a shelf.

When I wrote that note, what I was remembering was what the Dominican Nun, Sister Eulogia, had told us at Most Pure Heart of Mary High School: "There's always room at the top."

The note was short: "Did you make it?"

In the spring of 1966, as he prepared to leave the USS *Chicago* for his next assignment, he knew that getting to Vietnam—and leading a rifle company in combat—was crucial to making it. He volunteered to go there.

Vietnam was just getting started, the Marine units have just landed, and I'm a captain and getting somewhat senior. As an infantry officer, I told myself, "You better get in combat."

So I knew I needed to do that. I'm coming up for major, and maybe the war will be over and I wouldn't get a chance to have that on my record.

But then I found out there was a rule against consecutive overseas tours. I didn't know seagoing was an overseas tour, but they told me it was and I couldn't go to Vietnam because I was already on an overseas tour and you couldn't go from one overseas tour to another.

That's when he remembered General Fred Wieseman, who had endorsed him as a model of the African American Marine officer needed to integrate the Corps.

He was now a three-star and Chief of Staff of Personnel at Marine Corps Headquarters. So I sat down one day and wrote General Wieseman a letter. I explained my problem and how disappointed I was at not being able to go to Vietnam straight from the USS Chicago.

Now every officer has a monitor. You're a captain, so your monitor may be a major, and he may have fifty or one hundred officers that he monitors. One of their duties is to pick out the next assignment you should get. It turned out my monitor was just down the hall from General Wieseman. So he walked down the hall and spoke to my monitor.

A reply to Gary was not long in coming.

Dear Gary . . . I have been so proud of the progress you have made and will continue to make.

As a career Marine it is virtually essential that you participate in or directly contribute to any major undertaking that the Marine Corps becomes involved in. Otherwise it may cripple your advancement in the future and also as "professionals" we should expect that our services will be utilized to the best advantage of our country.

Since you indicated that you had made a specific request for duty in Viet Nam I took it upon myself to inquire as to your status. At HQMC they feel everybody will get a chance to serve there sooner or later but decided it would be expedient to order you out there when you leave the CHICAGO.

This is another opportunity to enhance your professional experience and your professional reputation—the latter an increasingly important factor as you attain higher and higher rank. I'm sure you know my hopes and good wishes go with you."[118]

So he had walked down the hall, spoke to my monitor, and both agreed that since I was already on the West Coast it would be much cheaper to send me to Vietnam than to send someone from Camp Lejeune. One week later, Cooper had his orders for Vietnam.

General Wieseman was one I never really got to sit down with and say, "Thank you, general." He had been of vital help to me twice, once when I was getting my regular commission, then when I wanted to get into combat.

It's amazing what a general can do.

5

Vietnam

The Marine Corps' expanding role in Vietnam had been underway little more than a year when Capt. Gary Cooper arrived, eager to pursue his own goals and confident in his ability to do so.

When I go to Vietnam, my main mission, the only one really on my mind, is simply to be an outstanding rifle company commander, leading Marines in combat.

Now in the back of my mind I know that a black man, a black Marine, had never commanded a Marine rifle company in combat, and a Marine rifle company is our basic combat unit. I understand a black officer, maybe a lieutenant, had a platoon in Korea, but I knew that never had a black Marine officer had command of a rifle company in combat.

Again, while I knew this and wanted to be the first, it was not at all the motivating force when I arrived at Da Nang in the spring of 1966. I just wanted to be the best Marine I could be.

Da Nang was not built up much when he arrived that May. In his recollection, he was greeted by little more than a muddy field with scattered huts, sleeping quarters, equipment sheds and offices not far from the air base. In one small structure—four walls and a window—assignments were being handed out. He got in line shortly after his arrival.[119]

They had a line for the senior enlisted men and a line for the officers, and so I go up to get the word. The major says to me, "Captain, you're going to the 3rd Anti-Tank Battalion."

The anti-tank battalion operated with a small, light vehicle called the Ontos. It was not what I wanted.

"Sir, this has got to be a mistake. I came over to be an infantry man."

"No mistake, Captain. You're with the 3rd Anti-Tank Battalion."

"Well, major. I can't go to the Ontos. I am six-foot-six. I can't even FIT into an Ontos."

"You don't have to worry about that. We're going to make you supply officer."

"Sir, I am sorry. I volunteered to come over here."

"I don't care if you're sorry or not. That's where you're going."

This was the nightmare Cooper had dreaded. It was a whiff of Jim Crow across the military divide, the longstanding Marine way of routing African American officers into motor transport, or supply—anything but giving them command over other men in combat. He had fought to get to Vietnam to lead a rifle company, and in an instant he made a decision that could be pivotal to his career as a Marine officer.

> *I did something that I'd never done before and never thought I would do. But there's something in the naval service that's called "Request Mast." And if you request mast, the senior officer must see you. So I said, "I'm going to have to request mast."*

To request mast is to ask for a hearing before the commanding general. It's an assertion that a complaint has not been properly handled, and it can be a form of brinksmanship. To request mast, in some cases, is to invite retaliation—or to put a blemish on a record that is fatal to advancement. In 2008, the *Marine Corps Times* reported that in a survey of active-duty Marines, 42 percent of men and 49 percent of women said they were retaliated against after they requested mast.[120] In the old-school days of the 1960s, the likelihood that it could be a career-ending step would have been even greater, particularly for a black Marine officer.

But it was the only option left for Cooper.

"You're requesting mast with the commanding general?"

"Yes."

"Get the hell out of here!"

I had a really big-time unhappy major on my hands.

Cooper did get the hell out, and he got a ride to division headquarters, a building on a ridge, then found his way to the outer room of the commanding general's office.

I told them that I was there to request mast, and they looked at me like I was crazy. Because you damn near never did that. But I figured, what the hell, this assignment is crucial to my career. So I sit down and it was maybe 11-hundred or noon, people go to lunch, nobody says a damn thing to me. I'm just sitting there. I had not eaten. So about 15-hundred or 16-hundred in the afternoon, people were starting to leave, and this colonel came up. I think he was chief of staff.

I jumped to attention.

"Captain, what the hell are you doing?"

"Well, sir, I came to request mast with the general."

"The general is a very busy man. What the hell do you want to talk to the general about?"

"Well, sir, I volunteered and it's been my dream to command a Marine rifle company. But instead of getting a rifle company, I was assigned to an anti-tank unit. I'm trained to lead a rifle company and want to request that assignment."

"Hell, is that all you want? Get the hell out of here. I'll send you down to the 9th Marines."

With this blunt, profane command, the colonel sent Cooper to a regiment where he had a shot at becoming commander of a rifle company.

I report to the headquarters of the 9th Marines. There's a mess hall and tent, and I go to meet the colonel who is in charge. He was a colonel and I was a captain. And that's like the difference between the Lord and the shepherds.

I can remember reporting in, saying "Yes, sir," standing at attention and us getting into a conversation. I don't remember any hassle at all. The colonel said, "We need some good company commanders."

And that was it.

Cooper was assigned to command rifle company M, "Mike Company."

The commanding officer then in charge of the 9th Regiment was Colonel Edwin H. Simmons, who later gained renown as a Marine Corps historian and retired as a brigadier general. On this day in May 1966 he had played a role in making Jerome Gary Cooper the first black Marine officer in command of a rifle company during combat. Over the years, this Marine historian would remember Cooper well, but at the time the precedent-setting assignment was a piece of Marine history that went unmentioned. It had happened, after Cooper's decision to request mast, in a decidedly offhand, unceremonious fashion.[121]

Cooper wasn't thinking about history anyway, or how a pivotal moment in his life had just occurred. He was savoring the challenge. In fact, what Cooper remembered years later was the way Simmons ran the officers' tent, being a real stickler for proper decorum even in the rough countryside of Vietnam.

> *He ran this officers' tent with so much protocol. Even though you were in combat, you stood up until the seniors came in, then you sat down, you made sure you ate with the right fork and knife. The guy next to you is saying, "Uncross your legs" and stuff like that.*

On July 5, 1966, Simmons was succeeded by a man to whom Cooper grew particularly close, Colonel Drew J. Barrett Jr.[122] His son, 2nd Lieutenant Drew J. Barrett III, died of wounds suffered in February 1969 in Vietnam, and in many ways Cooper felt that the elder Colonel Barrett was the person most responsible for helping him achieve success as a rifle company commander and later a Hill 55 civil affairs officer in Vietnam.[123]

"Drew saw [Cooper's] capabilities of leading others," said Barrett's widow, Betty Ann, many years later from her home at Daphne, across the bay from Mobile.

Cooper attended Colonel Barrett's funeral in 2003 and always remembered the vital role the colonel had played in helping advance a young black officer's career.

MEDIVAC MIKE

America's combat role in Vietnam had expanded in the spring of 1965 as the 3rd Battalion, 9th Marines, and other units began arriving to fight on the ground in support of the Republic of Vietnam.[124] The U.S.'s Southeast Asian ally was fighting Viet Cong and North Vietnamese in what increasingly had become an American war, one that would grow in deadly intensity and bitter controversy over the next decade. By the time Cooper arrived in the spring of 1966, the battalion numbered about one thousand personnel, including thirty-four officers, one of them the first African American with a Marine rifle company to command.[125]

The area where the 9th Marines were fighting —the I Corps region that included Da Nang—was known for its deadly difficulties. The enemy assault on Mike Company, which had become nicknamed "Medivac Mike," had taken a toll, as it had on other units. In a 1967 USMC historical account, Captain Francis J. West Jr. wrote:

> In the late spring and early summer of 1966, the most notorious area in I Corps was the flat rice paddy-and-hedgerow complex around Hill 55, seven miles southwest of Da Nang. In the Indochina War, two battalions of the French were wiped out on Hill 55; in the Vietnam War, a Marine lieutenant colonel was killed on the same hill. The 9th Marines had the responsibility for clearing the area and no one envied the regimental commander, Colonel Edwin Simmons, and his men their job. The enemy they hated, the enemy they feared the most, the enemy they found hardest to combat, was not the VC; it was mines.
>
> One company of the regiment—Delta—lost 10 KIA [killed in action] and 58 WIA [wounded in action] in five weeks. Two men were hit by small arms fire, one by a grenade. Mines inflicted all the other casualties. Only four of the wounded returned to duty. From a peak strength of 175, Delta Company dropped to 120 effectives. Among those evacuated or killed were a high percentage of the company's leaders: five platoon commanders; three platoon sergeants; nine squad leaders; and six fire team leaders.[126]

Cooper took command of Company M in May 1966.[127] It had just been engaged in the heaviest fighting of Operation Georgia, an initiative to secure the many hamlets around An Hoa, a base south of Da Nang, in order to construct an industrial complex on the Song Phu Bon River. In one afternoon firefight, five Marines were killed and fifty-four wounded while crossing a river and securing a hamlet; by the Marines' count, fifteen Viet Cong were killed and an estimated one hundred were wounded in that battle.[128]

A platoon leader with the company, then-2nd Lieutenant Charlie Tutt, recalled the May assault.

"There was a little bit of an industrial area the South Vietnamese were trying to develop," Tutt said. "There were Vietnamese engineers who lived down there with their families. There was an airfield that C-130s could land on. So on the morning of May the 3rd, we flew in there."

Amphibious armored assault vehicles, called Amtraks, were already there, moved down from Hill 55. For Mike Company, the river crossing was uneventful until they reached the north bank.

"In those days you went on top of the Amtraks because they went over land mines. It was not good to be inside of it," Tutt said. "So we're all sitting on top of this thing and, as soon as we pulled up on the north shore line, we got ambushed. The whole company. It was a pretty rough day. I remember F-4s coming in, right on top of us, dropping napalm and doing all kind of stuff. We took a fair number of casualties that day."

It was in this shooting zone across rolling high grass plains, jungle brush, hills, and dark meandering waters that Cooper first met the men of Company M.

Normally when you report in, you will spend a week with the outgoing company commander, where they will show you around, introduce you to people, brief you on your NCOs. But I got there and I report into the battalion commander. I don't remember his name. He's a little guy, maybe like a movie star, about five-foot-two or something like that. He said I would be going to meet Mike Company, taking over from Captain George R. Griggs.

"Captain Griggs has been ordered to go someplace else, and he's waiting on you," the commander said.

"What tent is he in?"

"He's not in a tent. He's out in the field. We're going to have a helicopter drop you off."

The helicopter took me into Vietnam jungle terrain. The company was in the middle of combat, dealing with weapons fire from VC.

I get off this helicopter and people are shooting at me. Goddam bullets are flying! I find the guy who I'm relieving. I think he shook my hand

and said, "Good luck," and got on the helicopter and left.

"Jesus Christ!" I thought. "What the hell have you done, Cooper?"

There was no time for introductions at that point. But eventually the company left the jungle and moved back to its An Hoa base camp, with tents for sleeping, a mess hall tent, and rope-bucket showers.

Cooper finally had a chance to size up his company, which by various accounts had at one point fallen to being about one-third short of the normal size. By mid-summer Cooper wrote his young friend Dan Freeman in San Diego that his company was attached to an 81 mm mortar section and "a few other small attachments for a total of about 200 Marines." It was mostly white, but included some blacks, a mix of draftees and regulars.[129]

"The unit was racially mixed and there was never any black-and-white issue," said Gary Dockendorf, a white who was a second lieutenant at the time. He later would earn a Silver Star for valor in rescuing two Marines—one black, one white—despite his own wounds. "The platoon sergeant I had was white. One squad leader was black."

Cooper didn't dwell on the fact that Mike Company, with its African American commander, would have a place in U.S. military history books. He had bigger concerns. Mike was riddled with losses.

"We were down to nothing more than a platoon, reinforced if that," said Gary Gretter, a first lieutenant who coordinated artillery with the company commander. "That was the whole Mike Company. Everyone else had been either wounded or killed. That's really awful when you think about it. That's what he took over and that's what he was left to build on."

Tutt said the company's "Medivac" nickname may have preceded the May assault, which added to its reputation of being hard-hit. He had arrived in February, a couple of months after finishing the Basic School, where instructors were beginning to get feedback on enemy tactics in Vietnam. One story he heard at the school was about a platoon that had swept through a village—which typically was in a rice paddy, with buildings atop dikes so they wouldn't flood—but had not cleared it of enemy hiding underground.

"We didn't really know about people digging in, about how they dug these spider holes and tunnels in the rice paddies," he said. As the story was told at the Basic School, he said, "the platoon moved out to sweep across the rice paddy to the next village, and the Vietcong came up behind them. They really ripped up that platoon pretty bad.

"The story was, the lieutenant was shot, wounded, laying there, and the Vietcong came up and picked up his pistol and shot him. True or not, it's what we got briefed in the Basic School."

When Tutt reported to Mike Company, he told that story to other lieutenants who had been in the An Hoa Basin a good while.

"They said, 'That's your platoon. You're the first officer they've had since that guy was killed.' I think that's the way Mike Company got that reputation."

Private First Class Joe O'Neill learned of the company's nickname shortly after he arrived in Vietnam.

"We got off the plane in Da Nang and got put in a quonset hut. There was guys in the quonset hut that were wounded. They were getting ready to go back into their unit," he recalled. "I'm sitting on a cot, talking to others on cots. One of them said to me, 'What company are you going to be in?' I replied, 'I'm going to Mike Company.' He says, 'Awwww . . . Medivac Mike! They just got hit down there near the river and they lost quite a few.' I guess that name stuck."

Cooper was determined to change it. Early on, he made it clear that Company M's method of operation would be different.

I got those youngsters together. It was a pretty interesting mix. Some draftees, some regular, a number of black Marines. So I got them all together and said, "You see what time it is?" It was like zero-seven-thirty. I said, "From this day on, do you know what our new name is? It's 'Fighting Mike.'" And that was it from then on. We were badasses.

"I have no idea why or how this worked, but he told everybody, You're no longer 'Medivac Mike.' You're now 'Fighting Mike,'" Gretter said. "In doing that, he became incredibly aggressive about things. He said, 'We're going after them. We're not going to sit around and have them come after us.'"

"The whole company changed when he took over," said O'Neill. "My morale was really low. When he came in, the whole company—the morale went up."

"I Must be Dreaming"

While morale was raised for all, it took on additional meaning for a young African American rifleman from Baltimore, Lance Corporal Ted Knight, who joined Mike Company in July 1966.

"I was still relatively new," he said. "I was assigned to a fire team. I saw this tall black guy walking by and I could have sworn he had on captain's insignia. I looked and I said, 'I must be dreaming.' 'Cause that would be the highest-ranking black person I had seen in the Marine Corps! So I said, 'No, it can't be.' But I started listening to a few other people in the unit and they said, 'Oh, yeah, Captain. . . . He's our company commander, he's a good guy.' And I said, 'Really?' I hadn't met him at that point.

"But then I met him probably several weeks later. I think he was introducing himself to new people coming in. I just was enthralled. It meant a lot to me to see a black guy—I was just eighteen years old, or just turned nineteen—to see a black guy in charge. And he had his act together. He just really seemed to have all his ducks in a row.

"Then I didn't see him too much after that, because I'm sure he had his things to do and I definitely had mine. I stayed out more than I stayed in. I was always on kill teams, a lot of out-posting. My platoon—I was the third platoon—we were a lot farther out than the rest of the company. I didn't see people back in the company too often.

"I think it was around September of '66 when I really saw Captain Cooper in action. We had a battalion-size operation. Of course the powers that be would know because I didn't exactly know how the intelligence reports came down. But I think our operation had to do with a large NVA [North Vietnamese Army] or Viet Cong presence in a particular area, in a village or a hamlet.

"We were on this large operation and were crossing this huge rice paddy. It was a BIG rice paddy, wide open. The entire battalion was spread out by platoon, and each platoon by company. I guess we were about two-thirds of the way across the rice paddy, most of the way over. That's when it looked like all hell broke loose. I mean bullets was flying, explosions. We was getting fired upon. When you're fired upon, bullets hitting all around you, your first instinct is to get down. So you're diving down, face-first into a rice paddy. You're down. I'm behind this rice paddy dike, bullets flying all around me. . . .

"It was getting bad. The rounds were becoming more frequent. Then suddenly I looked up, and who did I see but Captain Cooper! He was walking high-step. He wasn't running. He was high-stepping very fast towards where I was, but he was stepping over the dike and he had his .45 in his hand pointing forward and said 'Let's go!' I look up and said, 'Why in the hell am I down here behind this dike?' And I've got a rifle, he had a .45 and he's saying 'Let's go!'

"So I had a whole, totally different respect—now I already had respect for him—but I gained a lot more at that particular point. He led by example, put it that way."

Decorated USMC rifle company commander James Webb, a future Navy Secretary, U.S. Senator, and presidential candidate, described the Vietnam experience in an article he wrote years later:

> In the rifle companies, we spent the endless months patrolling ridge lines and villages and mountains, far away from any notion of tents, barbed wire, hot food, or electricity. Luxuries were limited to what would fit inside one's pack, which after a few "humps" usually boiled down to letter-writing material, towel, soap, toothbrush, poncho liner, and a small transistor radio.
>
> We moved through the boiling heat with 60 pounds of weapons and gear, causing a typical Marine to drop 20 percent of his body weight while in the bush. When we stopped we dug chest-deep fighting holes and slit trenches for toilets. We slept on the ground under makeshift poncho hootches, and when it rained we usually took our hootches down because wet ponchos shined under illumination flares, making great targets. Sleep itself was fitful, never more than an hour or two at a stretch for months at a time as we mixed daytime patrolling with night-time ambushes, listening posts, foxhole duty, and radio watches.[130]

County Fairs & Darts

"We operated around An Hoa, south of Da Nang," said O'Neill. "There was Viet Cong all over the place. There were booby traps. They'd hit us with ambushes. We built a place called Phu Loc Six. We had a tank on top there with infrared at night. You could see at night.

"Before that we were on a place called My Loc Five. That was really bad. I remember Captain Cooper being there. That was the first hill we had to take, cut the trees down, lay sandbags. In the heat it was really bad. We were out in the middle of nowhere. I remember Captain Cooper coming to our bunkers at night telling us there was a large force of NVA coming our way.

"He kept us pretty much on the ball, keeping our weapons clean. The morale was really boosted when he came in. He wanted to see action."

Mike Company had multiple missions. There were "County Fair" and "Golden Fleece" stagings aimed at increasing the influence of the South Vietnam government in rural areas ripe for enemy activity. The County Fair technique involved cordoning off a village and learning who they were or where they were, trying to enlist their support.[131]

"He came in and he had fresh ideas," said Tutt. "We did some things we hadn't been doing. County Fairs—he was big on that. For the type of combat we were in, it was really the beginning of this asymmetrical warfare to some degree. . . . A lot of booby traps, land mines—they weren't called IEDs then. You tried to flush people out. You tried to make the countryside secure.

"So with these County Fairs, you would move at night, or early in the morning, surround the village, then go in and try to flush them out. And do a lot in there to try to support the people in the village, anything you could do to make their situation better, and try to sort out the Vietcong if you can. The people that we dealt with in that area for the most part were Vietcong."

"We would move into a village for a day or so, then leave," he said, "and of course the VC were there and just come right in behind us. There were not enough of us, you couldn't cover every little hamlet that was there. There were a lot of them."

Mike Company also engaged in firefights during enemy attacks and ambushes and kept the road from An Hoa to the Liberty Bridge mine-free.

Then there were the search and destroy missions.

"Captain Cooper starts sending out 'Darts,' which were small fire-team patrols," said Gretter. "He would send them out there. They were aggressive. They were on this path waiting for the enemy—and that was not exactly what everybody did at the time—and they're out there and they ambush this VC patrol. . . . He said, 'Bring back their flag, bring back everything.' We brought it all back, and it boosted morale. It showed you could do things like that."

Cooper had another tactic, an approach not likely advertised in the military's combat handbook.

We killed so many VCs that I got a call from the regimental commander to come up, to explain to them how the hell we're killing eight to ten a night and other folks aren't killing any.

I told him that, what we would do in the villages, we would make our observations. We never saw any men. You would see little kids and you would see women. But no men. How about that? So what we would do is, we would send out patrols every night and they would report where they saw the good-looking women. Ah-ha. So we would set up ambushes there—about two in the morning. The men would start showing up by that hour.

That's how we did it. And it never damn failed.

Experience, Land Mines, Brothers

Cooper was cautious with his assignments. Gary Dockendorf, in combat for the first time, was a platoon commander in search of experience, but Cooper wanted it achieved the right way.

"You would go to a specific site that he would have approved," Dockendorf said, "and then he would send you your team of about five maybe, in conditions that offer you the advantage over anybody else, over the enemy, and that's where experience paid off.

"The sergeant knew how best to set people up where we could work as a team. I was a second lieutenant, but when somebody came down the trail, the sergeant would have had more experience as to when to actually start shooting, and that's what Captain Cooper was concerned about.

He was concerned that I would go out there and try to set something up, compared to a sergeant who was junior in rank but much senior in experience.

"But as a second lieutenant, I didn't want to sit behind the safety of a line and send people out to do something I've never done. I wanted to go out on a couple of these so I could understand what went on out there at night."

With Cooper's approval, Dockendorf was sent out and got experience in the field at night. And even more after the sun rose.

"The next morning a patrol was coming in. A signal was given to the friendly troops that this was a friendly patrol, but they didn't tell me that. They snuck up behind me and popped the flare—this was the signal and it scared the hell out of me! When it went off, I thought we were in the middle of an ambush and I jumped off the paddy dike into the rice paddy and came up soaking wet. When I looked up, I was sitting there in front of my platoon, and they were all just laughing that the lieutenant had panicked and jumped into the water."

Dockendorf also recalled how Cooper used his wits to avoid a public relations disaster.

"We had a case where we had come back after an ambush and accidentally killed a young civilian in a village. There was much grieving by the family and villagers. A CBS television crew was coming out for a visit, and the last thing you wanted was disturbing video of grieving Vietnamese family members. But Cooper handled the situation. He was pretty calm and had the grieving villagers taken to the north side of the mountain while he met the CBS crew on the south side.

"We made it through the day and took care of the family."

You get these Marines from all over the country, the fields of Iowa, New York City, from everywhere, many of them from different backgrounds. Boy, you let one of those Marines see one of their buddies get hurt, or somebody trying to kill them, you talk about a vicious, violent little sucker! I mean they are tough!

We worked to stop these youngsters from committing atrocities. They would cut an ear off in a minute.

In my unit, I demanded that if a Vietnamese woman came by, you stepped off the trail and greeted her. We taught respect, courtesy. But some people didn't. I went to villages where I saw people hanging upside down from trees. I can remember seeing a tank coming by with a head on the antenna. But that's when Marines got out of hand and their CO's weren't doing things the right way.

As company commander, Cooper was not expected to be in the thick of action.

If you're doing it the right way, and you're the commanding officer, you're not in the middle of that firefight. You're back a little bit so you can maneuver platoons. I can remember going into an area once and sending one platoon around and down in firing position on a dike of a rice paddy. I sent another platoon around to flush out the VC, and I can remember thirty of them running across in front of my Marines and I mean it was like a firing range. They were popping them.

But I'll tell you what was horrible. Land mines. Bungee pits. Sharpened bamboos in holes. So if a Marine stepped on it, the spikes would go up into his feet.

Probably what you hate most is, you're going along, and maybe half of your men have walked down this same trail, and you hear VRR-ROOOMM!, and you look back and you see black smoke. You know when you see that black smoke that some Marine has stepped on a land mine. Then you hear the sound, "Corpsman! Corpsman!" You talk about respected in a unit, that was the corpsman. Young Marines would get mangled legs and you'd have to call in the medivac helicopters to take them out.

One of the Marines whose platoon cleared land mines in Vietnam was a black engineer, 2nd Lieutenant George Walls. Cooper recalled meeting him on a trail out in the boondocks when Walls led a team of four or five Marines checking for mines. Walls actually had already seen Cooper for the first time in a different setting and had a vivid memory of it, too.

"At the time I met Gary, which was in the spring of 1966, there were very few black officers in the Marine Corps," Walls said. "At that point in my career—I was a second lieutenant and Gary was a captain—I had met two other black Marine officers. One was Ken Berthoud . . . and one of my instructors at Basic School was Captain Clarence Baker. So Gary was actually the third black officer I had met in the Marine Corps.

"I was a combat engineer officer and the leader of a platoon that was sent out in support of 3rd Battalion, 9th Marine—the combat operation was 'Operation Georgia.' The first night we were out on the operation, the battalion commander called all of his company commanders and his supporting unit commanders in for a conference before we got bedded down for the night. Everybody got to the meeting, except Captain Cooper had not arrived. I didn't know who Captain Cooper was. So we waited a few minutes. We were in this bamboo thicket, and all of a sudden this bamboo starts parting and crashing and here comes this six-foot, six-inch black Marine officer. It just blew me away."[132]

Like Petersen, Walls would become a friend of Cooper's for life—"I doubt that a week or two weeks has gone by since then that we haven't talked to each other"—and in 1991 Walls would join in making history as the third African American Marine general.

"We are like brothers," Walls told the USMC's oral history. "I'm an only child, and if I had a brother, Gary would have been my brother."[133]

PRIVATE WALTON

For Cooper, the Vietnam combat experience included being wounded twice, earning him two Purple Hearts.

> Both of them I believe were from shrapnel. One on the arm, one on the leg. A little scar, I was almost embarrassed to get a Purple Heart. They were minor scrapes, not life-threatening. I said "Thank you, Lord."

After the wound to his arm he wrote to Dan Freeman: *I move a lot faster and lower since I received my wound. Luckily the VC are horrible shots.*

While leading a rifle company carried with it danger to life and limb, it also placed on Cooper a personal burden: *The majority of my men are under twenty years old and are real hard-chargers. The hardest part of my job so far is having to be indirectly and directly responsible when my men are killed and wounded, but we have good days, too. I guess that is the story of commanding men in combat.*[134]

One of the men in his unit was eighteen-year-old Private Joseph Herbert Walton of Chicago. The company was at An Hoa on an August night, preparing for an early morning mission. The first sergeant told Cooper that Private Walton wanted to speak with him. Cooper waved him in.

"Sir. Private Walton requests permission to speak to the captain."

"Speak, Walton."

"Sir, I can't go in the morning."

"Walton, what the hell you mean you can't go?"

"Well, the Lord has talked to me, and I'm going to die tomorrow."

"You're going to die tomorrow? Well, you know, Walton, you're one of my machine gunners, and the Lord hasn't talked to me. Let me suggest you go pray over this and I expect your ass out there at formation at zero-four-thirty. You understand me?"

"Yes, sir."

Cooper learned later that Walton had put some of his premonition in a letter. And despite his fears, Walton joined the formation at 4:30 a.m.

We go out. We stop and we get going again. We're going to cross a rice paddy. Two platoons are already gone. Walton's platoon is in front of me. I'm behind. Suddenly there is enemy fire. And the first person down, the first person killed, is Walton.

It's a jolt Cooper felt for many years. A yellowing newspaper clip recounting Walton's death remains in Cooper's valued personal albums in Mobile.

Back in Chicago, according to the newspaper story that Cooper saved, Walton's parents grieved for their youngest son in their brick bungalow on the South Side. They had learned of his death from a Marine major who read from a small card. Just two hours after the major left, the news story said, the mailman brought a letter—written by Walton to a girlfriend. Prior to learning of his death, she had mailed it to his parents, feeling he would want it shared with them. In the letter, he wrote in part: "I realize that some of us must die, but God gave his only begotten Son that we may live in a free, sinless world."[135]

Cooper ruminated over the deaths of Walton and others in his company.

I had told myself that—I didn't have many Marines killed, maybe *ten, twelve, thirteen—that I was going to go and visit every family when I got back. So I was familiar with the South Side of Chicago, where Walton is from, because I went to Notre Dame. I knew where he lived, so I called the family one Sunday afternoon. I put on my dress blues, had my swagger stick, and I went to the family.*

I was overwhelmed by the family's grief.

They wanted to know everything about his last moments. What did he say? What did his face look like? Everything. And that was pretty traumatic.

SERGEANT KAPPMEYER

Walton's death occurred on August 20, 1966, a traumatic day for Mike Company all around. It had crossed the Song Vu Gia River that morning. Then, as Dockendorf would recall later:

"We had moved most of the morning, stopped for something to eat, and then moved down into a village. That's where we were hit by the Viet Cong. On that day it wasn't so much the North Vietnamese army as it was the Viet Cong."

Dockendorf was hit in the leg, had it wrapped and was continuing with the mission when others were pinned down, including a machine gunner who had been hit and called for help. Dockendorf's right guide, Sergeant Paul Kappmeyer, a twenty-two-year-old from Indianapolis, went out for the wounded Marine and was hit by enemy fire himself.

Dockendorf moved into action. First he pulled the machine gunner back to safety.

"Then I went back out to pick up Kappmeyer, who as best I can tell—in those situations it was hard—I was carrying him and was shot in the hand carrying him. And I think he was alive when I picked him up, because I remember him saying something—'I'd like to help out' or something. He said something as I was carrying him, and I think I got hit in the hand carrying him and I think he got hit as well, which was a fatal blow to him."

Kappmeyer was awarded the Silver Star posthumously for his heroics trying to save the wounded, pinned-down machine gunner. With hand and leg injuries, Dockendorf's first tour in Vietnam was over after just thirty days. But he would return for two more, thirteen months each, and also receive a Silver Star for "daring actions, inspiring leadership and outstanding devotion to duty" on that hellish day in the summer of 1966.

Along with Walton and Kappmeyer, at least three other Marines with Mike Company were killed in the August 20 firefight. All were nineteen years old.[136]

It was, said O'Neill, "an awful, wicked firefight. They set up an ambush in these trees. I had the point—my fire team did, I was the fire team leader in charge of three other Marines. You could hear the enemy fire up ahead, it was about three hundred yards up ahead of us at the tree line."

"Captain Cooper had us move double-time—me, Alton Smith, Doug Salyer—and he was right with us. He ran all the way up to where the tree line was, this was like three hundred yards, four hundred yards. There were some graves. They buried them above the ground, so there was these mounds. He got the machine gunner . . . to get it low and skip it along the ground into the tree line.

"He told the platoon—we were all behind the mounds—go fix bayonets. He gave the charge to go in, and we went in—he was right there with us—so we went to the tree line firing on semiautomatic. That's my most vivid recollection of Captain Cooper. It was very, very bad that day. He called in air strikes, he led the charge. . . . Whether it was the right decision or not, I don't know. But that's what we were taught to do. We went right up and into them."

"Captain Cooper was walking around, directing our fire, fully calm, composed," said another Marine with Mike Company, Ernest Murray.

An African American in the rifle company, Corporal A. Stephan Moss, said the August 20 battle was "the first movie-like firefight that I had ever been in. Me personally. Maybe somebody was in one like that before I joined 3-9. But I'm pretty sure this was one of the biggest battles we ever had.

"My radio man got shot in the head. I almost got shot in the head but the guy missed me."

Moss, like Cooper, had been drawn to the Marine Corps by a movie—*Battle Cry*, in Moss's case. He was just ten years old.

"For some reason, I guess as an African American kid, I wanted to test my courage," he said. "I was trying to figure out what I could do that would be the ultimate test. So when I saw this movie about the Marines—I didn't see myself in the movie, I think it may have had one African American—but for me, the idea was, 'What was I made of?'

"At ten years old I really don't know where that came from." But when the opportunity came—after he graduated from high school in D.C.—he enlisted. He was seventeen.

He arrived in Vietnam the same month as Cooper—May 1966—and was assigned to be a squad leader. He recalls his first real meeting with Cooper taking place after a firefight in which there had been a disagreement with a staff sergeant.

"Somebody came to see me and said, 'The captain wants to see you, Steve.' So now I'm going to see the captain and I'm walking down the trail. I see a tall African American guy coming from the other direction and I asked him, 'Where's the captain?'

"He told me he was the captain. So my first experience was not shock at all, but I didn't expect the captain to be black. I didn't expect the CO to be black. It just wasn't expected. So once he told me he was the captain, he gave me kind of like a football coach's lecture. Like a football coach talking to the quarterback about calling plays.

"Once he finished, he dismissed me and I was walking back and his exact words were, 'Moss'—and I turned around—'if anyone ever fucks with you, let me know.'

"After that, we got pretty close."

THE HOME FRONT

In letters throughout his Vietnam tour, Cooper kept up with family members, including his mother's sister, Geraldine, who had become a Catholic nun and taken the name Sister Hyacinth. She lived in a convent at Marbury, a village in rural central Alabama.

Gary wrote his mother: *Sr Hyacinth writes me often and I enjoy hearing from her. . . . I know their prayers must help us a lot because we have really had some close calls.*[137]

Back in San Diego, Cooper's young family also experienced the dark side of the war.

"I distinctly remember living in San Diego, in a complex, when he was shipped off to Vietnam. There were many single mothers whose husbands had been sent to Vietnam. I remember when they came and told us he had been injured in combat. I was six or seven, but I definitely remember it," Joli said.

"I had a friend whose father was in the Marines," said Patrick. "The families tended to live in the same area. What I do remember is my friend and I would go out to play, but one day he couldn't come out to play. It was a day when his family got up and found out his father had been killed in Vietnam."

But Gary tried to remain playful with his children, even from the war zone.

"Sometimes we'd receive a package sent from Vietnam, with a letter accompanying it," Patrick said. "The letter said there was a Vietnamese head in the package. So we'd open it and there was a coconut shell, with eyes and ears painted on."

In the killing zone of combat, though, mortality was no laughing matter.

Yesterday was a very sad day for me, Gary wrote his mother on September 5, 1966. One of his friends from San Diego had been killed in a battle the day before. Gary's mother had met the man's wife, Judi, and little daughter, Toni, on a visit to the base in California. *There will be much sadness in the neighborhood in San Diego. Here one really learns a lot about life!*[138]

No Bad Day

Cooper's tour as commander of a Marine rifle company in combat was coming to an end in September 1966. He had taken part in Operations Georgia, Liberty, Macon, Suwanee, and Mississippi. It went mostly unspoken, but he had made the kind of history that mattered most to him—no one questioned the leadership abilities or combat skills of the African American in charge.

Tutt, the white platoon leader with Mike Company, was one who was aware of the racial milestone. He had grown up in Atlanta, in a home that was tolerant about race, and had graduated from Georgia Tech.

"My parents were pretty much apolitical," he said. "Certainly I never heard any racial comments as I grew up. I didn't have any bias like some of the stereotype, which kind of gets my back up sometimes because there are people in the South who aren't that way."

In Vietnam, he was interested in talking to Cooper about race.

"You've got a white man from the South and a black man from the South," he said. "It was interesting. I think we got along well. In fact we had several conversations about that. One time we got a bottle of Scotch. We were back in An Hoa and we were drinking—not too much—and we were talking about it.

"I was aware, as he was, that he was the first. I don't know if he knew for sure that he was the first, but he said he thought he was the first African American to command a Marine rifle company in combat. We talked about it, because I had a lot of questions for him, about what it was like from his perspective, about what he faced as an African American in the South."

Tutt, who became a Navy aviator and flew missions in Vietnam, recalls his experience with Cooper as positive.

"I think we were both kind of cognizant of where we were from and learned from each other," Tutt said. "He was a good leader, a good company commander. He would push the company, he would innovate. We would do things we hadn't been doing, like the County Fairs, paying more attention to our movements, making sure we didn't get lax. That's really important in any situation but surely when you're in a combat situation you don't want to let standards down.

"But when you got back, when you put your hair down, he was a good guy. I talked to him and he had a good sense of humor and was fun to be around."

For Knight, the young black rifleman with Mike Company, a sense of Cooper's historic accomplishment didn't come until later.

"I had no idea and I didn't hear anyone speak of that," he said. "All I know is that all the guys were very proud of him, because he was a good guy. They all seemed to like him. He treated everyone genuinely. I'm speaking of the black guys, because there weren't that many of us there. At least not in my unit, it was third platoon. I think it was maybe six, seven black guys in the whole platoon."

Moss, as another African American in Mike Company, echoed Cooper and Knight in saying that making racial history was not on anyone's mind.

"That doesn't mean a goddam thing when you're in Vietnam," Moss said. "You're not playing rank. We never played rank."

Years later he spoke with Cooper about how he got to be in command of the rifle company, and learned that his old captain had to request mast.

"It's the same journey that African Americans go through, period," Moss said. "He had to do some wheeling and dealing just to have that unit."

The arrival in Vietnam of one white Marine struck a nerve for Cooper. It was the Marine who was a drill instructor at Quantico when Cooper was a young ROTC cadet in the summer of 1957, the DI who voiced racial slurs while making Cooper get up around midnight to do pushups until he dropped.

One day I'm at An Hoa, the first sergeant comes in. He says there's a new staff sergeant. I said send him in. He comes in. "Sir, reporting as ordered."

I knew immediately who it was. I said, "I know you from somewhere, don't I?" He said, "Yes, sir, you do."

That's when I told him: "You know what I want you to do? I want you to be a good Marine. Now get the hell out of here."

And we never ran into each other again.

But the incident was another reminder for Cooper of the multiple challenges he faced as a young black officer in a structure built by white men.

General Petersen and I talk about this all the time. People say, "How can you complain about the system? You folks became generals, and still you talk about how unfair it was." But the bottom line is, when I'd go to my rifle company in the morning, if white folks got there at zero-six-thirty, I knew I had to be there at zero-five-thirty. As a black officer, if you think that all you've got to do is do as good as everybody else, you're wetting in the wind. You can never have a "bad day."

6

Hill 55

Cooper's next stop in Vietnam removed him from his role commanding a rifle company in the thick of combat, but the threat of enemy attacks was never far away and a new set of challenges awaited him.

I didn't want to leave the men of Mike Company, but there was an unwritten rule that after you've been wounded twice, they want to move you out. Colonel Barrett and I talked about what I could do. He found out that I spoke a little Vietnamese—I had studied, at Barstow, conversational Vietnamese—and he was the one who made me Civil Affairs Officer at 9th Headquarters, known as Hill 55.

Cooper's outgoing, venturesome personality made him an ideal civil affairs officer. Part of his new job involved outreach, going to villages to offer assistance of various sorts, including medical and dental care, through a pacification program called "Hearts and Minds."

Your mission was to win the hearts and minds of the people. You would go out to the villages, and you had to be very careful, because these people who were VCs lived in these villages. You would never see them during the day. But you would have to be careful, in case one of them did stay home that day.

Under the "County Fair" operation, you would pick an area, and go in before dawn and surround the area. You would have people who were known as "chieu hoi" scouts—they were defectors from the VC; many of them were from the areas where you would go. So you would surround the villages and the chieu hoi scouts would get on the microphones and say, "We represent goodness" or whatever, and we would have medical teams. Basically you were there to let people know you were there to help them and also to make sure you got the bad guys out of there.

Carl Kachauskas, who met Cooper in January 1967 when he joined the 9th Marines on Hill 55, said the primary job of the civil affairs officer was to be a liaison between the Marines and the local civilian Vietnamese leadership.

"I went with Gary on some of his liaison trips to the local villages, mainly as a second hand, but sometimes for any problems dealing with communications, like the locals stealing our wire and telephone poles," he said. Later that year Gary's job took on a much larger role at Dong Ha, which was more populous and had the headquarters of a South Vietnamese regiment.

"One of Gary's favorite places to visit was the hospital and orphanage located in the Quang Tri area. I would go with Gary on some of those visits and the nuns, doctors, and nurses were very appreciative of the help and medical supplies Gary would provide. Gary was a very affable, polite and outgoing individual. He was a natural for a civil affairs officer," said Kachauskas.

John Styk, who arrived in Vietnam in October 1966 and shortly was assigned to drive Cooper, said they would leave Hill 55 in an American Motors Mighty Mite, a jeep in which Cooper had a two-way radio installed.

"He would tell me where to stop, and he would go on foot then by himself and gather information," said Styk. "There were a couple of different times we were out near Dai Loc and he had me stop up on top of a little hill. He told me, 'If you see anything suspicious—if any shooting starts—try to drive in and get me. I'll be in that church.' I don't want to say he wasn't cautious. He was very cautious about what he did. But he was a risk-taker."

Styk said Cooper had "Kit Carson scouts"—turncoat VC who had been repatriated under the *chieu hoi* program. "They would supply intelligence to the Marines. They would also go out and look for booby traps, show Marines where some of the stuff was. Captain Cooper's scout was in contact with him all the time. He had been a VC corpsman. He never carried a gun. When I first met this Kit Carson scout, that's what Cooper told me about him. He was my age, 18 years old. We used to take him in the jeep to different places, like down to An Hoa. We'd be driving along and the scout would say something to Cooper. Cooper would tell me, 'Stop right now.' The scout would jump out. He'd run out of sight. What he was doing was putting propaganda into the VC mail room. He had a price on his head."

THINKING OF FAMILY

As civil affairs officer, part of the job was to help the Vietnamese. You would go to the villages and meet the senior person. A great person in those areas was the Catholic priest.

I will never forget there was a Father Co. He came to see me one day. I had taken some courses in conversational Vietnamese, and Father Co said he needed some wood, for a school or something. He came back the next week and had learned to speak a little English.

I told him about my mother's sister Geraldine, who had become a cloistered Catholic nun and taken the name Sister Hyacinth. She was at a monastery in central Alabama, at Marbury—it was the first interracial convent in the South, the KKK used to burn crosses in front of it—and kept in touch with me and my family.

My aunt was fluent in French, and so was Father Co. I introduced them to each other, and they started writing each other. Through her, he wrote the Catholic church officials, and visited her at Marbury, and they helped him get a diocese in the U.S. He was able to escape Vietnam and get a job in this country.

The Vietnamese priest, the Reverend Phan Van Co—Father Co—later wrote a letter of thanks for Gary's help building a camp for more than three hundred displaced South Vietnamese. The letter also thanked him for helping Father Co move from his war-torn home country to Muskogee, Oklahoma, where a local Catholic priest was assisting him.

"Maybe you don't remember me," Father Co wrote, "but as for me, I never forget you. . . . You bring for my people food, clothes and everything. Today I am rescued from Communists in my country to come in United States. . . . I ask God to bless you and your family."[139]

Despite being in a war zone, Gary maintained contact and a semblance of normalcy with his family, as the correspondence with his aunt indicated. In letters, he noted that his own Catholic faith had not lapsed. In one letter from Hill 55 he wrote: *I've served Mass each Sunday for the last four weeks. Guess I'll never forget how.*[140]

His parents' divorce was on his mind at times, too, and his affection for all his family was easy to observe:

> *I'm very happy to hear that Mario did well in summer school. I pray that all will go well for him. I am happy that Mario is spending some time with Dad. Soon you will find that he will want to spend more time with him than you. It shouldn't worry you because for a boy it is a very natural thing.*
>
> *Charlie and the children are doing very well. She sent me some of Joli's school papers and they looked pretty good.*[141]

In another letter, he told his mother he was glad his siblings were writing her. But he had a question: *How do you get letters from Peggy? She has owed me a letter for over a month. I really enjoyed her visit to San Diego. I wish we could get together more often."*[142]

Gary even fashioned for his mother a gift from Vietnam:

> *I will save the picture of the suit you want until I get the measurement form back from you. I will mail it to you soon. Once the order is submitted, it takes six weeks to get it back. One problem—they will not be able to put the lamb collar on it. Do you want the collar plain—or another suit design?*[143]

For his young friend in San Diego, Dan Freeman, he mentioned another gift:

> *Have you heard of the Ho Chi Minh sandal? It's made of auto tire rubber. They are pretty cool! If you would like for me to send you a pair, trace your foot on paper and send it to me.*[144]

His brother Billy, the second-oldest of the Cooper children, had finished Notre Dame in 1963 and returned to Mobile to work in the family business. He married a beautiful Selma woman, Paulette Reid, and they had a baby boy, Christopher Reid Cooper, known as Casey, while Gary was in Vietnam. Gary inquired about Casey in a letter to his mother.

How is the baby? I'm happy that you get a chance to keep it once in a while. Don't spoil the kid. How is Paulette doing? She owes me a letter, too. Tell her I'm talking about her.[145]

DR. BARRY BOOTH

The "hearts and minds" program captured Gary's own heart, largely because of the prodigious efforts of an Alabama dentist, Dr. Barry Booth, who eventually would have a dental practice at Spanish Fort, across the bay from Mobile. Booth had graduated from Auburn University in 1962, joined the Navy Reserve and received his dental degree in 1966, the same year he volunteered for Vietnam and began his two-year active-duty tour.[146]

Booth arrived at Da Nang in November, about two months after Cooper had begun working in civil affairs. Initially operating a dental office out of a barge housing eight hundred sailors—"a giant floating dormitory," he said—Booth quickly signed up for the hearts and minds program. It sent dentists out on Dental Civil Action Patrols, or "Dent CAPS," in the villages. Cooper would accompany him on some. There was a foot-pedal-powered drill that could be carried by one person.

You would go through the villages and you would see no men, but you would see these little kids, and they would have cleft lips and they looked horrible. They were ostracized. Many of them died at a very young age because they couldn't suck their mother's breast.

"Most of the time," said Booth, "I would find places to go on my own to just get in the bush. Most of the time I would go by myself. But because I bunked on the barge when I was back at the pier, I would invite the supply officers to go along with me. There were a number of them who enjoyed going with me, but some of them were pretty discriminatory about which patrol they would go with me on.

"We went out in the bush, out in the villages. Sometimes with protection and many times with no protection. I would invite some of these supply officers to go with me because they were pretty much bored with their jobs, periodically I should say. At no time did I have a dental technician go with me. I was generally by myself. It was all dental extractions. It wouldn't be anything more than that—until I met Gary Cooper.

"I got attached to the 26th Marines on Hill 55, which was down south of Da Nang. Gary, a captain then, had more or less completed his stint as the combat officer. In civil affairs, he collected information about kids that had facial deformities, like cleft lips.

"At that time I was also working at a downtown civilian hospital on Hai Phong Street in Da Nang that was called Hospital C. I was doing general dental care, mainly extractions, not restorative work. Gary would bring the kids in, we would evaluate them. We didn't do cleft palates, we only did soft-tissue surgery with cleft lips. No bone surgery.

"But we would evaluate these children, schedule them into the hospital, operate on them and in three or four days we would turn them back to their villages. Unfortunately they were—just by virtue of the way they looked—somewhat outcasts in their villages and in their homes. But once we got to them and did our repair work, they were brought back into the mainstream of village life. It was a wonderful, wonderful procedure and certainly helped a lot of children."

Booth was pretty fearless about getting around South Vietnam.

"On Hill 55 I did go out on patrols. It certainly wasn't my job. I only did it on a lark," he said.

One night when he was with Cooper they came under attack.

"We were scrambling from—I don't know if it was rockets or mortars or whatever—but we did have to hit the deck. We jumped—it looked like a ditch—and we ended up in a latrine next to each other. A latrine! We've joked about that from then on."

LIBERTY ROAD

For Cooper, the tour with civil affairs entailed closer calls than jumping into a latrine.

One day we got the word we were going to Dong Ha. Where is that? Damn near walking distance from the DMZ. I can remember saying, "What the hell are we going to do in civil affairs in Dong Ha?"

We arrived there by helicopter, and had been there about a week. We were staying in huts—tin roofs, screens, plywood, a door at one end. We had a little hole in the ground to get into if there was an attack.

Boy, one morning all hell broke loose. We were in rocket range of the damn North Vietnamese, and they rocketed Dong Ha. You were in your bunk and you could actually see the shrapnel tearing holes in the roof and walls. A couple of people got killed in our hut. So we rolled off the bunks and crawled to the door and dropped down into that hole.

The hole was not very deep—at first. When the sun came up, about noon, that hole was TWICE as deep as it had been!

In civil affairs, you had to be very careful. Normally you would not have a lot of troops with you. A driver, maybe one Marine. You planned where you were going.

At night, you had to have your perimeter around Hill 55. You very often might be officer of the day. You'd have to get up during the night, make sure people were alert. You would send out patrols to make sure the enemy wasn't slipping up on you. They would often get in firefights out there.

Cooper had a certain respect for the North Vietnamese. He spelled it out in an April letter to Dan Freeman:

When last I wrote to you my unit was south of Da Nang City. About a week ago we were ordered north and are now fighting about six hundred meters south of the DMZ. Here, rather than the guerilla, we are fighting the trained NVA regular soldier. He is a good fighter and so far appears well led. He likes to assault our lines and our new M16 rifle has really been putting a hurting on him. When they assault they have a couple men assigned who shoot those who don't keep moving forward. I've seen it! They are all well fed and clean and their weapons are normally in good shape.[147]

One gruesome scene from that time is etched in Cooper's memory.

We were at Dong Ha, up near Con Thien. Sometimes helicopters couldn't get in because of all the weapons fire, and if there was a lull in the fire, they would put dead Marines, wounded Marines, on that helicopter. And if you wanted a ride, you better get on that helicopter. And I can remember getting on the helicopter and having it bank—and blood running out the side of it.

Con Thien and Khe Sanh were two of the famous battle sites. They were like maybe ten or fifteen miles from each other. We would fly up there. I'm not in combat, I'm a civil affairs officer, but I would ride up there sometimes.

Down where we were in Dong Ha they had these 18-wheelers, sometimes half full with dead bodies, because it was so bad the helicopters couldn't take off to remove the dead.

The Marines knew one area as "Dodge City" for its history of violent enemy attacks.

"Dodge City was off Hill 55, out what was called Liberty Road," said John Styk. "The saying among Marines was, 'If you got from one end of it to the other without being ambushed, you deserved liberty.'"

The well-known Liberty Bridge was also in the Dong Ha vicinity. As Cooper recalled: *One black Marine said, "I know why they call it Liberty Bridge. You go there and they're going to separate your body from your soul."*

Indeed, places along the road were called "Ambush Row," and even when there was no enemy fire, trips into the bush could be nerve-racking.

"We usually didn't travel Liberty Road," said Styk. "Cooper said we'll go the long way, we'll go into Da Nang and come down another road that weaves right into the lower end of Liberty Road to get to places like Dai Loc."

Even when being cautious, they could drive into trouble. Styk recalls taking Cooper and an assistant to a site, maybe a refugee camp.

"The place was deserted," he said. "There was something wrong. There was no livestock around. No people. Nothing. . . . Cooper took off by himself. He was gone for a while, fifteen minutes or so. He came back and we got out of there. I was never so glad to get out of any place as I was that. I had a real bad feeling about it. Nothing happened, but that's the kind of risk Cooper would take to gather intelligence."

Officers' Mess

Back at Hill 55 headquarters, the regimental commander held his morning staff briefing in the Officers' Mess over breakfast. This allowed each staff officer, such as those overseeing Personnel or Intelligence as well as Civil Affairs, to report plans for the day.

Major John Nichols, who attended these sessions along with Cooper, remembered him as "an earnest, happy person. He was serious and had a sense of humor." That sense of humor was evident during one morning meeting after Cooper had visited a nearby village.

"Captain Cooper related his description of the glee and delight the local villagers took in using a newfangled 'methane generator,'" Nichols said. "The people lined up, then used"—defecated into—"the device, which in turn generated electricity. The people had a first-time power supply" and the Americans had new friends.

"The regimental staff," said Nichols, "was also delighted in Gary's recital, in his usual humorous way."

The Officers' Mess was a favorite hangout, where Cooper was a popular figure, but there were security issues.

"It was located halfway up the ridge of Hill 55," Nichols said. "It was not the safest place, yet I don't recall any incoming rounds near there. It's two-hole 'head' was nearby, all alone on a near-barren slope. Along our portion of Hill 55, we manned 13 bunkers along a curved line. It was not unusual to be sniped at or have grenades thrown at us, generally during darkness. In front of our lines, incorporated within the barbed wire, were burial pagodas, which the enemy often hid behind. To destroy these monuments would worsen relations greatly, as ancestor worship was and is very dear to them."

One solution was to mount a 106 mm recoilless rifle on a "Mechanical Mule"—a flatbed truck—and aim it throughout the night at a prominent pagoda.

A bit later, Nichols said, Cooper got the village of Xuam Diem to dismantle the offending structure in exchange for ten bags of rice, ten bags of cement, and ten sheets of eight by four-foot tin. The downside: "The cement and tin had been stockpiled by our First Sergeant in hopes of building a swimming pool at the water point."

But life in this setting had its perks. At the Officers' Mess, said Nichols, the bar opened at 1630 daily. Drinks were generously sized and moderately priced. They were paid for with scrip known as "funny money" or "MPC" (military pay certificates). Ice was to cool the glasses, if it was available at all. When the sky darkened after dinner, the movie began.

"Captain Cooper and his ARVN Liaison Officer would stay after dinner, chat and tell stories and sometime see the movies." At least one film, said Nichols, starred one of Cooper's favorites, John Wayne.[148]

DEAR GOVERNOR

By May 1967, Cooper's year in Vietnam was coming to an end. His work with Hill 55 headquarters was praised in his Bronze Star citation. It noted, among other achievements, his facility with the Vietnamese language, skills in "developing a spirit of cooperation between the local people and Marine units," while also coordinating "civic action and psychological warfare efforts in connection with Operations County Fair and Golden Fleece."[149]

While Cooper rarely if ever referenced his race or the discrimination he had experienced growing up in Alabama, even while fighting a war in Vietnam he was aware of the civil rights protest movement back home. Most of the epochal moments in the 1960s civil rights struggle had occurred while he was on Marine assignments far removed from the marches and demonstrations. But he was still keen to what was going on, particularly in Alabama.

Lurleen Wallace had been elected governor in 1966 because her husband, arch-segregationist George Wallace, could not by law succeed himself.

> *There was a story in* Stars and Stripes, *and I don't know if I was in a tent or somewhere out in the woods. I read this article that the governor of Alabama had filed an appeal and was fighting an order to desegregate the schools. I said, "Hey, this doesn't seem right." So I wrote a nice, respectful letter saying, "Dear Governor, I'm very concerned to read this. Here citizens of Alabama are fighting for our country and our children can't go to schools of their choice."*

The newly installed Lurleen Wallace administration was basically an extension of her husband's political machine, which championed segregation. Her May 23, 1967, reply to Cooper's letter was right out of the Wallace playbook:

I believe that *Stars and Stripes* has misled you, or you have misunderstood my position regarding the school situation in Alabama. We have had freedom of choice for all races here for several years. Our objection to the recent court order is that it completely takes over control of our schools. We believe that parents, both Negro and white, should have the deciding voice as to what schools their children shall attend. We are very much against federal government control of local institutions of self government and education. We believe that you will agree that this is not in accordance with our constitutional system of government.

Governor George and I are proud of our men and boys serving in Viet Nam, and we remember you each day in our prayers.[150]

Cooper, unpersuaded, saved the letter.

7

Starting Over

After fourteen months in Vietnam, Cooper's next stop was Henderson Hall, the Marine headquarters smack up against the national cemetery in Arlington, Virginia. From his office he could hear the buglers playing "Taps" at funerals.

In other circumstances, the posting would have been ideal. The house on Fillmore was right down the street from his children's school. Like other military brats, they enjoyed the base swimming pool and other recreational outlets. There was shopping at the PX.[151]

But at home there were problems. Charlesetta had been left time and again to raise the children without their father around. Years later, she could say that she loved those Marine years—"I look back on it and I don't think I could ever have had those experiences on my own. It was courtesy of the Marine Corps—the travel, the people. Definitely."[152] But the long separations and perhaps other nagging resentments or personal problems caused her to drift away from family concerns. After more than a year apart, with her husband in Vietnam, the return to close quarters for Gary and Charlesetta led to quarrels, not affections.

The breakup had been in the making for a long time.

James Harrell: "Of course she stayed on him; she was always somewhat miserable and mad. The military life put a strain on her. And Gary had gone to a meeting. She was giving him all kind of hell. He said he was driving home. About six blocks from home he sees a little kid come out on the street with a military hat on. Driving on he sees one coming by with a uniform. About half a block from the house he sees a kid walking by with a sword. So he gets out in front of the house. She had set all of his stuff on the sidewalk!"

This was when I was stationed at Henderson Hall. We had a house on Fillmore Street in Arlington, maybe twenty minutes away. Charlie had gotten pissed off at me about something. She had put all my stuff out there.

In fact, when I came back from Vietnam, Charlie decided she didn't want to be married anymore. Now I've got to tell you, I was far from being a good husband. In addition to that, I was gone. Can you imagine, after being away on the USS Chicago *for two years, I volunteer to go to Vietnam?*

A possible career change surfaced during the Henderson Hall posting, but not the sort Cooper wanted. On the upside, the USMC was finally pushing to recruit more black officers. It had tapped a pioneering African American, Lieutenant Colonel Kenneth Berthoud Jr., to be a special advisor to the deputy chief of staff for minority officer procurement, and it established Naval ROTC units at a few historically black colleges and universities, including Prairie View A&M in Texas. Would Cooper be interested in being its ROTC instructor?[153]

I got a call saying they were going to establish, for the first time in the history of the Marine Corps, a Navy ROTC at a historically black school. It was to be at Prairie View, in Texas. That's the school my mother's sister, my Aunt Helen, had graduated from. I was told they needed a black infantry officer to head the Marine section, to be the Marine instructor for the ROTC unit.

Now, there were only three black infantry officers in the Marine Corps, and Prairie View was not a place that interested me. But mainly, I had never met a general who had been an ROTC instructor. So I said, "Well, sir, let me think about it." And when I got back to the general, I said, "Sir, let me make a suggestion. I've got the addresses and phone numbers of the other two!"

And they took one of them, a friend of mine, Clancy Baker.

Cooper, who advanced to the rank of major that October, enjoyed the job at Henderson Hall, but the routine was nowhere near as intense as the day-to-day of Mike Company or Hill 55. If Vietnam was far away for Cooper, however, for others it was coming home as the anti-war movement mushroomed and turned volatile.

In October 1967, an anti-war rally drew an estimated 100,000 protesters to the Lincoln Memorial, where speakers included Dr. Benjamin Spock, the widely read pediatrician. When thousands of the protesters marched on the Pentagon, chaos, disorder and violence ensued, with several hundred arrested. Cooper, who a year earlier was leading rifle company attacks on Viet Cong and North Vietnamese soldiers, was coming face-to-face with a side of the war he had not experienced.[154]

There were more riots in the nation's capital after the April 4, 1968, assassination of the Reverend Martin Luther King Jr. in Memphis.

I was in charge of troops on a day that riots started in Washington, D.C. I could see the smoke. I said, "Lord, please don't let me have to take these Marines over there in Washington." I said, "PLEASE, Lord." And the Lord answered my prayers—we didn't have to go.

Standing with the Marines in the parking lot of Henderson Hall, his concern was over what might ensue when they were confronted—or even attacked—by protesters.

I had these armed Marines, with loaded weapons, flak jackets. I was concerned that there would be violence, that I may have to order my Marines to fire on these protesters. Who knows what could have happened? Of course, I don't think anything good could have happened, that's for sure. But I was ready to go and would have if I had been ordered to.

That kind of confrontation was of a different order entirely than his mission in Vietnam.

Mike Company—that was the greatest experience in my life, leading Marines in combat.

I tell my daughter, Shawn, "You know, I'm really lucky. Just think, I've been in combat, I've been wounded, I've seen people killed, and it didn't affect me mentally." And Shawn says, "Daddy, that's a matter of opinion!" But seriously, one reason I don't think the experience in combat changed me was because I grew up around a funeral home. In Vietnam, I'd see people who had stepped on a mine and there would

*be pieces of them in a tree. I've seen people—you'd literally have to tie
them up, they'd go berserk. But that never affected me because I've
picked up bodies that had been drowned, and I really think that had
something to do with it.*

*I never went to a school for funeral home training, but as a little boy
I would cut the grass around the funeral home and go pick bodies up
and I would observe them in the morgue. I never did very much, but I
did some things that put me around the bodies.*

*Also, by the time I got ready to go into combat, I think I was really
mentally ready, I think I was the captain of my soul because I had studied, and I knew that opposing me was a person with the same objective
as I had—to kill me and my men.*

Over the years, Cooper would reflect on his Vietnam experience and
his view of those who opposed the war, including African American
giants of the era such as Muhammad Ali. Members of his own family,
including his brother Jay, were activists against the war; Jay joined New
York Senator Bobby Kennedy's presidential campaign in 1968, a campaign
that was passionately anti-war.

In time Gary Cooper could understand their arguments. As the war
dragged on for eight more years after Cooper left Vietnam, it became a
political crucible for Presidents Lyndon Johnson and Richard Nixon and
a flashpoint of anger for a generation struggling against racial segregation at home.

There were racial brawls, including one at Camp Lejeune in July 1969
where a twenty-year-old white Marine was killed, and one at the Kaneohe
Marine Air Station, where a fight involved some two hundred men.
Then-Lieutenant Colonel Hurdle L. Maxwell, who in 1968 became the
first black Marine officer to command an infantry battalion, was quoted
by *Ebony* magazine in December 1969: "The Corps says it treats all men
one way—as a Marine. What it actually has done is treat everybody as a
white Marine."

But Maxwell also said it was "only in the extreme higher grades that
you get great disparity in the proportion of blacks in grades," and *Ebony*
said that many black Marines, while not denying racial discrimination

exists in the Corps, "feel they get better treatment in the Marines than they did in civilian life."[155]

In Vietnam itself, however, the war took a fractured racial turn.

"It was very obvious that the type of Marines who were being drafted or entering into the Marine Corps would much rather have fought on the streets than fought in Vietnam, so to speak," General Frank E. Petersen would recall later. "Fragging was an issue. Quite often the closer you got to the shooting, the less of an issue there was. But one of my good friends was then a correspondent for *Time* magazine. Wally Terry. He wrote a book titled *Bloods*. And in it he outlined about eight different stories of individual black Marines who would rather kill whites than Vietnamese."[156]

Cooper saw none of that during his tour in 1966 and 1967.

My experience was different. You hear an awful lot about racial problems in the units. You hear about fragging, enlisted men throwing hand grenades at officers. You hear about the drug problem. But I was very lucky because I was there before that stuff started.

Of course something could have gone on that I didn't know about, but I talked to some of my enlisted men and we didn't have any drug problems. But we weren't close to anybody selling. We weren't close to a town. We were worrying about living. We were worrying about the VC.

During Cooper's time in Vietnam, black Marines displayed a quiet pride in African Americans in the officer ranks. Years later Cooper spoke with a black man who had served with Petersen, the pioneering black Marine aviator:

And he was telling me how they would stand in the back, and when General Petersen would take off, they would give the fist salute. So I asked the general about it, and he said, "Yes, I didn't tell anybody, but I'd see them back in the back giving the fist salute."

Petersen, when he was still a cadet in the early 1950s, had famously staged his own protest on the outskirts of Brewton, a small south Alabama town, while on training flights out of Pensacola, Florida.

"We would land at this small strip and go into this ramshackle restaurant to grab lunch," he recalled. "The white owner refused to let me inside the restaurant. So what happened, one of the other pilots went inside and bought me a sandwich and brought it out. I wouldn't eat it because I felt the owner had spit in it or something. I just sat there and stewed.

"Then I asked the flight instructor if I could be the last one to take off. He sort of smiled. I think he knew what I had in mind.

"The strip was right up against the front of the restaurant, so I lined up to take off and I swung the tail of my aircraft directly toward the entrance way of the restaurant and went to full power. And since it was a dirt strip, there was obviously a big cloud of dust and hound dogs running and the screen door flapping and then I released the brakes and took off.

"That was a standard place for us to go eat, and about a year later, another black cadet came through named Ed House. I said, 'Ed, when you go to such-and-such a field, bring your own sandwich.'"[157]

Again, in time Cooper could not only understand, but also find some room for mutual agreement with those who opposed the Vietnam War:

Think about it, these young African Americans over there fighting a war, and at home—it's kind of like the Montford Point Marines over in World War II saying, "Hell, we can't go in a restaurant but the German prisoners can."

But like those Montford Pointers, Cooper was guided by his firmness of military purpose. As he often said: *If they had sent me to Disneyland to fight, I would have gone to Disneyland. I was that kind of Marine. I didn't care who was president but I knew that I had volunteered to go, so that was it.*

James Webb, the former Navy Secretary and U.S. Senator from Virginia who was a Marine officer in Vietnam and later an accomplished writer, described the nation's post-war division:

In truth, the 'Vietnam generation' is a misnomer. Those who came of age during that war are permanently divided by different reactions to a whole range of counter-cultural agendas, and nothing divides them more deeply than the personal ramifications of the war itself. The sizable portion of the Vietnam age group who declined to support the counter-cultural agenda, and especially the men and women who opted to serve in the military during the Vietnam War, are quite different from their peers who for decades have claimed to speak for them. In fact, they are much like the World War II generation itself. For them, Woodstock was a side show, college protestors were spoiled brats who would have benefited from having to work a few jobs in order to pay their tuition, and Vietnam represented not an intellectual exercise in draft avoidance or protest marches but a battlefield that was just as brutal as those their fathers faced in World War II and Korea.[158]

To honor the Montford Pointers, who had fought selflessly in World War II despite injustices at home, Cooper joined some one thousand Marines and their wives in September 1967 at the New York Hilton for the third convention of the fledgling association of Montford Point veterans. The *New York Amsterdam News* paid homage to those who had opened the USMC door for blacks: "Thanks to those first Marines, they established a beachhead on an island of prejudice and never lost their nerve in the process."[159]

The newspaper carried a photograph of nine notables attending the convention. Two of them, sharply attired in dress whites, were Captain J. Gary Cooper and Major Frank E. Petersen Jr.

Cooper also attended the August 21, 1968, ceremony at the Marine Barracks, at 8th & I when Private First Class James Anderson Jr. was posthumously awarded the Congressional Medal of Honor—the first black Marine ever to receive the medal. A rifleman, he had died in Vietnam on February 28, 1967, pulling an enemy grenade close to his chest to absorb the explosion and save his Marine comrades.[160] Cooper had not been involved in his unit or operation, but it was important to his own sense of mission to be on hand when the award was handed to Anderson's parents.

There were very few black people who were senior in the Marine Corps at this time, but one was Ken Berthoud, who became a colonel. He was a sharp guy. Maybe Ken had gone to NYU, some Eastern school—almost none of the black officers in those days had gone to historically black schools.

Ken called me one day and said, "Let's go to Marine Barracks." He said the first black Marine is going to get the Medal of Honor posthumously. So he and I went. It was a solemn, great ceremony. I'm not sure we recognized the significance of it at that time. But after it was over I went down to shake the hands of the parents. I have in my office a copy of the citation that he received and a picture of the ceremony.

BREAKUP

Duty of a different sort called when he received word of his father's death, a suicide.

Algernon Johnson Cooper Sr. had left the bonds of Delaware Street years earlier. His departure occurred at the very time when his older children were on their way to making their emphatic marks in the world, including Gary with historic racial milestones as a Marine officer. Gary is convinced that his father's marital breakup and events leading to his death were set off by Bishop Thomas J. Toolen kicking Billy out of the white Catholic high school.[161]

When the other kids were growing up, Mama and Daddy were bitching at each other, blaming one for doing this or that and arguing in front of the kids.

Luckily I got none of that. I didn't know that Mother and Dad were having any problems until I was at Notre Dame, maybe calling sometimes and she's crying.

Mario was born, I think I was a junior in college. Peggy and others were in Mobile then, and they would stay with Mama I think most of the time because Mama probably hated the woman he was living with. You know how parents do when they don't have good feelings between each other. Surely that hurt all of the kids, not growing up in a stable home.

Mario tells me that they sent him to a boarding school in California by himself on a train when he was just ten years old. How sad.

My mother and I didn't talk about it. I can remember, though, coming home as a lieutenant in the Marine Corps and staying at home, and having a conversation with my daddy, telling him how disappointed I was with him. We just had a conversation and that ended it.

I don't think he and I ever talked again.

At the time of his death, the sixty-year-old A. J. Cooper Sr. had remarried and moved out of the Down the Bay neighborhood. He was in the

West Ridge Road home he shared with his second wife, Hattie P. Cooper, when he shot himself on November 7, 1968.

Last rites were held at the family funeral home on November 12 following a wake the night before.[162]

He had been secretary-treasurer of Christian Benevolent Funeral Home and Burial Association for some three decades. During that time, he shrewdly marshaled the sales force and sought to optimize profits and investment returns. Skilled in finance, he was successful and highly regarded—an officer of the National Insurance Association as well as a civic leader in the black community—but he had changed in his last years. Unlike the man who taught a rigorous financial ethic to his children, he was secretly stealing money from the company. The cost of sending his children to out-of-state preparatory and boarding schools and top-ranked universities had been more than he could handle personally. Without the knowledge of his Aunt Pearl Madison, who had been president and board chairman after her husband's death in 1963, he siphoned off company funds.

The funeral home had always done okay. The insurance company was doing great. When I came back, we sold more insurance. We had more than 100 employees, we had offices in seven cities, and I would visit those offices. I was the director, and we would have sales meetings. There were, during those times, thirty-five or forty black-owned insurance companies in the United States, and we had an association. A.G. Gaston was a part of it. And we used to out-sell all of them, maybe sometimes twice as much. We just ran a hell of a company. We had goals and meetings and a newsletter.

But it was a case of Daddy stealing money and depleting the reserves. You look back and say, "How in the hell did something like that happen?"

Well, we had a house in the Down the Bay neighborhood. I don't think the house was in trouble because I think my great-aunt helped him build the house. But can you imagine the cost in those days for a young black executive sending all those kids to boarding schools? That was what I'm sure was behind him ripping off the company. He didn't have any big Cadillacs. Just think, he had me at Notre Dame—I had almost graduated—but he soon had five other children, sending them to Marmion Military Academy [Illinois], the boarding schools, the universities and all. I think that drive to send them to good schools is what motivated him to do it.

Then he and my mother separated. Then he started living with another woman and you can imagine how embarrassing and troubling that was in a small town.

I am convinced—how can I say this?—I am convinced that that run-in he had with the church over Billy's enrollment at McGill changed him. I mean, we'd get home, we'd say the rosary around the bed every night, we'd say prayers, Daddy was at church every day. But, boy, once the bishop did that, the Catholic church was for him no more.

When he killed himself, A. J. had quietly put Christian Benevolent on the brink of bankruptcy, a financial problem that would take at least a few years to be resolved. In Washington, Gary's own increasingly rocky marriage to Charlesetta had come totally unraveled.

James Harrell: "Gary had to come back and take charge of the family business. Charlesetta said, 'To hell with it, I'm going back home, to the life of privilege like I had before in Chicago.' She had no interest in living in Mobile."

With a divorce, she headed to the Virgin Islands. Cooper mustered out of the active Marine service and returned to Mobile, a thirty-three-year-old single parent with three young children.

I had moved to Mobile. She had stayed in Washington. Shawn was the first one to tell her mama that she wanted to go live with her daddy. Then Charlie agreed to send the other two kids as well and I got custody of my children.

Patrick recalls their arrival in Mobile:

"When he first picked us up at the airport, my two sisters and I are arguing about who is going to sit in the front seat. He says, 'Look, Patrick is my only son. He's going to sit in the front seat and my two girls are going to sit in the back seat.'

"They were pissed. They were kicking the back of my seat. But within a year, I was in the back seat and one of them was in the front seat."

It was time to start over all around.

For Gary, resigning his regular commission in the Marine Corps was a difficult choice: *I damn near cried over that decision. But it was the best decision of my life, because it allowed me to do other things.*

MATT METCALFE

First up for Cooper was to save Christian Benevolent Insurance. With the help of Matt Metcalfe, a highly successful white insurance executive in Mobile, Christian Benevolent was saved.

When Gary sought Metcalfe's assistance, he picked well. For starters, Matt knew and liked Pearl Madison, the astute force behind the family's fortune. He also had been hugely successful as an entrepreneur building the assets of Loyal American Insurance Company.[163]

And he had no hint of racial bias.

"Growing up, I had no status," he said. "I was born in Montgomery during the Depression. My dad worked at little drugstores when he could. We would move along the L&N tracks. We moved first to Tuskegee. For some reason my dad and Dr. George Washington Carver were good friends. I would go out with my dad to the college and I met Dr. Carver on several occasions. I remember mostly all of the big carrots and potatoes in jars that were huge. You can imagine a six-year-old tyke looking at that stuff. Also I was impressed with Carver—of course I didn't know who he was, his importance or anything like that—but he was such a gentle, kind man that even I as a six-year-old kid picked that up. I don't know what the relationship was with my daddy and him. Dad was a druggist and of course he was a doctor, a PhD I guess in biology—whatever it was, they had a nice relationship.

"We moved from Tuskegee to Georgiana, then to Mobile in 1940, before the war started. I've been here ever since.

"I didn't go to college. I just managed to get out of high school."

In Mobile, Metcalfe worked on the docks before getting hired in 1955 as a clerk at Loyal American, a new firm that politically minded Jimmy Faulkner operated out of an antebellum home on Government Street. Four years later, at twenty-nine, Metcalfe was running the company.

"When Jimmy Faulkner and I started, it had a million dollars in assets. I made some seventeen acquisitions, and when I left we were in forty-nine states and eleven foreign countries, and we had a billion dollars in assets."

Like Gary, Matt has made connections far from Mobile. Among other things, he is a member of the Metropolitan Club of New York City, which was founded in 1891 by a notable group whose last names included Vanderbilts, Whitneys, and Roosevelts—and whose first president was J. Pierpont Morgan (as of 2013, Metcalfe had become the club's member of longest standing—he was inducted in 1964).[164]

The family company, Christian Benevolent, did not go bankrupt, but it was placed in a legal status where we were allowed to operate only as long as we had a judicial agent running the company. I remember that judicial agent was a white man, William Beckers, who had been close to my Aunt Shug. He became the judicial agent, we paid him a salary, and we continued operations. He really had no input on running the company, but was the agent for the court.

We were able to make payments, but our problem was not the daily operation of the business. The problem was we were supposed to have so much money in reserve, some percentage, and that had been hurt.

Metcalfe: "When I first met Gary, Loyal American had bought a larger building out on Government Street, a much larger, much nicer building. I looked out down the hallway one day and I saw these two giants walking down the hall. Gary is around six-foot-seven and Billy had to be the same height. They came down the hall—no appointment—they just said they wanted to see me.

"We sat down and Gary got right to the point—just as he does now. He said, 'I have a problem with my family's life insurance company, which is Christian Benevolent Life Insurance. It's owned by my aunt, Mrs. Pearl Madison.'

"Mrs. Madison is a woman whom I knew and had done some business with. She serviced some of the policies I had. A very aristocratic, lovely lady. Gary said his father had worked for Mrs. Madison, and was running the insurance company and the funeral home.

"He said when Billy got out of school—he had gone to Notre Dame also—he came down to help his father, to learn the business and get into it. He was gung-ho. His father had a habit of getting up early and going to the bank and getting the mail and bringing it to the office. One morning Billy thought he would show how interested in the business he was and got up earlier, went to the Post Office and brought the mail in and went through the mail. And he noticed on the bank statement it was $800,000 less—this is Gary telling me this—it was $800,000 less than the statements he had seen.

"So he went to his father and presented him with this, as a question. This was not an accusation. He just wanted to make sure his father was aware of the discrepancy and wanted to know why. And his father said, 'Billy, I have been stealing money from the company for years. I typed in CD's on the bank's statements to make up the deficit.'

"As I understood it, the statements would come out, and let's say they showed $2 million in the bank. If I recall correctly, Gary told me that his father just typed in 'CD's—$800,000'—or maybe every time he changed it. But that difference kept the surplus up, suggested the company had a surplus, which of course it didn't have.

"My thought to Gary was, 'How in the world could this avoid the examiners?' But it shows how loose the examiners were, and his father did this over those years. The examiners never went to the bank to verify it."

In forthrightly telling Billy that he had been taking the money, the fraud was no longer a secret. Algernon Johnson Cooper Sr. shortly went home, got a shotgun and killed himself.[165]

For Metcalfe, what Gary said next was revealing of Gary's character, the reason Metcalfe would try to help him then and always remain his friend: "Gary said, 'I resigned from the Marines and came back here because, even though I didn't steal the money, nor did Billy, we benefited. We were the beneficiaries of it. We got good educations. We got sent through Notre Dame and we got raised well.'

"He said, 'I have a duty to the policyholders to make this right and I've come back to do it. But the state is going to put Christian Benevolent Insurance Company in conservatorship, and I've been told you may be the one to talk to, to see George Wallace and present the story to George and see if he will give me a moratorium, give me a chance to see if I can't repair the damage internally through proper management.'

"So we did that, and Gary did restore Christian Benevolent to good health. It worked out well for the policyholders and of course for Gary and his family. But to me it shows such strength of character and determination—you don't find many men nowadays with that kind of mettle."

Matt felt much the same about Billy.

"He, like Gary, was reserved and carried himself well, just as the aunt did," Metcalfe said. "It carried through, the countenance and the stature and class that they all showed. Billy seemed to have that, too.

"My wife knew his wife Paulette much better than I knew Billy because my wife and his wife served together on some boards in town, child day care center or YMCA, something like that. Paulette—a beautiful woman, a beautiful lady, a very good person."

As for Gary's father, Metcalfe felt A. J. showed something like character in promptly owning up to his actions: "To a degree it showed—it's hard to use the word 'character'—but what would be the term for the fact that the father did not try to deny or cover it up but just shot straightforward and admitted it and then went and took himself out of the picture? What would you call that?"

While Metcalfe was helping Gary gain entrée to the state insurance commissioner, Gary was figuring out a way to rebuild the surplus.

One night in my sleep or something I had a dream that told me how to solve that problem, and it had to do with rearranging assets. So I came up with the idea, and I think I told Matt, but anyway, we were able to file a new annual report to make these changes, and we were able to get rid of the judicial agent.

One thing that helped us was that Matt was the president of a large, successful company, Loyal American, and Matt also knew the insurance commissioner. So Matt helped me get through to the Insurance Department, have them be friendly with me, give me ideas, allow us to do these things to rebuild the surplus. He really helped save the company so I could eventually sell it.

"I guess he managed the company frugally," said Metcalfe. "With life insurance companies, especially those well-established, they can be very profitable. Taxation is very low, I think the very lowest of any industry in the country, for the purpose of allowing reserves to be built. He may have injected some money—I don't know that—but he certainly built it back and the proof of that is that he was able to sell it for $2 million cash. Sell the equity, so that was the stock."

Pearl Madison died in 1975, at age eighty-eight. Gary became president of the insurance company and Billy chairman of the board. By then, the company's name had been changed to Christian Benevolent Insurance Company.[166] And in 1985, it was sold to Protective Industrial Insurance Co., a Birmingham firm owned by the family of J. Mason Davis, a prominent black lawyer.

ENTREPRENEUR

Along with trying to save the core family business, Cooper was simultaneously forging a new career in the Marine Reserves and launching new enterprises. Among them was Petal Pusher, a flower shop, and Black Star, a bail bonding company.[167]

My brother Billy and I were running the insurance company. My brother Jay was a lawyer. He had graduated from NYU law school and was back in Mobile. I would go to court sometimes, and I would see there were many black folks going to court, but no black bail bondsman. So I decided to start a bail bond company. I didn't know beans about it, but I did some research, and we started one—the old building is still down there. The first Black Star was located right on Davis Avenue, the middle of the black community. The little building is still there, on the corner of Martin Luther King—Davis Avenue was renamed—and Dr. E. B. Goode Drive. It's a little street named after the family doctor who circumcised me and brought my brother Billy into the world.

After we started doing well, we eventually moved the bail bond company downtown, on Royal Street right across from where the Renaissance Hotel is now. Black Star now was nearer the courts. The motto was: "You ring. We spring." We got plenty of folks out of jail. The big challenge then was people had to show up in court. If someone did not show up, the judge would forfeit your bond, meaning you would have to pay the court.

What made it so difficult for us is if one of the white bondsmen's clients didn't show up, the judge would give them another two months or so. Us? He'd forfeit our bond. We made sure we went out and tracked them down.

The other challenge was, the judges knew all the other bail bond people. They were their friends. They would actually use racial terms in court when addressing people back in those days. There was a judge who would call you the N-word in court. Luckily, with my background I was friends with most of the judges, too. So that worked out pretty well.

When the phone would ring, my daughter Shawn would say, "Oh, somebody's in trouble tonight!" I would put on my .45 and get my combat boots. I'd actually go out in town. I know businessmen—I'd go maybe to family-owned bars—they would point people out, and I would take them down to the jail.

In one case, when a man resisted, Cooper shot him—the flesh wound was treated at a hospital.[168]

This guy attacked me. Too many folks attacked would shoot to kill. That's what gets me so concerned. I shot this sucker in the thigh—where I wanted to shoot him. People who are trained, you don't have to shoot somebody in the goddam head.

Cooper's finance major at Notre Dame helped steer him toward involvement in a long-term proposal—the first minority-owned national bank in Alabama with a federal charter. It wasn't easy.

Back in Mobile in 1972 I got a call from William Powell. He must have been in his sixties then. He was a psychiatric social worker and one of the first two black policemen in Mobile. He had some friends, a couple of preachers, schoolteachers. None of them had any business experience other than maybe running a store. And they told me about wanting to start a bank.

Initially it was rough going. They couldn't get loans. People would talk to them like shit. So we formed an exploratory unit and they applied for a federal charter. We had to raise $750,000. This was huge.

We literally went door-to-door. We had so many shareholders—we had shareholders with five shares, two shares.

But they got a charter. They opened a bank.

At first the Commonwealth National Bank operated inside a trailer in a mostly black neighborhood. That didn't mean its operators won instant loyalty from blacks. The trailer raised suspicions.

Black folks would come out and look at the trailer and say, "That nigger's crazy. They put my money in there and a goddam truck comes and pulls that trailer away!"

At first it also was difficult to find blacks with experience to run the bank. Our first two presidents were a white woman—a super lady—and a white man. Then the young blacks started getting trained.

Commonwealth National was still a work in progress for Cooper but it was getting traction.

8

Single-Parent Days

B ack in the Port City where he was raised, Gary at first shared a home with his brother Jay, who had bought it and another property on Savannah Street, across from the historic Oakleigh house. A baby casket from the funeral home—filled with *Playboy* magazines—was part of the living room decor.

"They were trying to be cool bachelors," Shawn Cooper said.

Soon Gary moved his young family into a two-story home a couple of blocks away on Palmetto Street. It was also in Mobile's Oakleigh Garden Historic District, with its stately live oaks and prized older homes dating back to the 1800s.

Still with a Marine officer's mindset, Gary didn't tolerate slackers at home.

"He truly was a single parent. It's not like there were any housekeepers or anything else," said daughter Joli Cooper Nelson. "He was just into structure, discipline and order. Everybody got into the routine and rules."

"It was a culture shock," said Patrick. "My mom had been raising us for three or four years. During that period of time, we had very little contact with my father. Heading down to Mobile, it was a culture shock in terms of just being in the South and because we really weren't that familiar with him at that point."

In short order, they learned their new routine included Marine-style mornings.

"We woke up every morning to 'Reveille.' That may sound crazy, but we did," Joli said. "He would come in your room and say, 'Reveille! Reveille!' And you had to jump up. Then he would take us jogging in the morning down Palmetto and up Government streets, and he would sing that song, 'Here we go-oh! All the way-ay!' and I'd have curlers in my hair trying to get ready for school, running down there with him."

"We used to do that all the time," said Patrick. "He has always been kind of gung-ho. And with that gung-ho Marine Corps attitude comes some pretty stern discipline. So we had to learn to deal with a lot of discipline from him that we really hadn't had when we were living with our mother. That was a shock."

At times Gary took his morning run with a neighbor.

Ed Massey lived right down the street. We'd run in the morning. We'd run down by Magnolia Cemetery and the police precinct. Ed's white, and he always joked that he made sure he ran on the side of me because we didn't want the police to think he was chasing me!

Gary was not hands-off when it came to discipline. Corporal punishment was not just a threat.

"His recipe for success—I believe that fear was a motivator," said Shawn. "There was no doubt that you knew expectations and you knew what had to be done. And if it didn't get done, you knew you were going to be dead."

With respect to my kids, I got custody of all three of them when I returned from Vietnam. They were in the sixth, fifth, and fourth grades at the time, but it was important to me to be there. Many kids lack this stability in their lives.

I actually regret we no longer have the draft because there are inner-city kids who do not get the leadership and discipline they need. The draft would help them.[169]

For Patrick, Joli, and Shawn, the structure imposed by their father was a home-based boot camp, and their mother, Charlesetta, was not often a factor.

"She was not in our lives for a couple of years," said Joli. "We saw her maybe once or twice. In the high school years, we would spend time in the summer in Chicago when she'd left the Virgin Islands and moved back to Chicago. I wouldn't say we saw her regularly, no."

"Neither of my parents really had maternal or paternal instincts," said Shawn. "Dad did it because he had to, because Mom wouldn't do it."

"He was very much chauvinistic, in my opinion," said Joli. "There was a place for men, there was a place for women. He had extraordinarily high expectations. He articulated those and he showed that for the most part we were on the same page. He would never allow in the household, ever, the sense that you were average. There was nothing average about us.

"When I think about my involvement with my children's lives today, going to all their social activities—none of that stuff with him. I cheered and played sports. I don't remember my father being at anything. That is, I think, a generational thing. But he was always encouraging, always supportive.

"He was very much an entrepreneur. He worked a lot, and so did we. . . . So growing up, there was always the expectation that you would support yourself. We were always taught financial management perspectives: You pay yourself first. Always your goal is to be your own boss. Fiscal management."

A House with Add-ons

While he wanted his children to shoot for the highest marks, Cooper also wanted them to practice humility.

"It could have been because at this point in time he was in the Reserves, and he was in politics," said Joli. "In politics, the perception of the people is critically important, so he always, always taught humility. Both the folks you meet going up and the folks you meet going down, you treat everybody with respect and dignity."

"In our household there was never an ounce of elitism or 'better than' or 'different from,'" said Joli. To her mind, this stemmed from her father's Marine experience.

"I don't know this to be the case but I've always heard that when you're a Marine, depending on other Marines, you're as strong as the weakest link. So there's a real focus on teamwork and co-dependency. I think that was very much how we were raised. It was never 'us' and 'them.'"

With the Cooper family's burial insurance business on the rocks when Gary's children moved to Mobile, there was no sense of their being among the black elite, as had been true for Gary and his siblings growing up.

"It was very different. That was not part of our life in the least," said Joli.

"Where my father grew up," Shawn said, "Gladys had the big brick house, and all those other houses were these little shotgun houses. So here Dad is, this handsome, tall guy. Handsome, but he didn't have pretty hair—he had nappy hair—so he just had to kick ass.

"All the other black kids who did not come from the means that he had, he had to make sure—I mean he already stood out—but he had to be regular. That was a trait. Everybody says my grandfather was a regular, regular man. Loved to hang in the projects, had his woman over there, you know, just very social and made people feel good about themselves. And I think that's where Dad got that from."

Looking back, Patrick said the Cooper family was understandably part of Mobile's black elite in the early part of the twentieth century when the burial insurance company was formed and flourished under the Madisons.

"There are some very old, established, highly educated black families down in Mobile," he said. "Our family had been around for such a long time, it went back to the early 1900s. One of the things that distinguished us—I won't say distinguished us, but made us a little different in the black community—was our family had a couple of businesses. We had the Christian Benevolent Insurance Company, which wasn't an insurance agency, it actually wrote its own policies and had actuaries to determine mortality rates and was probably the largest employer of African Americans in the Mobile area.

"So they had that business, and because your family owned a business, your image is a little different. I think that's the case in the white community, too: If your family owns a business, it's a little bit different environment.

"But Shawn, Joli, and I didn't grow up in a wealthy environment. We grew up in a very intellectually rich environment, but it wasn't a wealthy environment. Take a look at the house that Gary lives in now. It's the same house he's had for forty years, with some add-ons."

CULTURE IN BLACK AND WHITE

Despite the divorce and the insurance company's financial difficulties,

Gladys Cooper remained a regal figure who set about in 1969 to form "Culture in Black and White," a far-reaching program to teach music, theater and the arts to children of all colors.

Her daughter Peggy, off at college, had begun a workshop in the arts for young people, giving her mother the germ of an idea for a similar project.

"My sister Peggy, she's an optimist," said Dominic, the younger of Mrs. Cooper's two daughters. "She started the first black student union at George Washington University, and when she graduated she started careers in the arts for kids. She went on and started the Duke Ellington School of the Arts. All of this was for the poorer kids, and my mom got the idea. She got the determination that she could do that and she started 'Culture in Black and White.' They had this great program for kids, to learn to dance and all sorts of creative disciplines.

"I think I came home one summer, and I did one. I was a dance major, so I did one of the dance classes."

Gordon Tatum Jr., writing in the *Press-Register*, explained the concept:

> Her idea, 'Culture in Black and White,' was to educate, make all of the art forms available to children, then watch the community reap the rewards of her hard labor and the work of many others. . . . Blacks and whites have come together to do what was necessary. That says something about Gladys Cooper's determination.[170]

She was the president of "Culture in Black and White." Joaquin Holloway Jr. was vice president.

"There was not any one incident that prompted it to be formed," said Joaquin, who recalled the initial meeting in the living room of Mrs. Cooper's big house on Delaware Street: "The whole idea when we had our first meeting—my mother and Gladys were the co-founders—we were sitting around talking and said we wanted to expose the young people to various aspects of culture that they might not normally have been exposed to because there were still pockets of segregation. This would train them in dance, music, karate, that sort of thing.

"A training program—what were we going to name it? We wanted to expose young people to various aspects of culture, but we wanted people to know that it wasn't just exclusively for black young people. It was for people who needed an opportunity to be involved in those activities. When it came time to come up with a name, we decided to call it 'Culture IN Black and White.' I may have been the one who coined that name."

Joaquin produced all thirty-two annual spring festivals that allowed parents to see what the kids had been practicing on Saturdays at Bishop State Community College.

"'Daybreak in America' was the first festival," he said. "My mother came up with the name of that festival. It was in the spring of 1970."

Joaquin's mother, Lucy Ariel Williams Holloway, was a natural complement to Mrs. Cooper for the launch of "Culture in Black and White." With degrees in music from Fisk University and the Oberlin Conservatory of Music, she already had made an impact on the lives of many young people in Mobile as a teacher at Dunbar High School.[171]

She was, as Edward O. Wilson described her, "an inspirational figure whose presence and high degree of excellence showed everyone what education and leadership could accomplish in the black community, even when smothered by a deeply segregated society."[172]

One of her early students, Walter Hugh Samples, told of a precursor to "Culture in Black and White"—a fundraiser for the high school that Mrs. Holloway initiated. It was known as "Dunbar Night."

"Dunbar Night was tantamount to a course in Music Appreciation," Samples told Wilson. "This program included singing, dancing, reciting, some musical instrumental numbers, solos, duets, and choruses. Its repertoire included work songs, folk songs, jazz, popular music, classics and some operatic numbers. This annual activity plus the school song did much to engender school spirit, pride, and morale. Each program usually ended with the singing of a Negro spiritual or a medley of Negro spirituals."[173]

After she retired, a school in Toulminville was named the Ariel Williams Holloway Elementary School in her honor.[174]

Mrs. Cooper encouraged the news media and arts community to get behind the new program. She invited Tatum and Charles Manchester, executive director of the Allied Arts Council of Metropolitan Mobile, to her home for a briefing.

"Gladys Cooper was black and proud," Tatum later wrote for the *Press-Register*. "Mobile was full of racial tension in the late 1960s and early into 1970. She was looking for a common denominator. Because the arts appealed to her and to some of her children, she decided that might be just the thing to draw people together."[175]

The first festival was at the municipal auditorium, Joaquin said, "but that venue got to be price-prohibitive, and the show moved next to the Saenger Theater.

"I've got pictures in my files of the buses bringing the schoolchildren to the Saenger. The door at the Saenger that's now all boarded up, it used to have a sign: 'Colored Entrance.' When we had our festivals, the area around the Saenger would be just packed. Cars everywhere."

Gladys Cooper, as president of "Culture in Black and White," helped give it citywide notice and cachet in the community. She didn't teach classes in music or the arts, but she was key to its success.

"Mrs. Cooper was not one to take 'no' for an answer," wrote Tatum. "She pushed beyond that, especially when she thought 'her' kids could gain something."[176]

With three grandchildren being raised in Mobile by their dad, Gladys Cooper also was able to connect with them in ways that had been impossible when they were moving from one far-flung military post to another.

"We saw her all the time," said Joli. "My father was in the state legislature, so he would be gone three or four days a week during the session. So she would drive her yellow Cadillac over—we called it the 'Yellow Submarine'—and take care of us.

"She was very, very much a part of our lives."

"In terms of our life, she definitely wasn't a primary caretaker," Joli said, "but when my dad traveled she would come over and stay with us. I think she was just trying to get through the day with three rambunctious teenagers. I'm sure her nerves were frayed by the time you were finished with her. But we saw her all the time, every week."

With dark hair, dark eyes, and a light brown coffee complexion, Gladys

Cooper reflected her Mouton ancestry in Lafayette.

"She was Creole," said Patrick. "She looked Creole, and in that area of Mobile, Down the Bay, you had a number of Creole families."

Also, if the family's finances were in trouble, Gladys Cooper didn't show it.

"She was always immaculately groomed," Tatum wrote, "and in the latest fashions which she wore well on her slim figure. Hats were a passion." But there was more to Gladys Cooper than the exterior.

"She spoke well, was dressed to the nines, and could be very persuasive."[177]

"She was my surrogate mother growing up," Patrick said. "When I was just having a hard time dealing with my father's discipline, I would end up staying with her for a month or two. I'd spend my summers with her.

"I was extremely close to Gladys. She was just a very sweet, loving person."

"Wow. This is the Reality."

For Gary's children, the move to Mobile brought into play racial issues that they had been largely oblivious to while in the military environment. For Shawn and Joli, the eye-opener occurred when they joined the downtown Mobile YMCA swim team. Shawn was about nine years old.

"I think I was the only black—you know historically black folks don't swim—and we had a meet at the Country Club of Mobile," said Shawn. "The Country Club of Mobile at that time, unbeknownst to me, did not allow blacks to participate." When told she couldn't take part because she was black, she took this new information home to her father. She said she was puzzled to be called black when, by her lights, she was Hawaiian!

"My teammates told me that I was Hawaiian, because of course I was born in Hawaii. So I informed Dad that that wasn't right, that I should be able to swim because I was Hawaiian."

Her father laughed—and set her straight.

"Let me share a little knowledge with you," he said. "You're a colored girl. You will always be a colored girl."

Shawn, like her parents and siblings, was indelibly black under the racial calculus of segregation, but in person, she is a creamy tan not easily pigeonholed. She would understand this more fundamentally as an adult, but as a child, spending a lot of time with her grandmother Gladys, she began to sense how the color of her skin could define her.

"I was at my grandmother's program, 'Culture in Black and White,' at Bishop State," she recalled. "It was there that I had people say, 'Are you black or are you white?' . . . They would say, 'You white?' 'No. Really I'm not,' I'd say.

"So I really got it a lot from these black kids. But I also now have to go back and recognize they had such limited exposure. I'd just come from living all over, a military brat. So that was my first experience with recognizing something with race."

For Joli, there was the time when her downtown YMCA swim team traveled to Birmingham for a meet, but the Birmingham pool was segregated. Joli said she was told she couldn't compete because she was black, but her teammates stuck by her—they refused to swim if Joli couldn't and left the meet early.

She doesn't recall mentioning it to her father.

"I don't remember a one-on-one conversation, but I think, for me, it was this lost innocence," she said. "Remember, I had been to Hawaii and California and Chicago and Virginia. And then to come down to that, it's like I'm trying to soak it in and understand the rationale behind it. I think it was more a loss of innocence. Like, Wow, this is the reality."

"For me it was a little later, in high school," said Patrick. "I liked to play chess a lot. A buddy of mine, who is white, we went to high school together and sometimes he would come over to my house and we'd play chess. We'd have another guy come over, and we'd play chess for hours. He always wanted to invite me over to his house, but he says his mom has a problem with that, she won't have anybody black over to the house. So that was probably my freshman or sophomore year of high school.

"Then I remember walking to school. We typically walked from the house to my high school at McGill, and you had to walk through a couple of white neighborhoods. You had some kids yell racial epithets at you. That was not uncommon."

9

Political Milestones

By the early 1970s, racial change was afoot in Mobile, and the impact of voting rights protests in the 1960s had increased the chances for blacks to campaign successfully for political office. This change was not lost on Jay Cooper or, later, Gary.

The slowly improving racial climate in Mobile was thanks in large part to the efforts of John LeFlore, leader of the local NAACP chapter, which he revived in 1926.[178] LeFlore's activism had been galvanized as a young man when he was arrested after a scuffle with a white passenger on a segregated streetcar. His offense: he had refused a demand to give up his seat.[179]

His unrelenting push on a range of black issues—equality, jobs, voting rights, schools—antagonized the segregationist power structure in Montgomery. With the NAACP growing in numbers and playing roles in such cases as the Rosa Parks arrest and the attempt by Autherine Lucy to integrate the University of Alabama, then-Attorney General John Patterson went to state court in 1956 and won a quick ban on the NAACP conducting business in Alabama. Through a variety of delaying tactics by the state, it took eight years before the U.S. Supreme Court struck down the state ban with finality. Long before then, LeFlore had continued his work against racial injustice by moving under a different banner, the Non-Partisan Voters League.[180]

He opened doors of political cooperation with progressive whites, most notably Joe Langan, who served at various times as a Mobile city councilman, mayor, and legislator. The work of leaders like LeFlore and Langan helped Mobile avoid the notorious violence erupting elsewhere in the state during the civil rights movement. As Alabama historian Harvey H. Jackson III wrote in a history of Mobile:

> When compared with other Alabama cities, Mobile seemed the soul of racial accommodation and toleration. Although the city remained segregated in most activities, the first black policeman had been hired in 1953, and there were twenty-six African Americans on the force a decade later. Spring Hill College had admitted black students the year of the *Brown* decision. Segregated seating on city buses ended in 1963, and soon afterward black drivers were hired. Sit-ins in other cities moved local leaders to agree quietly to desegregate lunch counters, and white fears of a drop in business proved unfounded.[181]

In July 1963, in a *Wall Street Journal* article headlined: "An Alabama City Builds Racial Peace Elsewhere," Mobile was viewed as a placid antidote to racial turmoil.[182] This came at the midpoint of the same year that newly elected Governor George C. Wallace "stood in the schoolhouse door" at the University of Alabama, and four black girls died in the bombing of Birmingham's Sixteenth Street Baptist Church.

But by the mid-1960s, LeFlore's efforts to work with white moderates and progressives like Langan had begun losing the support of more militant black activists in Mobile. And long under the threat of violence by white supremacists, LeFlore and his wife, Teah, escaped serious harm as a dynamite bomb tore apart their home on the night of June 28, 1967. No one was ever arrested.[183]

The bombing was a signal that Mobile was far from immune to racial turmoil. Over the next decades, the city's image of serenity was marred by the "mock lynching" of a black suspect by white police in 1976 and by the murder of a black teen who was abducted, beaten, and slashed to death by two Ku Klux Klansmen who then strung up his body on a tree near downtown in 1981.[184]

But LeFlore and civil rights lawyers had been relentless with litigation and found federal courts receptive where change could not be wrought politically.

With the help of the NAACP Legal Defense Fund, LeFlore sued to desegregate Mobile's public school system. The 1963 suit, known as the Birdie Mae Davis case, remained in the courts for decades, while other suits challenged city and county government structures that kept blacks from winning elective offices.[185] Similar legal efforts at the state level led to legislative redistricting, which opened the door for blacks to serve from majority-black House and Senate districts.

While the black vote had increased in Mobile and elsewhere in the South, many white candidates were loathe to court it—with the notable exception of Langan. Along with being aligned politically with LeFlore, Langan was a brigadier general in the Alabama National Guard and a friend of Gary Cooper's. Invited by Cooper to his Marine birthday ball, Langan not only accepted but stood side-by-side with Cooper—both in uniform—for a photograph.[186]

Jay, Peggy, and Mario

LAW & POLITICS

Although he had attended a military prep school, Jay Cooper was thinking about making a different kind of history than his oldest brother when he graduated from Notre Dame in 1966. While Gary was setting a racial milestone in combat in Vietnam, Jay headed to law school at New York University, where he was one of only nine blacks among some 600 law students.

But there were mentors and inspirational figures for him—three black law professors, in particular, were important to Jay's legal education and future: Leroy D. Clark, a civil rights lawyer who later taught for a quarter of a century at the Columbus School of Law (Washington, D.C.); Haywood Burns, who became dean of the City University of New York School of Law; and Robert Carter, who became a federal district judge in New York.[187]

"These three men made a difference in my life," Jay said years later. "They taught me what a powerful tool the law could be for black folks. They taught me to be creative. And they taught me that we had an absolute obligation to other black people and that, no matter what we did, we should never stop giving back. Giving back was the debt we had to pay for the opportunity.

"These men also taught me the meaning of excellence. That rhetoric cannot replace research. That writing well was more important than waxing eloquent. They showed us that failure was not the result of less talent but of less work."[188]

They taught that black students were at NYU law school to be educated,

Jay said, "not to be assimilated. That to be black was a blessing, not a burden."

Partly with the guidance of those three, Jay founded the Black American Law Students Association, or BALSA, which later changed its name to the National Black Law Students Association, reflecting those of color from other nations.

Along with the study of law, Jay was drawn to the emerging role of blacks in American politics in the 1960s, taking a post with Senator Robert F. Kennedy's staff in New York. Soon he was on board with Kennedy's campaign for president in 1968, working in the candidate's campaign headquarters in the Watts section of Los Angeles. It was on-the-job training for a future political candidate: getting voters motivated and organized, planning speeches, handing out literature.[189]

"In terms of mentors, in terms of someone to model yourself after, there's no one better than Bobby Kennedy," Jay said years later.[190]

On the night of the California primary, the exhilaration of Kennedy's victory over Eugene McCarthy was shattered by Kennedy's assassination in the kitchen of the Ambassador Hotel in Los Angeles. Soon Jay was back in New York, escorting Coretta Scott King from the Kennedy funeral at St. Patrick's Cathedral, to the train to the capital, and later to the gravesite at Arlington National Cemetery. It was barely two months after her husband, the Reverend Martin Luther King Jr., was assassinated in Memphis.[191]

Despite the tragedies of 1968—including his own father's suicide—Jay Cooper was keen to the possibilities of a political career when he got his law degree from NYU and returned to his hometown in 1969, joining the firm of Vernon Crawford and pitching in with lawyers doing battle over school desegregation.

Jay told reporter Steve McConnell: "I was a civil rights lawyer, criminal defense lawyer, whatever-the-dog-dragged-in lawyer."[192]

"Vernon Crawford was one of my mentors, really a hero in my opinion," he told another interviewer. "Vernon graduated from Brooklyn Law School and came home when he was the only black lawyer in Mobile, opening his practice on Davis Avenue. Vernon had set high standards and really had represented people who had no representation."[193]

"Since high school I've wanted to be a lawyer," Jay said after his return to Mobile. "I guess it dawned on me that there was only one black lawyer in Mobile, my hometown. As the first national director of the Black American Law Students Association, one of the things I had said to black law students was that they should return home after graduation. I would have been sort of hypocritical if I hadn't come back here."[194]

PRICHARD MAYOR

On the political side, Jay Cooper set his sights on adjacent Prichard, a gritty industrial town that was still closely mixed racially—with whites in the voting majority—in 1972 when he ran for mayor. With a population once approaching 50,000, Prichard had begun to feel the pinch of an economic downturn, and the number of residents, as well as its sense of prosperity, was dropping.[195]

Racial segregation kept the city largely polarized, with segregationist Governor George Wallace making a Labor Day speech in Prichard part of his routine. Few blacks held city government jobs.[196]

But the president of the Prichard NAACP chapter, John Langham, saw the possibilities of a Cooper candidacy for mayor, and Langham was a man Jay admired.[197] Jay took the challenge. It was a far greater challenge than if the city was heavily majority black; for an African American to win and run a Deep South city with an evenly divided racial population—that could have a more lasting impact.

Jay was able to attract well-skilled campaign staff. John Dean, former head of the Democratic National Committee's Minorities Division, arrived to serve as campaign manager. Targeting the city's unmet needs, the campaign cast incumbent Mayor Vernon O. Capps in a negative light. With difficulties raising funds from cash-strapped local blacks, Jay got much of his $22,000 campaign war chest from friends around the nation.[198]

Jay received the endorsement of the *Mobile Beacon*, a black paper, and the Port City's dominant white daily, the Mobile *Press-Register*. As *Ebony* magazine writer Alex Poinsett noted, it was "the first time in Mobile's history that the *Press-Register* had endorsed a black man for public office."[199]

With the nonpartisan August election in Prichard approaching, white voters generally were quiet and didn't raise race issues publicly.

Poinsett found an exception: "At least one white woman voter was open enough, however, to tell Jay: 'I wouldn't elect you dogcatcher.' He refused to be equally frank. He merely thought to himself: 'I wouldn't put you in a kennel, either.'"[200]

"That was really the beginning of politics in the family, Jay running for mayor of Prichard," Gary's son Patrick said. "All of us worked in his campaign, going out and knocking on doors, canvassing. We'd go out with these chitlin' buckets and stop on the corner and ask people to contribute to the campaign, allow us to put bumper stickers on the backs of their cars.

"Chitlin' buckets were the ones that chitlin's had come in. We'd wash them out, and that was the bucket we'd use to collect money on street corners . . . even a nickel, whatever they could give to the campaign."

Jay's campaign put Prichard on the map. With Gary, sister Peggy, and other Cooper family members taking part, Jay's candidacy drew wide notice.

That was an interesting campaign. Maynard Jackson came down and campaigned for him. Andrew Young came down, Muhammad Ali, some other folks.

Those other folks, the *Washington Post* reported, included "New York lawyers who had been roommates of Jay in college, aides to several northern black mayors and state senators, black public relations firms in Washington, some white volunteers." "We laid on Jay everything a presidential campaign would have had,'" Dean said. "We had poll watchers, drivers, transportation people, press people, issues people, everything."[201]

It was a rough campaign, but there were lighter moments.

Peggy, while she's in law school, decides there are many poor children in Washington who would stay in school if their curriculum involved something to do with the arts. So she started this program—this is prior to the Duke Ellington School, the Duke Ellington School evolved from this. It was called the Workshop for a Career in the Arts.

Jay's running for office. Peggy sends me something saying, "The Workshop for a Career in the Arts will perform in Mobile for the A. J.

Cooper campaign. Gary Cooper coordinator." So here comes about 25
of these little black kids from Washington.

Mamie Sinclair ran the Malaga Inn, and she let those kids stay at the
Malaga Inn. So these kids come in—I'm living not far from there—they
come in about four in the evening. About ten o'clock at night I go down to
see how they're doing. I'm exaggerating, but the Malaga is like a square,
with an open courtyard in the middle, and it looked like I could see
green smoke rising from there as I arrived. All those kids down there
smoking joints! I said, "Peggy, you better get these guys into their rooms!"

But Jay got elected. It was close and that was some election—both
sides signing arrest warrants against each other for illegal votes.

With his victory, Algernon Johnson Cooper Jr. became the first
black to defeat an incumbent white mayor in modern Alabama history.
Among the first blacks elected mayor of sizable Southern cites in a wave
of victories, he helped found and was the first president of the National
Conference of Black Mayors.[202]

"You should have seen the kids running up to touch him when he got
here," a black schoolteacher in Prichard told the *Washington Post.* "They're
so proud one of us got elected mayor."[203]

For Jay, the hard part was just beginning. When Alex Poinsett visited
him two weeks after Jay took office, he described the new Prichard mayor
this way: "Tall, twenty-eight, so tense he sometimes squeezes his hands
together to keep his fingers from shaking."[204]

Prichard was beset with enough financial problems to set off shaking
by anyone with a hand in its finances. It was poor, with more than half
of its residents on welfare and in substandard housing. Its tax base had
eroded, and its debt had grown—and the mayor himself was giving up a
busy law practice for a smaller pay check and bigger headaches.

A dynamic, outspoken, and eloquent politician who sought to win
white as well as black support, Jay Cooper was not without critics and
antagonists from both races during his at-times tumultuous two terms.
But he pulled political levers to attract badly needed state and federal
funds to rebuild the city's infrastructure. He understood how to pick up
grants from government agencies and could tick off his successes. Among

them: a new jail and city hall and a rebuilt drainage system.²⁰⁵

Jay was an emerging political figure who tried to improve Prichard's financial future but was in the crosshairs of opponents, literally—shots were fired into his home, and the father of a police officer Jay had suspended was charged.²⁰⁶

He won a second term, then had to fight back in court when a federal indictment accused him of wrongdoing in a land transaction. Cooper supporters saw the federal case as a misguided, racially motivated attempt to bring down a rising black political star. With Jay testifying at the trial before an almost all-white jury, he was acquitted.

"When this began, one of the things we said was, 'Know ye the truth and the truth shall set you free,'" he said after the verdict. "I want to say that I appreciate the jury for recognizing that truth. It is particularly rewarding, and a sign of Mobile and where we're going, that eleven whites and one black could return this verdict."²⁰⁷

His exoneration at trial, along with his exhausting work to improve the city, put an upbeat stamp on his second term, but the toll of it all was heavy.

"I've had an impact," Jay told the *Washington Post* prior to his acquittal, "but in terms of my life and my psyche, I've got grave doubts that it was worth it. I feel like I just want to get the hell out, maybe practice law in a place like Crested Butte, Colorado."²⁰⁸

In fact, he went on to practice law in a much bigger venue—the nation's capital—and his political achievement in the city of Prichard remained an enduring racial milestone of the 1970s.

"AN ANGRY YOUNG BLACK WOMAN"

Like her older brothers, Peggy Cooper came of age in the still-segregated South of the 1950s and early 1960s when the modern civil rights movement was building momentum. Her family's home on Delaware Street was a planning venue for black leaders and civil rights lawyers. The power of protest and activism was evident all around.

Like her brothers before her, she learned early that segregation's indignities extended into almost all aspects of life.

"I was furious," she told an interviewer. "I couldn't go anywhere. If you went to the movies, you had to sit on the balcony and move to the last row if there were so many whites that they had to occupy the front rows. Even at the mass, we should sit in the last four rows. I was pretty pissed off."[209]

That edge of combativeness did not diminish as she left Mobile for a Catholic high school out of state, Saint Mary's at Notre Dame, and then George Washington University in the nation's capital.

Peggy arrived at GW in 1964—"a very angry young black woman," as she said at the school's 2011 commencement—and wasted no time confronting racial discrimination. On her second day on campus, she picketed racially segregated sororities and fraternities, a protest that eventually led the Greek organizations to change their charters. Peggy also spearheaded the writing of a student bill of rights and organized the black student union.

When the university's president, Lloyd Elliott, asked if the black students wanted a black studies department, she and others at that time said they didn't—"because we wanted every department to have black studies."[210]

After chairing a cultural arts weekend workshop at GW for "very talented but very raw" young minorities in the summer of 1968, she co-founded, with dancer and choreographer Mike Malone, a training project, Workshops for Careers in the Arts. With logistical support from GW's president—and eventually $6 million raised by Peggy—it grew over the next six years into the Duke Ellington School of the Arts, a renowned cultural fixture in D.C. that became part of the public school system in 1974, with Malone as its first artistic director.

Ellington, who had died earlier in 1974, was a Washington native whose legendary career as an innovative jazz genius made the selection of his name for the school a natural fit, but for Peggy, the connection was almost personal: a memorable photograph of her parents was taken with Ellington at the Blue Note in Chicago.[211]

The school's beginnings were modest. On the Monday after Malone suggested that she start the arts workshop, Peggy went to President Elliott with a three-page proposal. It would be a summer arts training program at first. Only later, while she got her law degree at GW, would it begin hatching into something bigger, finally a four-year high school.

"Mike and I decided to start the program incrementally because if we told anyone that we wanted a high school, they would think we were nuts," she said.[212]

Her experience in the segregated South was also a motivating force behind the school's creation.

"Just the kind of rage that gets into you, you have to do something with that," she told Cathleen Medwick for *O, The Oprah Magazine*. "And I saw the arts as a ticket to opening up worlds for kids. Their purchase of a train ticket to a broader life. And I thought, 'What better revenge in an unjust world?'"[213]

The Ellington School grew in the early 1970s into a full-scale high school with a range of arts training courses. Its students have dreams, Peggy said, "so big and real that they've propelled these kids out of difficult, poor, often illiterate families and into some of the finest artistic arenas in America."[214]

Peggy's own dream was being realized as well.

"I left George Washington as a woman who had transformed from black to African American, I'm sure. And I was not so angry anymore," she said, "because I saw how my energies could be directed through institutional help to create, and change, and give opportunities to others."[215]

It was after she had begun law school at George Washington and kick-started the Ellington School's arts program that her father's suicide shook the family. With the revelation that he had been taking money from the insurance company, the Cooper family financial bounty she had enjoyed was over.

"I went from having whatever I wanted," she told author Burt Solomon, "to zip."[216]

But like other Coopers, her drive to excel and challenge the era's racial barriers was undiminished. While she earned a law degree at George Washington and became a member of the D.C. bar, Peggy's interests ranged far from the courthouses and private practices of typical new attorneys. During this time, she began a six-year tenure as chair of the executive committee of the D.C. Commission on the Arts and Humanities, an important community panel. Along with art, her interests included education, culture, media, politics, social networking, and philanthropy.[217]

She had a gift for connecting with people in many fields who mattered, not just people of means, but she was good at connecting with them, too.

"Brashly bright, brimming with ideas, and willing to pursue them, Peggy was catnip to white liberals looking for promising young blacks to help along," Solomon wrote.[218]

In 1972, after earning her law degree, she became at twenty-five the youngest person ever selected as a fellow at the Woodrow Wilson International Center for Scholars; as a fellow, she chose to study how the arts could positively impact inner city lives.[219] She also received the John D. Rockefeller III Award, which was given each year to a young person making "an outstanding contribution toward the well-being of mankind."[220]

It was also during this period, on a trip to Paris, she was attacked by a gang of men, but eventually she was able to regain her full sense of mission, creating avenues for gifted young people to pursue careers in the arts, and beginning one of her own.[221] She worked as a programming executive for Post-Newsweek Stations (now Graham Media Group) and produced documentaries for WTOP-TV, winning Emmy and Peabody awards—one a documentary on the history of black dance, her sister Dominic's chosen artistic field, the other a piece on racial discrimination at the *Washington Post*.[222]

"Through the Eyeballs of My Siblings"

For Mario, the youngest in the Cooper family, the route to law school and politics was different than that of his older siblings. Born in 1954, nearly twenty years after Gary, his parents split when he was a boy, and the strict home life and resolute Catholic faith that Gary had known was missing.

"By then, I think a lot of things had slipped by the wayside," Mario said.[223]

Mario in his youth enjoyed the largesse of the family fortune, though, and at age 10 he was put on a train—alone—to travel to California to attend a Catholic boarding school, St. Catherine's Military School, in Anaheim.

This was in 1964, a time when all of Mario's siblings had basically left home for college, boarding school, or to start careers and families.

"I think I was ready to go, in a psychological sense," Mario said.

When back home, Mario usually stayed with his mother in the family house on Delaware Street. His father, in the years leading up to his death, did not share with his youngest child any of his private thoughts.

"No, no. He would never talk to me," Mario said.[224]

His mother seemed to Mario more reserved after the breakup with his father.[225] But there was nothing reserved about Gary, Jay, or Peggy, who were each a force field of energy in a confrontation with Jim Crow. In many ways, they provided Mario with a sense of expectations and were the source of his own drive for achievement, eventually at the highest level of government.

"I think that is a good analysis," he said. "It maybe was more because of my siblings than my parents. For me, my sense of it all was really through the eyeballs of my siblings, less so from my parents. My father literally never talked to me."[226]

With Peggy and Dominic already in Washington—Dominic had followed Peggy to St. Mary's and then to George Washington University—Mario was drawn to the capital's emerging black political scene. In 1971, he spent a little time working for the campaign of Marion Barry, who successfully ran for a seat on D.C.'s school board, where he served as president. Still in his teens, Mario was around many of the black political and artistic notables of the period who flocked to Peggy, but he had made no career choice.

"I think I needed a job when I joined the Barry campaign," he said. "I volunteered for a position in the summer. It was absolutely great. It was clear Barry was going to win and that just made it even more fun."[227]

Still, Mario's journey to become a national Democratic Party player was not direct—attending college at Middlebury, in Vermont, he shunned any role in campus politics and did not feel he was being steered by Peggy or Jay toward any particular role in the civil rights movement.

"Being the youngest, I was pretty much given as much rein as possible," he said. "They would have supported anything I chose."[228]

But his interest in politics had been heightened by his experience in Barry's campaign. The next year, he pitched in for his brother Jay in the Prichard race, and later volunteered to work in Sergeant Shriver's 1976 presidential primary campaign.

"A friend of mine was working for a friend of his in the Shriver campaign," Mario said. "They needed volunteers, and I said I would pick the quarter in the last part of the school year and volunteer. So then I met the whole Shriver family. The balloon from there puttered out, but they were certainly an interesting collection of people."[229]

It didn't putter out completely. The Shrivers helped Mario land a job with the Democratic National Committee when he graduated from Middlebury College, the alma mater of the man who would later become Mario's political mentor, Ron Brown.

"That was really my first job outside of college," he said. "The Shriver people helped me get that job."[230]

As the 1960s turned into the 1970s, the achievements of Gary, Jay, and Peggy were already of note in military, law, political, and cultural circles. Mario, the youngest, was just getting a taste for politics in the early 1970s, but he was ably gifted and in time would become an important national Democratic Party figure.

For Gary, a decision to forge an electoral campaign of his own would take him into politics and a new venue: the Alabama Statehouse.

10

Goat Hill

fter settling in as Prichard mayor, Jay Cooper encouraged Gary
to make a little political history of his own. "Gary," he said, "have
you ever thought of running for the Legislature?"[231]

Gary had not. He was not at all familiar with statehouse politics in
Montgomery or what needed to be done at the local level to get there:

I really didn't have a clue.

But with the help of federal court challenges, the first two blacks
since Reconstruction had been elected to the Alabama House in
1970—Fred Gray and Tom Reed, both from majority-black districts
in Macon County. And by 1974, newly drawn districts in Mobile and
other parts of the state opened the possibility for more blacks to win
seats in the Legislature.

Gary had been active in community affairs, which can be crucial to a
political career, but it had not all been clear sailing. Returning to Mobile
after serving in Vietnam, the business-minded Cooper wanted to join the
Junior Chamber of Commerce, but his application was turned down. He
tried again, then went to see the Jaycees' president.

"What happened to my application?"

*"Gary, the members have decided that you're not qualified to be a
Jaycee."*

*"Look, why don't you get me the applications of your mem-
bers. . . . Anyone who is more qualified than me, I'll eat the goddam
application."*

It was galling—here was Cooper, a University of Notre Dame graduate,
a Marine major with a chest full of medals, twice wounded in Vietnam,

and from a prominent, civic-oriented, business-minded family that went back decades in Mobile. Not qualified?[232]

He did get accepted to the Bienville Club, a tony private club with dining on a floor atop a downtown bank building that offered sweeping views of the Mobile waterfront. Established in 1967, it was all white initially. Cooper recalled being one of the first blacks, if not the first, to be invited to join. [233]

> *During Mardi Gras, some good-looking girls came from Atlanta, and I was a bachelor then, and I got my buddy and we took them up to the club. This white family came in with their grandmother. She was really old, and she said, "When did they start letting niggers up here?" This woman's children were mortified. They apologized. We of course were very accepting of the apology.*

On the political side, Cooper in 1969 became one of the first blacks appointed to the Mobile Auditorium Board. The appointment came after lengthy protests and boycotts led by Neighborhood Organized Workers, or NOW. The issue was the lack of blacks in higher level jobs with the city and downtown businesses. So as the protests continued, the auditorium board was expanded from nine to 12 members, with Cooper one of the three new members.

Cooper was not associated with NOW, which was a more radical group than John LeFlore's Non-Partisan Voters League. NOW undercut the League's role in politics in the black community, although NOW's protests drew the active support of the Dominican Sisters from Most Pure Heart of Mary Parish. NOW's influence later waned amid criminal investigations, but initially it had stirred action to boost blacks in the port city.[234]

While on the auditorium board, Cooper enjoyed conspiring with E. B. Peebles—a prominent white civic leader—to bring some uncharacteristic off-color glitz to Mobile's theatrical scene.

> Hair, *the musical, was coming to Mobile and they were advertising it. When I was on the board, one of the white board members was a great guy, his name was E. B. Peebles, a shipping executive, real active, the city's football stadium, Ladd-Peebles Stadium, was renamed in his honor. Well, we sat next to each other. There was a lot of hell-raising*

about not wanting Hair *to come to Mobile because of its nudity. This was the 1970s. "We can't have this in Mobile!"*

So E. B. said, "Cooper, let me tell you what to do. You call for a secret ballot, and I'm going to vote for you. I want to see it."

And we voted secretly and Hair *came to the auditorium.*

When Cooper was not tapped for a second term on the auditorium board, he was displeased that a black was not picked to succeed him, and let it be known. He told reporters:

I think it was time I was replaced, but I think someone from the black community should have replaced me.[235]

Cooper also took aim at one of Mobile's most cherished sporting events, the Senior Bowl. Long a stage for college seniors to be eyed by pro football scouts during a week of practices and a pretty meaningless game, the Senior Bowl was a prized civic venture—but apparently only for the white establishment.

Cooper, however, got on the Senior Bowl Committee:

I don't know how I did, but there are no other blacks except me. And they have this luncheon, and here are all these football players—about 70 percent of them black— and no kids from our community.

It prompted him to write a letter to the editor of the *Mobile Press-Register*, dated January 8, 1972:

Dear Editor:

Amid the laudations that abound this week for the Senior Bowl Committee, I must comment on their most unsatisfactory performance in the area of the involvement of the Black community.

Is the Senior Bowl Committee such an elite and qualified group that local Blacks cannot be included?

Civically yours,

J. G. Cooper[236]

While Gary's active role in the community was helpful, he also had a campaign ace in the hole—his family's role in the mortuary industry for fifty years.

Having been in the funeral home business, I knew a lot of the ministers, and this was an important political advantage. They could spread the word. They could get out the vote. A lot of these speeches I made were at Sweet Pilgrim Baptist Church, those kinds of places.

I started driving around. I found where the boundaries were for my House district. I looked at the racial mixture, which was somewhat even back in those days. So I decided to run. I was so lucky to come up with an opponent like Pat Eddington. Pat was an absolute charmer, just a gracious opponent.

Patricia Eddington and her husband Bob lived a few blocks from Gary Cooper in the Oakleigh Garden District and were devout liberal Democrats. Unlike Gary, they were involved in party building and organizing at all levels—and would continue to do so, raising funds decades later for Bill and Hillary Clinton's presidential bids. For Pat, a champion of black voting rights, facing a black candidate in the 1974 Democratic primary was awkward. She and Gary chose to make the campaign exemplary. There would be no negative ads or attacks from either side.

We made agreements what to do, and what not to do.

Black voters were largely backing a black candidate trying to make history—no black had been elected to the Legislature from Mobile since the Reconstruction era. However, Gary also had support from whites. This was at a time when the Democratic Party was still dominant in the state and winning its primary election was tantamount to a general election victory. Conservative whites voted in the Democratic primary—there was no Republican opponent in Gary's House district—and many of them voted for Gary Cooper.

His victory was all but assured, but there was a last-minute hitch. The Corrupt Practices Act required candidates to file certain paperwork on campaign finances by a deadline, and when Cooper made his run for the House seat in 1974, the deadline loomed, and he had overlooked the need to file.[237]

This was not optional. Paul Kirkland, the Mobile County probate office clerk at the time, recalled that two county commissioners, Howard Yeager and Coy Smith, had to be appointed after the same law kept them from taking the office even though they won the vote. "This would be a huge embarrassment for Gary if he didn't file," Kirkland said.

But Gary was away and couldn't be reached immediately. So Kirkland called Jay Cooper and told him that Gary may be about to make history—but in the wrong way.

"I told them to come to my house and they would meet the deadline if they got there before midnight. And they did."

With disaster avoided, Gary's victory made him a potent political figure, one who had support from blacks as well as conservative whites.

Pat's challenge was that she was the liberal, I was the conservative. I was on the board of the Red Cross, a Marine veteran, had fought in Vietnam. My politics were conservative, in almost all areas.

This had not escaped Bert Nettles, a Mobile Republican who helped build a two-party system in Alabama. In the summer of 1974, interviewed by Southern historian Jack Bass, Nettles described Gary Cooper as "a very, very attractive fellow . . . very influential with the black community, very well accepted by them."

Was Gary like his brother Jay politically or philosophically?

"No," Nettles answered, "I think philosophically, Gary, the older one, is more of a Republican and probably would have run on the Republican ticket if he felt like he could have gotten elected. Jay is younger and, I think, more of a Democrat. I'm talking about national philosophical basis now."[238]

Another astute political mind in Mobile also saw Gary's potential, his huge upside as a new leader in Port City circles. This was Jim Atchison, a white lawyer who in the early 1970s began forging a political team to challenge the Old Mobile establishment. He had a kind of street credibility: "I'm from Mobile. As they say, I was born and raised here. I came back after law school in Tuscaloosa. I wasn't part of Old Mobile. Something that stuck with me was that I was raised around my father's furniture stores on Davis Avenue and Dauphin Street. Our clientele were primarily people in the black community.

"I was raised in this environment, and I understood. I would deliver things to their homes at Christmas and whenever, so I had an understanding in relationship with the minority community. It was a natural thing for me. It helped me with people like the Coopers."[239]

Atchison was returning to Mobile after law school around the same time Gary was coming back from the Marines, and Jay was doing the same with his NYU law degree and political aspirations.

"My first recollection is when Jay Cooper ran for mayor of Prichard," said Atchison. "I wasn't real actively involved, but peripherally I knew about it and kind of supported that. Then Gary was instrumental in that campaign, helping Jay. As it went on, after this I became real involved in local elections.

"A fellow named Gary Greenough ran for city commissioner and I got involved in that. I agreed to help him as soon as I finished what we called 'the summer trial thing' with the courts. So I got started helping him, we got involved raising money, and Gary Greenough won.

"As things went on, we got involved in other races and elected other people. We didn't know any better, so we just kept going at 'em. Sheriff's races. County commission. All sorts of things.

"All of these people kind of came together, and this *Birmingham News* writer, Sandra Baxley Taylor, did a news article about it. She dubbed us the 'Young Turks' of Mobile. I was mentioned in there, of course, about all the races we had gotten involved in and how we were taking on the establishment. A friend of mine in Birmingham called and said he had just read an article in the Sunday paper about all of us down here. We were kind of rebels."[240]

Atchison thought Gary Cooper had unique gifts that made him not so much a rebel as a political natural.

"I saw him first as a Marine," Atchison said, "because he was a Marine business type—I call it 'Marine business.' I don't know if I thought about it that way at the time, but Gary was no-nonsense. If a black was acting foolish, he would tell them as quickly as he would someone else. I saw him as very conservative fiscally, but also very concerned about minority rights, about being a leader.

"His stature is so important. Jay's tall, too, but Gary has a commanding presence with people."

The Young Turks may have been taking on Mobile's establishment, which was mostly white, old money, with a lot of holdover racial bias, but Gary was offering a different kind of politics for the black community, too.

"John LeFlore was about marches, about confrontation with the white community and the business community," said Atchison. "Gary was about a different approach. It was more sophisticated, more business-wise, more 'we're not going away' type of thing. John LeFlore was of course a significant leader here and was working at things long before Gary, but Gary had much more presence than John did."

Much as LeFlore and Langan had formed a biracial front, the Greenough race gave Cooper and other blacks a white political partner.

"During that race Gary Cooper and Jay—and I think some others—took Gary Greenough into the black communities, took him to some black nightclubs, because the black vote was going to be very important."[241]

The extent to which Gary Cooper could help bring a new political calculus to the black and white vote in Mobile was evident in that race. Greenough, a political newcomer who had served in the Marine Corps, was challenging incumbent City Commissioner Joe Bailey.

At one time there were a couple of older individuals in the black community—John LeFlore was one—who would pass out a "pink sheet" all over the black community before time to vote. So black folk would follow their pink sheet, which was under the name of the Non-Partisan Voters League, when they would go vote. But there was an election, not long after my brother got elected mayor of Prichard, when a new young guy named Gary Greenough ran against the establishment. I worked with Greenough and I helped him win.

The *Press-Register* took note of the development. It had been long known that the Non-Partisan Voters League was supporting the white incumbent, Bailey. But, the paper said,

A new breed of young black political activists had been working perhaps even harder for Greenough. Most of them, including business-man Gary Cooper, had been involved in the successful campaign last year to elect A. J. Cooper mayor of Prichard. Bailey won in most of the black wards, but his overall margin was a thin 1,659 to 1,592. In years past, the pink sheet endorsement would have delivered better than 90 percent of the vote.[242]

Atchison said that black leaders like Gary and Jay looked beyond the pink sheet. They started saying, 'We can't have our folks being dictated to by a very few people.' The pink sheet went away slowly. What happened was, some people started getting together a few outsiders and putting together their own pink sheet. So you would have competing pink sheets. Some skullduggery was going on, but it slowly went away."[243]

Those seeking more progressive politics in Mobile viewed the split vote in the black wards that helped Greenough win as a watershed moment. But it also had its skeptics, according to the *Press-Register*:

> While the Cooper group feels the split was a real breakthrough against the old guard in the black community, other black leaders are concerned that it could represent a diminishing influence by blacks.[244]

Black political leadership was indeed evolving, but when Mobile's first black legislators since Reconstruction were elected in the 1974 race, one was John LeFlore and another was Gary Cooper.

CROSSING POLITICAL LINES

Conservative, maybe even the type of conservative who feels at home with Republicans, Gary Cooper also remained popular in the black community. And with good reason—he had been outspoken in pushing for more black representation in local government and civic offices. His successes in the military and the business sector were sources of black pride.

So he was an agreeable figure in the mostly white conservative mainstream as well as among the emerging black political leadership. He was no card-carrying Republican or Democrat, but he could find common purpose with both. This was a duality that would define him at all levels of his career—in the military, and in politics, business, and diplomacy—a forceful but pragmatic black voice who knew his way around the more prosperous white world.

This was evident when he reached Montgomery. He was a member of the inaugural Alabama Legislative Black Caucus that formed after seventeen African Americans won election in 1974 to the redistricted 140-member Legislature. Along with Cooper and LeFlore, the caucus included another highly regarded House member from Mobile: Cain Kennedy, who later would become Alabama's first black circuit judge.[245]

We formed the caucus in meetings at the Harris Bel Air, the restaurant near Alabama State's campus. There was one guy who didn't want to be a member. I don't know what his trouble was, but we all thought he was crazy. In this day and age, you don't want to be a member of the Alabama Legislative Black Caucus? At least we can have a forum to talk about things and identify things that need to be done.

The caucus included State Representative Alvin Holmes of Montgomery, who was as short as Gary was tall but one of the quickest wits and most outspoken members of the entire Legislature. In keeping with the style of the times, Gary sported an Afro, which made him loom even taller around Holmes, who took notice: "Your 'fro is bigger than mine!"[246]

Almost in the same time sequence as the forming of the black caucus, Gary agreed to be a floor leader for the political nemesis of blacks, Governor George C. Wallace. Cooper's engaging personality and pragmatic politics—as well as his being a strapping six-foot-six Marine officer who had fought in Vietnam—allowed him to play both roles without alienating either side.

"A couple of times when I was up there I worked as a page," said Gary's son, Patrick. "It was interesting. People were incredibly polite and friendly. He was pretty popular up there because of his military background. And Gary always had a pretty good relationship with people whether they were black or white, whether they were Republican or Democrat. He always had this ability to cross these lines."

James Harrell: "Gary is a fascinating guy. He has all those elements that are kind of atypical. Pretty intellectual, sort of stern and militaristic, but he has a big sense of humor. He loves to laugh."

Among his ways of poking fun at legislative colleagues: "Notre Dame had been challenging Alabama for a national championship in football in 1973, and had beaten them in the Sugar Bowl. And did it again in '74," Harrell said. "Gary had a sign made up: 'God made Notre Dame No. 1.'"

Cooper did not overlook the history that was made when he was among the first blacks elected to the Alabama Legislature from Mobile since Reconstruction. Or the history that lives on at the Capitol, the old domed building on a grassy hill, known as Goat Hill because goats once grazed it, where landmark events of the Civil War and the civil rights movement took place.

He described it in a speech years later:

I often sat in those hallowed halls after everyone had gone and I would look above the Speaker's desk and see on the wall a marble plaque that stated "In this room in 1865 Alabama voted to secede from the Union." I would then walk across the Rotunda and enter our historic state Senate chamber and above the desk where the Lieutenant Governor guides the sessions is a marble plaque that states "In this room in 1865 Jefferson Davis was inaugurated as the first president of the Confederacy." I would then walk and stand on the steps of the Capitol and look down Dexter Avenue and on the left hardly a block away is the Dexter Avenue Baptist Church where the greatest social revolution in the history of man started.

What a feeling of awe.

The Alabama Capitol, of course, was the place where former Governor Lurleen Wallace was serving when she replied somewhat dismissively to Marine Captain Gary Cooper's letter from Vietnam in 1967. She had died of cancer the next year, and now her husband was back in command, albeit as a crippled figure. Shot by a would-be assassin in Maryland as he campaigned for the Democratic presidential nomination in 1972, George Wallace was rolled around the Capitol in a wheelchair and sought to modify and soften his once-rabid segregationist storyline. Getting a black to serve as a floor leader was a move in the new direction. It could help with his next bid for president in 1976.

He of course had a horrible reputation in our community. But I can remember him telling me that he thought he made a lot of mistakes and if he had to do it again . . . he was interested in letting people know those were not his true feelings.

So the pragmatist in Gary responded when another Mobile politician, Representative H. L. "Sonny" Callahan, asked if he would join him as a Wallace floor leader. A conservative Democrat who would later become a long-serving and powerful Republican congressman, Callahan coupled an easy-going, friendly manner with a quietly ambitious political mind, much like Gary himself.

"Governor Wallace suggested that I approach Gary and ask him if he would be interested in being a floor leader," Callahan said. "So I went and asked him and he agreed—and he made a good one. On racial issues, I don't recall any problem in that respect at all. Governor Wallace did what he wanted to do on segregation, but he was fair to all and I think Gary realized that, and realized at the same time that there's an opportunity there to have input in the decisions. But Gary did ask what a floor leader does. I said I didn't know, but we'd just have to jump into this together."

Floor leaders generally took issues in which they had an interest and helped move Wallace administration proposals through House channels. In return they could expect Wallace's help on their local bills. Cooper, of course, had received help from the Wallace administration when the family insurance company was in trouble. Still, he had his concerns.

At our first meeting, I said, "Governor, surely during this time there are going to be some things we disagree on. You may have some ideas that I don't support and vice-versa."

"Let's work it like this," Wallace said. "We will agree that if we come up with something that we disagree with, we will just excuse ourselves, and we will ask no questions, but we will also agree not to criticize what happens in the media, the press."

And we all shook on it, and that was the way it worked.

James Harrell said Gary's military background may have helped him gain access to the Wallace team. "A good friend of mine, Bill Jackson, went on to become George Wallace's legal advisor and a general in the National Guard. The military background gave Gary a lot of recognition. It was somewhat controversial for Gary to be a Wallace floor leader. Wallace during that time was reaching out to offset a lot of things he had done."

Patrick recalled, "When he was a floor leader for Wallace, he liked for me to ride up there with him. I think this was around the time I was learning how to drive, so I was pestering him about driving the car. The big issue in the black community was really whether Wallace had changed. At the same time I think the interesting point was, there were two sides at play: one was that a black was representing George Wallace, and the flip of it was the whole idea that George Wallace would actually extend himself to somebody in the black community. I met Wallace a few times when I was a kid up there. I'd go into his office, and he was just super nice. Still, the big question was, 'Did he really change?' I think Gary believes that he had really changed."

Gary, in fact, did get to see another side of Wallace, the private man who had begun as a progressive but opted to be an arch-segregationist when that was politically popular. In Wallace's last years, it weighed on him.

I on a number of occasions had a chance to sit down with him, and he expressed a great deal of regret for some of the steps that he took. I got so I kind of liked him. The challenge was his actions had caused so much suffering. But he was a feisty little guy.

They had their differences, but Cooper remained on good terms with Wallace. At times this was by accident.

Once when Cooper was at Camp Lejeune in North Carolina for summer training as a Marine reservist, Wallace and his entourage arrived nearby as part of his final campaign for president in 1976.

He was having a major fundraiser and a rally in North Carolina. As it happened, the Marine officers, myself included, were staying in the hotel where Wallace was having an event. In civilian clothes one evening at the hotel, I'm going to dinner and I come down, and here's the governor's election team. Boy, were they thrilled! To think that I traveled all the way to North Carolina to support the governor! The governor saw me and hugged me and said, "Cooper, I'm so happy to see you!"

I didn't tell them anything about why I was there. And when I got back to Alabama, the governor was my best friend.

FOES & FRIENDS

Being a Wallace floor leader gave Cooper a different political bearing than most others in the Legislative Black Caucus. But Cooper said there was never any friction over his work with Wallace, and the caucus was united on most issues of racial fairness. The need for unity was apparent from the start.

On their first or second day in the chamber, Cooper recalled, a white legislator from northeast Alabama walked up to the podium where House Speaker Joe McCorquodale was conducting chamber business.

"Mr. Speaker."

"The gentleman from Calhoun, you have the floor," McCorquodale said.

"It's a sad day in the Alabama House of Representatives," the white legislator, Representative Ray Burgess of Anniston, announced to the chamber.

"Why is this a sad day?" McCorquodale asked.

"Look, if the Lord wanted black birds and white birds to fly together, he wouldn't have made different flocks."

The chamber fell quiet. State Representative Chris McNair, a black legislator from Birmingham whose daughter Denise was killed in the Sixteenth Street Baptist Church bombing in 1963, walked from his seat at the back to take the floor. He noted that all in the chamber were duly elected, and he had a request.

"While we're here, can't we at least sip out of the same ladle?" Mc-Nair asked.

"Yes," Burgess said. "You sip out of your side, we sip out of our side."

Burgess also mocked McNair after the black legislator proposed having at least one black physician on a newly structured Alabama Board of Health. Burgess followed by proposing that doctors also must be from China, India, France, and Germany; the McNair proposal was defeated.[247]

Burgess carried a holstered .38-caliber revolver into the House chamber until it was disallowed by colleagues. A warning sign went up when Burgess responded angrily to a proposal in 1975 by Holmes, the black lawmaker from Montgomery, to remove the Confederate flag from the pole atop the Capitol dome. "He went temporarily insane," Holmes said.[248]

The flag remained at the time, but eventually, in a continued drive by Holmes, came down. Several months after the House contretemps, Burgess died from a shot to the head during an argument with his wife at their home; the shooting was ruled accidental.[249]

The comments by Burgess at the start of the session in 1975 were an introduction to statehouse racism that Cooper would not forget. But he also remembered all the friendly, helpful people. One was former state Senator Pierre Pelham, a Mobile lawyer from a prominent family in rural Washington County.

A graduate of Harvard Law, where his associates included boxing promoter Bob Arum, Pelham was a brilliant mind, an eccentric personality—he befriended gonzo journalist Hunter S. Thompson after being aligned politically with Wallace[250]—and an eloquent, riveting speaker. He also liked to farm. Gary got to know Pierre's mother, who was as much a character as her son: *She used to tell me, "Lord, if Pierre's daddy knew he went to Harvard to raise tomatoes!"* But it was Pierre's oratory that made him a statehouse star. He drew throngs to the Senate gallery when he took the microphone. He had some advice for Gary on elocution.

In his youth, Gary shied from public speaking.

I can remember being frightened to death to give a public speech. When I went to Notre Dame, I took a course in public speaking. That course helped me overcome that fear. Then you learn how important your delivery is in being an effective leader.

But I could never give a very effective speech that someone else wrote for me. I would always take it—not all the time—but I would rewrite it, practice it, and make it mine.

When I took that course at Notre Dame, I was terrified. What made me so damn terrified, every time I would open my mouth people would start laughing. Because here I was from Alabama, I would say, "How y'all doin'?" and that would set off the laughter.

Pelham helped hone Gary's delivery at the Statehouse:

"I want to give you some advice," Pelham told me. "You may not need it, but listen to it and try practicing it. What I'm going to recommend

is: never stand up in the Legislature and open your mouth and say
anything, unless you have written it down and practiced it and really
understand what you're saying."

Too many legislators go to the microphone haphazardly and start
talking to a disinterested, preoccupied chamber, their points lost amid
loud chatter and the shuffling of papers around the room. Cooper was
no Pierre Pelham, but he knew how to pick his spots.

Every time I got up, the House got quiet as a pin. Because I didn't
do it often, but when I did, I would do it right.

"WE'LL STIR THINGS UP"

Cooper may have been a Wallace floor leader and adroit among
Republican-leaning conservative businessmen, but he was keen to act
or speak out against vestiges of Jim Crow.

At a news conference in Mobile, he raised hell over the failure of the
Mobile police and fire departments to hire blacks in top posts. It had come
to his attention that no blacks had been added to those departments for
the last five years. Cooper said he had learned from a black secretary with
the Personnel Board that any time a black passed the employment test,
the grade would be changed to failing.[251]

It made for a spirited Cooper news conference—one that remained
memorable for his friend Jim Atchison, the emerging political kingmaker
for new leaders in the Port City.

"We started looking at the Personnel Board," Atchison said, "how it
was controlled by certain people, older political types. There were very
few minorities in the police and fire departments that were higher-ups.
Very few were getting in. Gary was in the Legislature by then. I was setting things up and he said, 'We'll stir things up.'

"We called a news conference in front of the Personnel Board on Government Street. Gary came to my office that morning and we prepared
for it. Then he and I rode over to the Personnel Board. All the newspaper
people were out there, along with the electronic media, because he was
threatening legislation. Things were going to have to change.

"During the course of it, I had become real involved, out front with the

Young Turks. I was getting too much publicity. So I stood on the side of the building when Gary held the news conference. And there was a little local newspaper called the *Azalea City News*, a weekly. Their reporter was there and wrote a funny article. It said, 'As Representative Gary Cooper held a news conference in front of the Personnel Board, attorney Jim Atchison was on the side of the building behind an azalea bush listening.' Never forgot that one. But eventually advances were made that helped the fire and police departments. Gary was very determined on that."

TURNING THE TABLES

Gary's election to the Legislature gave him an opportunity to revisit a matter he had found insulting. In 1973, he was preparing to marry his second wife, Gloria Giles, a registered nurse. Her family home was in the Plateau community, only a few blocks from where an African American Heritage Trail monument was placed in recognition of Africatown.[252] The settlers of Africatown were among more than 100 Africans kidnapped and forced aboard a ship, the *Clotilde*, in 1860, a half-century after slave importation had been made illegal in the U.S. It was the last ship to make that voyage with kidnapped human cargo.[253] Gloria was from a working family, Gary said, but all the children in her family went to college.

She was breathtakingly beautiful. She was super.

When he went to the probate judge's office at the Mobile County Courthouse to obtain a marriage license, however, he was told to sign the "colored register." The office kept one for blacks to sign and one for whites to sign.

Gary balked. He explained that he was a Marine officer, back from service in Vietnam, and that he did not want to sign such a register. Probate Judge John L. Moore, in another room, apparently heard Gary's remarks.[254]

Moore, appointed in 1963 by his friend from law school, Governor George Wallace,[255] had kept separate marriage license registration records for "colored" and "white" and was not about to end the practice. Cooper recalled hearing a racial insult as Moore shouted from the other room for Cooper to either sign the register or "get the hell out of the courthouse."[256]

Gary signed it—to get the license and marry Gloria—but did not forget the humiliation. Elected to the Legislature the next year, he would shortly have a chance to turn the tables on Moore.

The probate office clerk at the time, Paul Kirkland, said in an interview years later that Moore needed to get a bill passed for his retirement as probate judge. Kirkland said the probate judges in Mobile and Birmingham, unlike others, had to be lawyers and had legal responsibilities that made them the equivalent of circuit judges, but they weren't under the circuit judges' retirement plan. So a separate bill had to be enacted into law for Moore.

As it happened, the bill had to be passed by a House committee whose members included one state Representative Gary Cooper of Mobile. And the objection of *one* member could block the retirement measure. It was safe to assume that Cooper was likely to block it.

Kirkland, warned of the problem by state Representative Sonny Callahan of Mobile, conferred with Cooper before the committee met. Cooper reminded Kirkland of the separate marriage license registration books for blacks and whites in the probate office. Cooper was firm: he wanted that changed.

"Would the bill die if it isn't?" Kirkland asked.

Not mentioning the bill, Cooper repeated that the practice of having racially separate registration books needed to end. Now.

"Give me ten minutes," Kirkland said.

He called Moore and advised him that Cooper wanted the marriage license books combined. He said he didn't think Moore's retirement bill would get out of the committee otherwise.

Moore said he would change the practice. There would no longer be racially separate marriage license books to sign in Mobile County.

"How soon can it be changed?" Kirkland asked.

"Consider it done," Moore said.

It was.

THE BEGINNING OF A FRIENDSHIP

Part of Cooper's connection to the Wallace administration came through James Harrell, a new friend at the time. Harrell was from Bessemer but had gone to Alabama State University on a basketball scholarship, gotten married, and stayed in Montgomery. Like Cooper, he appealed to the Wallace team at a time when the governor was trying to change his stripes at least slightly on the race issue. New opportunities were opening up for blacks with professional skills.[257]

"I had just graduated from Alabama State and was working as a consultant for a firm called Urban Consultants run by an urban planner named Gene Brock," Harrell said. "He was a good friend of the Wallace administration, and the Alabama Development Office under the Wallace administration at that time had no blacks. ADO's division of state planning got 99 percent of their money from Housing and Urban Development, a federal agency, and HUD had been on ADO about hiring black professionals. They didn't even have a black secretary.

"Gene Brock asked me would I take a cut in pay to become a state planner with ADO. He said that if I didn't like it, I could come back. He thought I had the temperament to do the work. So I went down, interviewed, and got the job.

"A guy named Red Bamberg was head of the Alabama Development Office. He was a segregationist, but he was fair with me. During that time I interacted with the Attorney General, Bill Baxley—not so much Baxley but his lieutenants, Myron Thompson, Sally Greenhaw, George Beck."

Those three were part of a "Who's Who" of the Baxley team of the 1970s. Baxley had hired the first black attorneys for the AG staff, including Thompson, and expanded the number of women. Thompson became Alabama's second black federal judge, Greenhaw became a state circuit judge, and Beck the U.S. attorney in Montgomery.

"My job was in a little division of ADO called the Office Of Small and Minority Business Enterprise. It was really about zoning regulations and approving grants, planning, a lot of studies that we had to review so they could get their money. The only minority in that agency, I got to do a lot of things for the governor, going out and meeting groups, reading proclamations. This was under Governor George Wallace, around 1973. That's when I started off, knowing Jay Cooper when he got elected mayor of Prichard. Jay was an avid pursuer of federal funds. He had pulled some strings to get some grants coming to the state that would help Prichard. Some of the grants, I was the administrator of. Got to know Jay real well.

"When Gary got elected, I got to meet him. A representative of the independent business association came by to see me. He had met Gary because he was pushing some legislation for independent business people. He asked, Did I know Gary? And Gary came up to my office and said maybe we can get this bill passed. That was the beginning of our friendship."

As their friendship grew, they eventually joined in business ventures, but not all were successful.

"We formed a group and got a contract to sell railroad crossties," Harrell said. "There was a government program that had to do so much with minority businesses. We sold fifteen thousand crossties to what was then the Northeast Corridor Federal Railroad Administration. Fifteen thousand. It was a pretty big contract. But when we added up expenses, I think we each wound up making about six dollars."

JOBS, DRINKS & PRISONS

As a new House member, Cooper was not expected to introduce and pass major bills, but his legislative agenda was far-reaching and unusually progressive for the state. Among his initiatives, he wanted to restore civil rights to those former convicts who had completed their sentences in misdemeanor and felony cases—a restriction that denied the vote disproportionately to blacks and would remain a roadblock to the ballot for decades.[258]

Notably, he pushed successfully for state funding of Opportunities Industrialization Centers, at that time a rare instance of a state supporting OICs. Known as the OIC Assistance Act, it was a job-training initiative founded and turned into a nationwide program by Reverend Leon Sullivan, a prominent black organizer who fought apartheid in South Africa.[259]

The Reverend Leon Sullivan was the one who came up with the principles to help cure apartheid in South Africa. They were known as the Sullivan Principles. I remember he came to speak in Montgomery and we got his OIC program started as a state project in Alabama. Connie Harper had founded a private, nonprofit OIC for Central Alabama. We followed up with one of the first state-funded OIC programs.

OIC sought to give poor people the tools and training to compete for jobs. It was the opposite of a handout, encouraging self-motivation, and much to Cooper's liking.

What made it good was, we would talk to people in the inner city and say, "How would you like to prepare for a job?"

They would say, "Great, how much do you get paid while preparing for a job?"

"We don't pay you a damn thing," we'd say.

So we had people sign up for job training, for no pay, and because they were motivated we got almost everyone of them hired.

Cooper, who enjoyed a drink, also pushed for an end to the state's monopoly over the sale of liquor, proposing a phase-out of the Alabama Alcoholic Beverage Control board and its state ABC stores, gradually turning the business over to private enterprise.[260] The system in place was difficult to budge, however, and ABC stores live on, although Cooper's position in time led to widespread legal sales, particularly of wines and beers, by private stores and supermarkets.

Cooper's route between Mobile and Montgomery took him past the road at Atmore leading to two major state prisons, Holman and Fountain. From this he developed an interest in the corrections system and its inmates. The severe deterioration of prison conditions had become an issue for the Legislature.

People in prisons would be sleeping with crap on the floor. You'd go in the prison kitchen, they'd have food with eyes floating in the soup, like pig eyes. If you committed an infraction, they had these little tin huts that they put you in, in 90-degree weather. The place was filthy and it was horrible. That was something I was interested in, because I had run some brigs in the Marine Corps. I ran the brig at Barstow, and one aboard the USS Chicago.

So after I got elected in '74, I volunteered and I handled some bond legislation for the prison system and got them passed. So they liked me, and I could go down and knock on the door and they'd let me go around to the cells. I used to go on death row and talk to people—the

warden even let me sit in the electric chair—Yellow Mama, it was called.
What a chilling feeling THAT was!

But his effort to put a black in a top prison system post, despite the disproportionately large percentage of blacks behind bars, was thwarted by Wallace. Cooper, feeling he had Wallace's promise to select a black, helped push for passage of a bill creating a new deputy commissioner post, but in the end it went to a white man, a Wallace ally. The man chosen by Wallace had been sent to federal prison before he was exonerated and his conviction overturned.[261]

Wallace's explanation to me: "At least we appointed someone with prison experience."

11

Making Welfare Work

W hile maintaining his military ties as a Marine Reserve officer and overseeing family enterprises in Mobile, Cooper ran successfully for a second term in the House in 1978. His civic resume was impressive—the board of the United Fund, Dearborn Street YMCA, Community Chest, Mobile Mental Health Center, and the OIC job training center hatched by anti-apartheid activist Leon Sullivan. Among awards, he had been selected Man of the Year by the Non-Partisan Voters League.[262]

Gary was now a recognizable name in Mobile and Montgomery, and at the Capitol, change was afoot. Wallace, unable by law to seek a third straight term, left the state's political spotlight and a new face, Fob James of Opelika, took over as governor.

A one-time Auburn University football star, James had made a fortune by introducing plastic-coated, easy-to-grip barbells to America's expanding fitness and sports equipment world. A warm, convivial man, he had a down-home way of talking that charmed voters. He also was making his first statewide political race, emerging as a fresh voice in a gubernatorial campaign full of political veterans. It was supposed to be a fight between the politically well-traveled "Killer B's"—Attorney General Bill Baxley, Lieutenant Governor Jere Beasley, and former Governor Albert Brewer. James swept past them all, defeating Baxley in a runoff and taking the oath of office in January 1979.

There was a lot about James that Gary liked. He was a highly successful businessman. He talked conservative politics. As a former Republican, he didn't have Wallace's Southern Democrat segregationist baggage. His campaign theme: "It's time for a new beginning."

That theme rang true for Gary Cooper, too. He soon would give up his legislative seat to take on a new challenge—joining the James administration as commissioner of the Alabama Department of Pensions and Security, the sprawling welfare agency that reached into every county and was the largest agency in the state. The appointment made him the first black to be put in command of such a vital and massive agency in Alabama since Reconstruction—easily the highest-ranking black in state government in nearly a century.

James wanted to break with the Wallace legacy, and putting a black with Cooper's credentials in charge of the welfare agency was one of his first steps. A little providence may have played a role, too.

Cooper and James Harrell went to the Governor's House Motel on the night of the gubernatorial primary runoff between James and Baxley. Both candidates had scheduled their election night parties in large conference rooms at the motel on Montgomery's South Boulevard, and Cooper and Harrell went to mingle with the Baxley crowd. As the evening unfolded, James surged comfortably ahead, and Cooper and Harrell left the disheartened Baxley room—only to meet Fob James in a hallway heading to his victory celebration. They followed, and the exuberant James declared, "Representative Cooper, y'all are doing a great job for me in Mobile!" With that, Cooper and Harrell went on into the James event and mingled with his supporters.[263]

"Stroke of luck," Harrell said. "No way Gary was supporting Fob James."

But James invited Cooper to join his administration as head of Pensions and Security.

> *Fob James called me one day and said he wanted to talk to me. I was impressed because he wanted me on his team. I recognized how important it was to be elected to the Legislature, but I also realized that none of us had ever had a Cabinet position, at least of this magnitude, that would allow us to help the poor, orphans, people in need.*

Any agency head can be a Cabinet member if the governor declares it a Cabinet post, and Wallace had made Birmingham weekly newspaper publisher Jesse Lewis the first black Cabinet member in modern times as head of the state's transportation safety unit.[264] But it was a small agency with nowhere near the responsibilities, impact and personnel of Alabama's welfare system, a department with more than four thousand employees.

It happened pretty quickly—it seems like in just days or weeks after winning the election.

In his speech upon becoming commissioner, he spelled out his goals, and he concluded with these words:

I ask for your help. I ask you to tell your friends that you have met the Commissioner of the State Department of Pensions and Security. If there was ever any racism in that department, it ended on the 5th of February. If there were people in that department that did not speak courteously to our poor and disadvantaged, they are not going to be there long. But the only way I can do this is with your help, your support, and your prayers.[265]

Publicly, Cooper was quick to announce plans to seek innovative ways to better assist the poor and elderly and cut out waste and fraud in the Department of Pensions and Security. Privately, he found the agency in a shambles, with low morale inside its stale bureaucracy and little love for it outside.

The department had a horrible reputation. The legislators hated it; to some it was welfare, giving money to lazy-ass people who didn't work. The employees didn't like it because they had to deal with these people—some of them smelled, looked like hell. The press didn't like it. And the people who got the money didn't either. They were always complaining because the workers would come by their house and do inspections and they would not treat them with respect.

Cooper had a plan. He also had help. Two women on his staff played key roles as he began his attempt to turn the department around.

One was his administrative assistant, Mary Ann Venable. The other was J. D. Schremser, hired to help improve the department's image.

J. D. had a degree from the University of Wisconsin. We sat down. If something is not right, let's do something about it. Let's come up with a plan. And J. D. came up with this plan—to change the image of the Department of Pensions and Security. We decided who our customers were: legislators, the press, the people who got the aid and the department employees. We came up with a plan for each one.

They made a file for each legislator, noting their birthday, where they went to college, short but personal notes that served as a tickler system to send out birthday cards and other goodwill contacts.

Good public relations extended to the press, too.

I knew most of the big guys. We let them know how open we wanted to be and how we'd never not tell them the truth. There was a bar called Cooley's, on the south side of Montgomery, a black bar in a black community. Maybe every month or two weeks we had a happy hour for the press. We had little paper bags, and in these paper bags we didn't have food stamps but we had booze stamps. So they would each get five booze stamps!

With the employees, we did the "Dare to Care" campaign.

Cooper traveled to every county—many employees at county offices had never seen a DPS commissioner, ever—and began a motivational campaign, recognizing top employees, sending them handwritten birthday cards. There were staff Halloween parties: Cooper showed up in an XXXL Superman costume for one.

James Harrell: "He wanted to be in every county, and I would ride with him. Morale in that department was low. You're dealing with poor people all the time. He tried to instill in the department the mindset: Yeah, these people are poor, but they're the reason you have the job. You should serve them with some gratitude. Be a professional. He did do that."

For those receiving welfare, there was another change: *We started calling them "Yes, sir" and "No, ma'am." And we started mailing the food stamps.* Gone was the humiliation of a long wait in line—lines Cooper experienced firsthand.

"We actually would go and stand in line with the people and ask them what kind of service they were getting," Harrell said. "Some of course would moan, others would say the service is great."

Cooper single-handedly engineered change in the department when it came to the medical needs of those who were poor and diabetic. Will Campbell, a Legal Services lawyer in north Alabama at the time, was preparing to sue the state to provide syringes to diabetic patients on Medicaid so they could inject insulin. Medicaid law required that "medically necessary" supplies must be provided, but the state's welfare rules prohibited payments for syringes out of conservative fears that the needles would be used to inject heroin. When Cooper learned of the problem and possible litigation, the state's rule promptly disappeared. Syringes suddenly were covered.

"He just changed it," Campbell said, still recalling years later the rare act of swift state action to help Alabama's needy.[266]

It did not escape Cooper that he was blazing another trail for black men and women. In a speech shortly after taking command of the huge state agency, he noted how much had changed for blacks over the past century.

> *Many years ago in Lowndes or Sumter County there was an old black man—he may even have been born in Africa—sitting on a plantation with black children around and them asking him, 'Tell us what should we do? We have undergone the suppression as long as we can. When can we ever get any power? Should we fight now? What should we do?"*
>
> *And I am sure the old man told them, very wisely, too: "The time is not right, we don't have the power, we don't have the law. Let's wait until the time is right."*
>
> *Today, ladies and gentlemen, you and I know that the time is right. The time is here for us to assume the power to control our own destiny that has so often escaped us. But as we gain affluence, as we gain in power, we must also gain in our sense of responsibility.[267]*

Cooper was meticulous. Along with visiting offices in every county, he personally inspected them, even to see how well the equipment was dusted. Phillip Browning recalled the tall Cooper "looking at the top of Coke machines to make sure they were clean."

Browning, a P&S staffer who went to California to direct the Los Angeles County Department of Public Social Services, overseeing a staff of 14,000, viewed Cooper as a mentor. In a letter years later, he told Cooper that "your training lives on in both me and my son."[268]

Early in his tenure with DPS, Cooper shrewdly saw the vital but still marginal role of women in the political process. In a 1979 speech on the topic of "Racial Minorities in Politics" at the Taft Institute Seminar at Auburn University, Cooper covered a lot of ground on getting eligible blacks registered to vote and then turning out to vote for worthy candidates.

Right now our task is to get more minorities to participate in politics, whether through running for election, working in campaigns for either blacks or whites, or simply by pulling the lever at the polling place. And while we're encouraging more blacks to run, let's not forget a too-often overlooked segment of our black population—our women.

There are some rare Barbara Jordans and Shirley Chisholms, but generally black women are not coming to the forefront in either national or state politics. It's unfortunate, too, because they have a lot to offer—and a lot to fight for. Black women have the poorest-paying jobs, the poorest educational opportunities, and the heaviest family responsibilities. The men who are representing these women have not begun to meet their needs, so they may well have to do it for themselves.

It also came to Cooper's attention that some women receiving support from his agency were not getting required financial aid from divorced or absent fathers of their children.

One of the biggest challenges when I got there was that people couldn't get child support. I got a bill passed that connected child support to tax returns. It stated that if someone owed child support, they could not get their tax refunds until they paid up.

Cooper, while running the far-reaching department from Montgomery, still had family responsibilities at the Palmetto Street home in Mobile. He and Gloria had divorced—*We were married about five years. I was not a very good husband, but she was a super lady and we remained friends.* Gary was a single parent again. A note to himself spelled out one day's priorities.

How many fraud cases were prosecuted last year and the year before?

List on sheets the items of a major nature that we must commence work on.

Then:

Tell Shawn to turn the thermostat down and open curtains in living room so flowers may get light.

Left and above: Gary's maternal great-grandparents, Julie Andrus and Paul Mouton, who lived together in Lafayette, Louisiana. Below left: The twin sisters, Julia and Julie Andrus. Below: Julie's daughter, Agnes Mouton, Gary's maternal grandmother. All photos taken on unknown dates in Lafayette, Louisiana.

Right: Algernon Johnson "A. J." Cooper Sr. and Gladys Mouton Cooper. Below, the Coopers with 7-month-old Gary.

Above right: Gary playing outside the Christian Benevolent Funeral Home in Mobile. Left: Gary and his cousin Marilyn [now Funderburk], 1937. Right, Gary and Billy standing, Jay and Peggy seated, late 1940s.

*Left, Great-Aunt Pearl
Madison with her
husband, William
Madison. Above, their
home in Mobile's "Down
the Bay" neighborhood;
around 1940 A. J. and
Gladys Cooper built next
door. Below, Gary and
cousin Judi [Stephenson],
Mobile Bay, 1953.*

Above, Gary at Notre Dame, 1954–58. Left, Charlesetta and Gary on their wedding day, Chicago, 1958. Below, Charlesetta and Gary on the weekend when he was commissioned a lieutenant in the U.S. Marine Corps, graduated from the University of Notre Dame, and married. To the right of the couple is Gary's grandfather, Osceola Osceola Cooper.

Above: Gary, Charlesetta, Patrick, Joli, and infant Shawn in 1962 during Gary's first assignment at Marine Base Kaneohe. Below: Captain Gary Cooper swears in 1st Sgt. Jim McCargo, a Montford Point Marine, aboard the USS Chicago.

Above, from left: Unidentified air officer, Captain Cooper, and Gary Gretter, during their service with Mike Company, a rifle unit, in Vietnam in 1966. Below: Gary in Vietnam with two South Vietnamese children during his tour in 1966-67.

Above, from left: Billy, Gary, and Jay Cooper, with Great-aunt Pearl Johnson Madison, in a 1979 photo accompanying a Mobile Bay Monthly *retrospective on the 1970s, when the Coopers made their marks on local and state politics. Inset: Gary and Jay look over returns after the 1972 Prichard mayoral election when Jay became the first black to defeat a white incumbent mayor in Alabama since at least Reconstruction.*

Right: Gary stands beside one of Mobile's most revered political leaders, Joe Langan, a former mayor and legislator who worked with black political organizer John LeFlore to fight segregation and push for economic progress for blacks and whites. A brigadier general in the National Guard, a uniformed Langan was photographed at Gary's Marine Birthday Ball. Below right: Gary's cousin, Marilyn Funderburk, and his sister, Peggy, who would become co-founder of the Duke Ellington School of the Arts in Washington, D.C., a prominent philanthropist and collector of African-American art, and president of the district's school board.

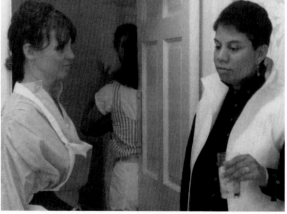

Above left: Pat Eddington and Gary Cooper exchange friendly comments after he defeated her in 1974, making him one of the first blacks elected to the Alabama Legislature post-Reconstruction. Above right: Cooper sits in the Alabama House chamber. Below: Governor Fob James named Cooper commissioner of the Alabama Department of Pensions and Security, 1979. He was the first black to serve in a Cabinet post for such a huge agency.

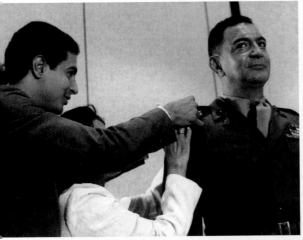

Top left: Son Patrick, pins on new insignia with help from Gary's mother, Gladys (obscured). Top right: Cooper as commanding general of the USMC 4th Force Service Support Group based in Atlanta, 1986. Above: Gary with three of history's most prominent African American military officers, from left, Marine Lt. Gen. Frank Emanuel Petersen Jr., Air Force Gen. Benjamin O. Davis Jr., and Vice Admiral Samuel Gravely Jr., at a meeting in Washington, D.C., engineered by Cooper while he was serving as assistant secretary of the Air Force, 1991.

Left: Nettie Stewart became a vital part of Gary's businesses in Mobile, including Commonwealth National Bank, the family funeral home, and Gethsemane Cemetery.

Right: Ambassador Cooper and wife Beverly at an evening reception in Jamaica. Below: Beverly relaxes at the ambassador's residence in Kingston during Gary's term as U.S. ambassador to Jamaica.

Top: Gary with son Patrick and grandchildren Sam and Celia on a Cooper family vacation in Jamaica, 2014. Center: Gary with his daughters, Shawn (left) and Joli (right), on the same vacation trip. Bottom: The Coopers became the first African American family with three generations graduating from the University of Notre Dame. Pictured in 2009 with Notre Dame President Emeritus Theodore Hesburgh are Gary ('58), daughter Joli Cooper-Nelson ('81), and her son Ashley Cooke III ('11).

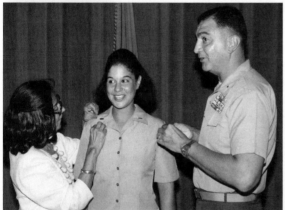

Top: Gary joins daughter Shawn on her graduation day from Officer Candidate School at the Marine Corps base at Quantico, Virginia, 1985. Left: Grandmother Gladys Cooper pins on Shawn's gold bars after her commissioning as a 2nd lieutenant. Below: Astronaut Neil Armstrong golfs with Cooper in a fundraiser for several Mobile charities. Armstrong and Cooper became friends while serving on corporate boards.

Above: The USMC's first three African American generals share a laugh together; from left, Lt. Gen. Frank Peterson, Maj. Gen. Gary Cooper, and Brig. Gen. George Walls. Below: Gary, Beverly, and Gary's friend from their Vietnam days, Marine Corps Brig. Gen. George Walls.

Left: Mario Cooper, Gary's youngest brother, was a key figure overseeing the Democratic National Convention in 1992 and a leading HIV/AIDS activist. Bottom right: Gary's sisters, Peggy, at left, and Dominic, stand behind maternal aunts, Helen, at left, and Marvel, two of the four "beautiful Mouton sisters" of Lafayette, Louisiana. Left: Casey Cooper with his wife, Amy, and sons Leo and Lincoln after his investiture as a federal district judge in Washington, D.C., in 2014. Bottom left: Jay Cooper with nephew Casey on the same occasion.

Joe Geeter

Cooper with Montford Point Marine Ted Britton at a Montford Point Association's Atlanta event in 2015, shortly before Britton's 90th birthday. Like Cooper, Britton served as a U.S. ambassador in the Caribbean, holding the diplomatic post in Barbados and Grenada.

∼

SOURCES OF PHOTOS

Unless otherwise indicated, all photos are courtesy of Gary Cooper from family archives. The photos on page 1, the bottom left on page 2, and the bottom photos on pages 3 and 6 are courtesy of Judi Stephenson. The top and center photos on page 12 and the center and bottom left on page 15 were provided by Shawn Cooper. The photo on this page is courtesy of Joe Geeter, national president of the Montford Point Marine Association.

A PARTING OF THE WAYS

Over the next two years, Cooper accomplished much of what he had set out to do, but he began to find out that not all of it sat well with the governor. Cooper initially had thought James to be a "nice, fair, regular guy."[269] But with President Ronald Reagan and the Republicans taking power in Washington and roundly denouncing "big government" and "welfare queens," he felt that James had begun to show different colors: *I was really kind of shocked at the underlying attitudes that he had.*

One point of disagreement was over mailing food stamps. When Cooper had begun to visit county offices, he found that an overriding concern of the poor—particularly those who were elderly or infirm—was the requirement that they wait in line outside the building to get the food stamps in person. *It didn't matter if it was raining, freezing, you're in a wheelchair—you were outside in a line.* He got a team to review the pros and cons of mailing food stamps and found there was very little or no loss or fraud in the process. So the department started mailing them.[270]

When word of the change got out, an irate James confronted Cooper.

He said, "Why didn't I know about it?"

I told him, "I thought you were the governor, and I was the commissioner."

It would not be long before their differences became insurmountable. In March 1981, a time of tight revenues, James wanted budget cuts, including cutting Pensions and Security jobs at the central office in Montgomery. Cooper balked; he felt James was reneging on a promise made in September 1980 to protect the DPS budget.

In comments to the *Anniston Star*, Cooper said:

> The governor and I agree on a number of issues . . . but we disagree on how the cutbacks should be made. . . . When the price of cutbacks is employees' jobs and human suffering among DPS recipients, I can't go along.[271]

Their differences led to one of the most embarrassing episodes of James's first term. James summoned Cooper to the governor's office in the Capitol. The *Anniston Star*, quoting Cooper and an unanmed source, reported that Cooper

> was never given an opportunity to discuss the cuts. . . . James said, "I think you and I have different philosophies of how to run state government."
>
> Cooper replied, "I agree. We ought to discuss that."
>
> "That won't be necessary," said James, who then pulled from a file a resignation letter he required of all cabinet appointees when appointments were made.[272]

At the time and years later Cooper had no recollection of signing such a letter, and he told the governor he would not be bound by it. His reason: the commissioner legally serves at the pleasure of the DPS board. It would take a vote of the board to remove him, once the governor sent the board a request to fire the commissioner. And, at least at that point, James didn't have the votes on the seven-member board, which included its first two black members and two white members who supported Cooper.[273]

Signing a letter of resignation? Maybe I did, but the reason I don't remember signing a letter is because when he brought up that we were going to have a parting of the ways, I'm not even sure at that minute that I knew the board had to fire me, not him. I'm not sure that dawned on me until I got back to my office. But that was the law, and he was pissed that it was a board decision, because I had the votes. Doris Bender, the mother of the Bender Shipbuilding owner in Mobile, was the chairperson of the DPS board. She told the governor: "I am not voting to fire Gary Cooper."

COOPER'S TROOPERS

James also didn't have the support of much of the news media, which generally found it unseemly for the governor to abruptly fire the highest-ranking black in state government, particularly one of Cooper's stature who was fighting on behalf of the poor.

Some editorials branded the governor's actions "ill-advised," "bush league," or "poorly handled."[274]

"The policy that Cooper violated would appear to be that of feeling sympathy for the poor and working to get more money for his department," wrote *Birmingham Post-Herald* political reporter Ted Bryant.[275]

The *Montgomery Advertiser* even saw the clash as a potential springboard for Cooper politically.

> Mr. Cooper's abiding faith is inspirational. In order to bring him down in the first place, Gov. James replaced two black P&S board members with white ones who would vote to remove Cooper, who was well liked by the working staff. More intriguing is what might become of the statewide popularity accumulated and fostered by the wealthy and articulate Mr. Cooper. He argued Friday his concern was to protect about 1 million Alabamians affected by a weakened department. Contrary to stereotype, not all of them are black.
>
> That's not enough for a serious run at the governor's chair, but the way we sometimes field 10 or 15 candidates for lieutenant governor, the chance to make it into a runoff in that race might be tempting. Still, he was thought to enjoy his time in the legislature, and was never, up to now, troubled by flights from reality.[276]

On the governor's side, there were also columns pointing out that, in fact, Cooper was a gubernatorial appointee and should abide by longstanding political decorum and step down. Veteran political commentator Bob Ingram said Cooper should have "departed quietly," not create "a racial issue" that drew backing from black political activists.[277]

While pro-Cooper protesters carried signs that said "James is racist," Cooper dismissed any racial aspect to the contretemps in comments to reporters: *I honestly don't believe the governor is a racist. I don't think he's too smart, but racist he is not.*

Blacks were energized in support of Cooper, and they included Alabama Democratic Conference Chairman Joe Reed, even though Cooper had never joined the ADC. At an event in Selma, where voting rights marchers had been clubbed violently by troopers amid clouds of tear gas at the Edmund Pettus Bridge in 1965, Cooper was not overlooked.[278]

The church was packed with people, and Joe Reed saw me sitting at the edge. He said, "Here's a man who would rather not serve on his knees, but stand on his own." I got a big cheer out of that.

Ingram saw only the downside: "All Cooper did was make it unlikely that any future governor would use Cooper's talents."[279]

The welfare agency also rose to Cooper's defense.

Some four hundred people from across the state held a rally on the Capitol steps to protest cuts to welfare programs and seek repeal of sales taxes on food and medicine. Organized by the Alabama Coalition Against Hunger prior to Cooper's firing, it turned into a pro-Cooper event, with some chanting, "We want Gary!"[280]

Many DPS employees publicly supported Cooper at the rally, wearing ribbons that said "Cooper's Troopers."[281]

Also, the Alabama Conference of Social Work presented Cooper with an Outstanding Service Award in recognition of the "leadership he has shown as an advocate for the poor." Cooper was named recipient of the award the week before his firing. *"I never knew firing could be so much fun," Cooper said as he accepted the award.*[282]

The steps to fire Cooper took place on April 3, after James had removed the only two blacks ever to serve on the DPS board. He replaced them with two white men just minutes before the board met behind closed doors and voted 5–2 to fire Cooper.[283] James had run for governor promising "a new beginning." But in a state viewed by critics as a segregationist backwater, he opted for a secret meeting to kick out the highest-ranking black in state government since Reconstruction.

Harrell said the next commissioner James appointed had state trooper protection. "He was really afraid that the department was going to strike and there would be some chaos there," Harrell said.

There were difficulties for the department but not chaos, and Cooper moved on. Although his years in the Alabama political spotlight were over, his role on the national stage was just beginning.

12

Moving On

Through his years back in Mobile as a businessman, politician, and single parent, Cooper had continued to set milestones for African Americans as a leader in the Marine Reserves.

When he took command of the 13th Force Reconnaissance Company at Mobile, the USMC's historical calendar for 1971 noted that on February 21 Cooper became the first black Marine officer to command a Reserve unit in the United States. In 1977, he added to his resume another milestone: the first black to command a Marine Reserve battalion, the 500-man unit headquartered in Birmingham.[284]

Cooper said his Reserve experience was an unexpected boon in a number of ways.

I really didn't know much about the Reserves. I found out that in my hometown we've got a Reserve unit, based right here in Mobile. So I applied to be the commanding officer. The man holding that post, his time was up. And lo and behold, here I am a few months off active duty and I become the commanding officer of a Recon company in Mobile, Alabama.

And I didn't even know you got paid!

This company had about 190 people in it—just two of them were black folks, and one was me.

Why so few blacks? A past commanding officer, from Mississippi, came to me years later and wanted to get something off his chest. He told me that it was his policy not to let any black Marines in that unit, and if any of them got in there between drills, he would work to run them off.

The Reserves under my command, they were a challenge. They did not want to see me show up—here I was a regular officer just off active duty. The first time I ordered the men to fall out in formation, I didn't know whether to laugh or cry. They were the scroungiest looking goddam Marines I had ever seen. They had on tennis shoes with their scroungy-looking uniform and their long hair and all. But underneath they were sharp Marines, and that experience went very well. I was a major at that time, and we got a trophy for being the best marching unit in the parade.

Next up: Birmingham. When his assignment was announced—command of the 4th Battalion, 14th Marines, 4th Marine Division—Cooper told the *Mobile Press-Register* that his race was of little concern: *I have always felt that it's the quality of leadership that counts and not the color of your skin. My experience has been that most all Marines feel that way.*[285]
In fact, race was a factor in his selection.

In Birmingham, I took over an artillery battalion. The battalion had a firing battery in Joliet, Illinois, and one in Chattanooga, Tennessee. I would visit them along with operating out of headquarters in Birmingham, which also had a firing battery.

Now they were having big-time trouble because about 65 percent of that unit was black. This was during the time of our racial consciousness, and they wanted to wear their Afros, and those white officers didn't know what to do with the brothers up in Birmingham. This was an issue that developed in the early 1970s, somewhere in there.

So I was asked to be the commanding officer of the artillery unit. They came and found me. I was not an artillery officer. I was infantry and all I knew was how to call the artillery in. Normally an infantryman wouldn't go to an artillery unit, but I wanted a command, so I said I would do it. And I knew this unit was in deep kimchi up in Birmingham.

So I interviewed with this colonel, a great big guy, Colonel Bjorklund. He was the regimental commander. I'd made lieutenant colonel by then, this is 1977, and he said he wanted me to be the new commander. He went on to tell me they were having some challenges. These were times of racial tensions, and they were having some challenges, and he thought that I could really help the Marine Corps.

But I had a concern. I said, "Now, Colonel, one thing we must re-member: I am not an artillery officer. So when the time comes to give fitness report grades, you can't judge my technical proficiency against your artillery officers. So if we have that agreement, fine."

We got that agreement.

I go to Birmingham. I could tell why they were having trouble. The Marines in the battalion looked like hell—bushy Afro hair under the Marine Corps covers. I didn't say anything the first time around. I talked to them and inspected them. Most or some of the senior enlisted were black also. I had to figure out a way to do this without seriously hurting morale.

Maybe I didn't do anything the second drill, but I found a way for these sergeants to meet with me after the drill, and I said, "You know, do you LIKE being a sergeant? Or would you like better to be a PFC? Let me suggest to you that when Colonel Cooper comes back, I expect to have some goddam haircuts on these Marines. And them looking like Marines!"

It didn't fail. I got back, and they were squared away. They even won a prize as the top marching unit in Birmingham's Veterans Day parade.

All these young Marines needed was some leadership. We could talk real good. It wasn't long that we had a good understanding. I had a few I had to change their status in life from sergeant to PFC and a couple I had to put out, but overall, they were just waiting on someone to provide leadership.

Now, I go later to headquarters in D.C. and I look at my fitness report. When it talks about "regular duties," I got "below average." So I go to see this colonel at headquarters. I said, "Colonel, this isn't what you told me."

"That's right," he said. "You're right. We'll change it."

So I go back a year later. It still hasn't been changed. I said, "Colonel, this isn't what you told me."

"Well, well, we . . ."

I said, "Don't change it. Leave it. Because when the promotion board looks at that, they're going to know YOU fucked up, not ME. Because I'm not 'below average' in anything."

So I left. I don't know if he ever changed it. But one day several years later he called and said, "I see you just got selected to be a brigadier general. Can I come to your ceremony? I'd like to meet some of those generals."

Well, we had moved on. "Colonel," I said, "You're welcome."

BAD NEWS, GOOD NEWS

The supply officer with the Birmingham battalion was Joe Wilson, a white Marine reservist who in private life was a professor at the University of North Alabama and a businessman. Wilson had been with the Birmingham battalion about a year when Cooper arrived. They hit it off. Typically, Wilson learned, Cooper moved quickly on behalf of someone who impressed him.[286]

"We went to summer camp, I guess in 1977," Wilson said. "When we got back from the fire exercise, he told me, 'I want you to be my XO"— executive officer. "So I became XO of the battalion. Six or eight months later, I think he relieved the Lima Battery commander. We had Kilo, Lima and Mike batteries, and the Lima Battery was in Birmingham. At any rate, the Lima commander was gone, and Gary told me, 'As XO, Major Wilson, I'd like for you to recommend three or four individuals, and put them in priority order, to become the commander of Lima Battery.'

"I did that and went back to his office. I had them lined up. I'll never forget this. I said, 'Here's my list. Here's my first individual, my second, my third. Here's the rationale for the first individual,' . . . second, third, on down the line.

"He said, 'I agree with you 100 percent.'

"I said, 'Well, thank you, sir. Should I inform the first individual?'

"'No. You're going to take it. I want you to command Lima Battery.'

"I said, 'But I'm not an artillery officer.'

"He said, 'You will be shortly. It's yours.'"

End of meeting.

For Wilson and Cooper, not every Reserve weekend or exercise went as planned.

Once we went to a firing range. This was at Fort McClellan in east Alabama, near Anniston. We were doing live fire—boom, boom, boom—the round was that big. Joe Wilson came up to me.

"I hate to tell you this," he said, "but I've got bad news and good news."

"What's the bad news?"

"We just hit a farm house."

We hit a farm house! I was mortified. I thought my career was over.

"So what's the good news?" I asked.

"Wasn't nobody home."

The line can bring a laugh now. But not then.

"I remember it just like it was yesterday," Wilson said. "You don't forget something like that. That was our Mike Battery commander. Both Lima and Mike batteries were at the fire exercise near Anniston. When they started that morning, they didn't do everything they should have done. Didn't run their safety checks, didn't validate everything. And the first round they fired went off the base. That's one neither Gary nor I will ever forget."

No Showers

"At Camp Lejeune," Wilson said, "we had been on a very successful fire exercise, one of the best exercises we'd ever had. We had finished everything. This would have been on a Thursday or Friday, and we'd be flying out on Monday to come back to our Reserve center. The Marines, when they have a pretty good relationship with their commander, they want to throw him in the shower.

"Gary and I were filthy, dirty. We had been out there four or five days on this fire exercise. So when we got in, we both got cleaned up. We put on spit-shined boots. We both liked spit-shined boots. We liked squared-away uniforms. This is back in the '70s.

"He was sitting at his desk. We were in the barracks—they assigned us barracks to work out of—and he comes running into my office. We were trying to get all of our fitness work done, all of our paperwork done. He says, 'Major Wilson, I see a group of Marines coming. There must be at least fifty to a hundred of them. They're coming, and they're going to throw your ass in the shower. And they're going to throw mine in, too! You need to go out there and stop them!'

"I thought, 'Well, crap.' I get up, and I walk out, and there are two steps on the barracks. I stand on the top step. They're about fifty yards away. He had seen them coming—and fifty yards is a pretty good ways out—and I'm trying to think of what exactly I'm going to say.

"They just keep marching. They get about twenty yards from me, and about that time Gary steps out, to my right, directly beside me. He said, 'Just stand there—I'll handle this.'

"I said, 'Yes, sir.'

"About that time, he said loudly, 'DE-TAIL . . . HALT!'

"They stopped. They weren't even in formation. They were coming to throw our butts in the shower. But they halted.

"And he said, 'AH-TEEN-SHUN!' And they all came to attention.

"He said, 'Marines! We've been off on an exercise, and as I explained to you when we finished in the field, we were able to come in, and we all got dressed. We're getting all of our maintenance work done. We're getting all of our paperwork done. And we're going to go home and celebrate. I'm so proud of you, Marines! . . . AH-BOUT . . . FACE!'

"And they all about-faced.

"He said, 'FOR-WARD . . . MARCH!'

"And they marched off. And we never saw them again."

Patrick

Gary's son Patrick, born at Quantico, Virginia, could have emulated his father with a military career—he had a potential offer to go to West Point but chose the Ivy League instead. Neither had seemed a possibility at first.

"I was a really awful high school student," Patrick said. "My freshman year and part of my sophomore year, I just had no interest in studying or doing homework. It was reflected on my grades. I think I was on a perpetual punishment from my father."

But Patrick was intellectually gifted. Even while blowing off school-work, his flair for chess was evident. He was ranked one of the top fifty players in the country under the age of eighteen. He would even write his college essay on chess.[287]

James Harrell: "It just came easy to him. Talking to Patrick, you would think this is just a street kid. But he tested very well."

His aunt, Peggy Cooper, who had begun a relationship with Washington, D.C., real estate developer Conrad Cafritz around this time, saw Patrick's potential.

"Aunt Peggy came down for Mardi Gras. I had taken the PSAT, a preliminary test with the SAT, and had scored pretty high. That caught her interest. She just said, 'Look, Patrick, if you study and get really good grades from here on out, all A's, it'll help you in the whole college process, and I think get you into Harvard or Yale with your board scores.'

"I believed her and got A's the rest of the semesters."

The Ivy League beckoned. Cafritz, whom Peggy would marry in 1981, helped steer Patrick to Yale, his alma mater.

"I could have gone to West Point, got the same free ride there, and my father wanted me to go to West Point, but I was just . . . my Aunt Peggy was just absolutely insistent."

New Haven, however, was a far remove from Mobile.

"Like going back to Alabama had been a culture shock, going to school in a New England area was a culture shock," Patrick said. "Dress was different. Speech patterns different. Weather different. It was somewhat intimidating.

"My aunt was insistent that I look like someone who was at Yale. So I go up a couple of weeks early, and she sees all my clothes—polyester pants, polyester shirts, bright colors with sailboats on them. She gets a big Hefty garbage bag and throws all my clothes into the garbage. Then she takes me to this D.C. store called Britches—it's kind of like Brooks Brothers— buying me khaki trousers and blue blazers, things I'd never had before. She had me totally prepped out even though I had never gone to a prep school.

"I get there early for an orientation program. I'm sitting in my khakis and blue blazer. There are a couple of black freshmen sitting across the way. They're speaking fluent Spanish. I said to myself, 'Oh my god, how in the world am I going to be able to succeed here when they've got kids fluent in Spanish?"

Then it dawns on him. There's a reason they're speaking fluent Spanish: "They're Puerto Ricans."

But succeeding at Yale was not just a matter of keeping up academically.

"I think the real issue for me was that you go from a strict environment, being raised by my father, to an environment where you have total freedom. If you want to stay out till five in the morning, you can stay out till five in the morning. The adjustment of going from a Marine Corps household to an environment where it was total, complete freedom—and yet enough rope to hang yourself—that was tough."

Too tough at first. By his sophomore year, Patrick had had enough.

"At that point I really just didn't like the environment," he said. "I decided to drop out. I left Yale early in my second semester and didn't take a single final exam. "I went back to Mobile and stayed a month or so with my grandmother until my father gets some report from Yale that says I received five F's for my second-semester classes. I was suspended.

"He is just beside himself. He tells me, 'No son of mine is going to be a dropout in any state I'm living in.' I was given the orders to pack up and leave.

"So I moved to D.C. to live with my Aunt Peggy for a short bit. Then she got really upset with my antics. She packed up all my stuff and put it on the porch and told me to find another place to live by myself."

Patrick was hitting bottom. It was a landing that turned into an inspiration.

"I worked as a laborer for about half a year," he said. "It was pretty tough, getting up at three and four in the mornings. Literally I'm digging ditches and being a laborer. It was really through that experience that I realized I was squandering an opportunity. There were a number of kids I worked with—and I was pretty young at that time, I was like nineteen or so—but they were incredibly smart. Some of the most amazing, innate intelligence, intellect that I ever came across. They didn't have the Yale opportunity, and they were just shocked that I blew that chance."

He also began to realize that a degree would be a ticket out of the ditches: "You don't have a degree, this is what you're in for. So I was motivated at that point."

Having connections helped. He got a job on Capitol Hill working for Senator Donald Stewart, an Alabama Democrat who had served in the Legislature with Patrick's father before winning a special election for the U.S. Senate seat in 1978. "I did that for about a year and a half. And I had to take courses and get A's or B's in order to reapply to Yale. I took the courses at Georgetown, got two A's, and reapplied. When I went back—by then I knew I wanted to go to law school—I also had a grade point average that looked like Donald Duck had gone to Yale. I realized I needed to make A's, so for the next five semesters, I made the A's."

He majored in economics and political science, subjects he took to almost by nature. There was much to be gained as well: "Some kids from some pretty powerful black political families were there."

He also excelled in an area that his father had not—basketball. Unlike Gary's brief, almost comic tryout at Notre Dame, Patrick was good enough to catch the Yale coach's eye. While not a starter, he was a key substitute and lettered.

"Dad was never really an athlete. Where we lived in Mobile growing up, there was a park not too far from our house. They used to and still do have basketball courts there. I didn't start playing basketball until seventh or eighth grade. But I found I loved it and spent all my time at Crawford Park playing basketball. At night, sometimes I would sneak out when I was grounded. All the kids were just terrified of my father, so they would climb over the fence and run off in the other direction if they spotted him.

"I played a lot of playground ball. I had never gone to basketball summer camp or played any organized basketball. I think I tried out for maybe the high school freshman team. I didn't have many skills, and when I graduated from high school I was maybe five-ten, five-eleven. But when I got to college, I started to grow, and then when I took some time off from Yale, by the time I came back I was six-five.

"The way I ended up playing, I was playing with the varsity before the season started. I knew a couple of guys on the team. I was kind of doing my thing, and the coach saw me and asked if I wanted to play on the team. So I lettered in basketball that year. I would have played again except I didn't have any eligibility—you have to use your eligibility within five or six years. So I couldn't play my senior year because I didn't have any eligibility. But it was a lot of fun, something I wanted to do. It was a great experience. Some of my best friends now are folks I played with on the basketball team."

Applying to law schools, Patrick was accepted at Harvard and Stanford as well as Yale. But by then, he had become comfortable in that New England environment, and he stayed at Yale for law school.

13

National Stage

In private life, Black Star and Petal Pusher had been jettisoned, but Cooper still pursued multiple endeavors along with the funeral home and insurance company. These included attending a special program for senior managers at the Harvard University School of Business, and in 1981 he became vice president for marketing with David Volkert & Associates, a Mobile-based architectural and engineering firm with clients around the region.[288]

His work with Volkert & Associates was a direct result of his ouster as state welfare commissioner by Governor Fob James. When the firing occurred, Matt Metcalfe's friend and business associate, wealthy Baldwin County newspaper publisher and politician Jimmy Faulkner, told Cooper: "If Fob fires you, I've got a job for you."[289]

The job was at Volkert & Associates, which sought contracts with government building projects as part of its business. Faulkner, a politically connected former mayor and state senator who twice ran for Alabama governor, was a Volkert consultant. Cooper, as a well-known African American from Mobile, played a key role in lining up black officials with local governments to give Volkert a better shot at their architectural and building contracts. He also helped steer the firm to opportunities in the nation's capital.

We built the visitors' center at Arlington National Cemetery. I helped them get that job. I also helped them get some jobs at National Airport.

Already providing assistance to administrators at Spring Hill, the Jesuit college in Mobile that had been a leader among Southern campuses in integrating its student body, Cooper also was named a trustee at Talladega College, a natural fit for him. He had been asked to join the board by J. Mason Davis, a black attorney in Birmingham who was active in state Democratic Party politics. Davis's family owned the insurance company that eventually bought Christian Benevolent Insurance from the Coopers.[290]

Talladega was a historic traditionally black campus. Formed after the Civil War when two former slaves got help from the Freedman's Bureau to educate the children of slaves, it eventually became home to the famed *Amistad Murals* by the African American artist Hale Woodruff, depicting scenes from the uprising of captive Africans on the slave ship *Amistad*.[291]

It was during a trustees meeting at Talladega College that Cooper's role on a national stage would begin. The date was October 27, 1983. A phone call for Cooper required him to excuse himself from the board meeting. On the line was the assistant commandant of the U.S. Marine Corps, Lieutenant General D'Wayne Gray.[292]

Four days earlier, a suicide bomber had driven a truck loaded with explosives into the four-story Marine barracks in Beirut, Lebanon, setting off a massive explosion that killed 241 American servicemen, 220 of them Marines.[293] Gray needed Cooper at headquarters in Washington, D.C., to help coordinate information to the families.

"When can you be here?" Gray asked.

"Well, sir, it's Thursday. I'll drive back to Mobile, get my uniform packed, and I'll be there Monday morning."

That was three days too long for Gray. "Good," he said, "I'll see you at zero-seven-thirty in the morning."

Cooper's attendance at the Talladega College board meeting was over. His marketing services with Volkert & Associates were put on hold. Calling home, he was able to get his uniforms and gear packed and flown up for a prolonged stay in Washington. His friend, James Harrell, joined him and took the wheel for the long drive to D.C.

"We left Montgomery at like two o'clock," Harrell recalled. "It got dark. He said, 'I should have told you, I can't drive at night, I don't like to drive at night.'"

So Harrell wound up driving day *and* night, and Cooper was in place and ready for service ahead of the seven-thirty deadline the next morning.

Cooper's job as Casualty Control Officer was to oversee the pressing task of verifying the casualties—the names of those Marines killed and those wounded, as well as the severity of the wounds. Family and relatives had to be notified in a professional manner. The commandant's office needed to be kept on top of developments.[294]

I was the senior person. I had a staff. We always make sure that officers do this.

The work was carried out by phone and with the use of charts—*I don't remember us having many computers in those days.*

The extent to which Cooper succeeded in his task was spelled out the next month when the man who had called him—assistant commandant of the Marine Corps, Lieutenant General Gray—wrote Cooper's next fitness report:

10 Nov 1983

Washington Navy Yard

In the immediate aftermath of the 23 Oct bombing of the BLT head-quarters in Beirut, I recognized a need for help in keeping myself and the CMC completely informed of the situation regarding the casualties of the bombing. At my request, Col. Cooper abandoned his civilian pursuits and came to active duty to assist me in this complicated and delicate task. Simply stated, as a result of his efforts, the leadership of the Marine Corps was kept completely informed, immediate action to improve systems was made possible and many opportunities for false steps were avoided. In his willing, able and timely response to our need, Col. Cooper personified all that is best in the Marine Corps. His myriad activities in business, government and education all took a back seat when his Corps called—and his active duty service was handled with just the right combination of sensitivity and aggressiveness. He is pre-cisely the type of reserve officer who ought to be promoted to brigadier general at the first opportunity and given the broadest gauged and most demanding responsibilities possible.[295]

The fitness report gave Cooper confidence that he would in time follow his friend Frank Emmanuel Petersen as a general officer in the Corps. Petersen had been the first African American Marine awarded a star, in March 1979.[296]

> *I learned later that General P. X. Kelley, who would become Commandant, was key to General Petersen getting the star. Kelley told me he would not sign the list for promotions if Petersen was not on it.*

For Cooper, word that he would become a brigadier general came five years later in a phone call from that same General Kelly.

> *In the Marine Corps, when you get selected to be a general, it's such a small outfit, the custom is that the commandant will call you himself. I was in a hotel in Atlanta, had been out half the night, and I get this call one morning saying, "Cooper, this is P. X. Kelley, the commandant of the Marine Corps." I was about sitting at attention in the bed, and I thanked him, and after it happened I got on my knees and said, "Thank you, Lord!" Because I knew what an honor that was—an honor for anybody, but for a young black kid from Mobile, Alabama, it was a special honor. Here I was, the first African American infantry general in the Marine Corps and the first African American general from the Marine Reserves.*

> *And I remembered the note I wrote to myself one night at sea on that ship, the USS Chicago. I had sealed it and put "Do not open for twenty years" on the back. That was June 1964—not to be opened until June 1984—and I put it in my scrapbook and kept it on this shelf.*

> *Every few years, I'd look at this sealed envelope, and I had an idea what I had written to myself, but after the commandant called me—my promotion was May 18, 1984—I went home, I went and found this note. It was about ten days off from when I said I could open it. I opened the envelope, and it said: "Did you make it?"*

> *I told my kids about it, and when I got my star, my mother pinned my star on me at the Marriott Gateway in Arlington, and my kids got that note I wrote in 1964 and had it framed for me, and for a long time I had it hanging in my den at home. Now it is on display at the National African American Archives and Museum in Mobile.*

Sometimes when I give speeches to youngsters, I tell them that story, about writing the note and opening it twenty years later, about how important it is to write down your goals.

Cooper was also mindful of the significance of what someone else had written down about him—that 1983 fitness report by General De'Wayne Gray.

That was absolutely key. In the Marine Corps, there are some of us who think that getting to become a general in the Reserves is a lot more difficult than getting to become a general on active duty, because in the entire Marine Corps Reserves, there are only ten generals. They say as a Reserve officer to get selected brigadier general is like the spaceship Columbia hitting you when you're standing on the corner. To have the opportunity to go before that board that had that fitness report in my record, signed by the commandant and the assistant commandant of the Marine Corps, was probably almost unheard of.

$\star$ $\star$ $\star$ $\star$ $\star$ INTERLUDE $\star$ $\star$ $\star$ $\star$ $\star$

Joli

For Joli, the allure of the University of Notre Dame and later the world of finance, both paths previously traveled by her father, would be potent influences. But not at first.

"I don't recall visiting Notre Dame early on," she said. "I did go visit during high school, but it was probably my second choice behind Brown."

For Gary's children, the desegregated Catholic high school in Mobile was McGill-Toolen. The McGill part of the name was from the old McGill High, the boys' school that was all-white before Gary's brother Billy quietly enrolled in 1955—and was subsequently banished. The other part of the school's name was in recognition of the bishop who expelled Billy, Thomas J. Toolen, later archbishop of the diocese.

"The high school was completely integrated by the time I went there," Joli said. "A couple of years before I entered, it was actually an all-girls school called Bishop Toolen and the all-boys school was called McGill. And they combined them maybe three years before I came. It was probably 10 percent African American when I went. All the African Americans who went to the Catholic primary schools fed into McGill-Toolen."

Patrick landed at Yale. The choice would be different for Joli.

"My dad in his influential way suggested strongly that Notre Dame be one I consider. So I ended up there. But it had not been my lifelong dream."

In time, however, it became a springboard, professionally and culturally, much as it had for her father. It had been about a quarter-century since Gary Cooper rode from the South in the train's Jim Crow car to South Bend, but the impact for Joli was similarly strong in 1977.

"Going up to Notre Dame from Mobile, it was such an eye-opener," she said. "Despite being well-traveled, we had seen nothing. So I remember going to Notre Dame and literally had on my white knee socks. I had never seen a bagel in my life. I went to the cafeteria and it was like, 'God, why are these donuts so hard?'

"We grew up a black Catholic family and had limited access to other cultures. So culturally it was—it was not a broad-based school, but it was broader than what I had been exposed to in Mobile. At Notre Dame I saw my first yarmulke, and I said, 'Wow!' It was great diversity."

While blacks were more prevalent at Notre Dame than in the mid-1950s when Gary attended, they were still distinctly in the minority. Joli was one of only twenty-five African Americans in her graduating class. But she found the social life agreeable, perhaps because the historically all-male university had just begun accepting female students in 1973, a few years before she arrived.

"The ratio of men to women was five to one, so there were no issues there," she said with a laugh.

Jolie had worked at her father's various businesses during high school years, making finance a familiar topic and a possible major in college. But it wasn't a foregone conclusion that she would opt for a business major at Notre Dame, as her father had.

"At that stage, you don't know what you don't know," she said. "They didn't have a multitude of majors like they have now—entrepreneurial studies, information technology, stuff like that. . . . I don't think there was a lot of method behind the madness of why I selected finance."

But with a finance diploma, she made a short initial stop for graduate work at the Wharton School at the University of Pennsylvania, then took a job with Aetna. When her father was promoted to brigadier general and assigned to a Marine base in Georgia, however, he asked her to come home and help him run the family business.

"So I left Philadelphia and worked full time for him at the insurance company and the funeral home," Joli said. "I did that for two years. Then I went back to Wharton. Going back to grad school was when I really began to evaluate my professional options."

14

Flag Rank

While Cooper's sense of achievement as a path-setting black Marine officer continued to grow, it was still not hard for him to recognize that color remained as much a demarcation line in the Marine Corps as it was in most of American life.

When I was a brigadier general, I came up to Washington, and they have a place for us to stay at the Navy Yard. They call them Flag Quarters. These are wonderful apartments where the generals and admirals stay. Whenever I go up and sit in them, I say, "Just think, white folks have been living like this all the time."

But I was there one day, and I was to be picked up at zero seven hundred in the morning by a Navy vehicle. So I'm out there and I get in the car, but at the same time, there was a white general in town whose name was Cooper, too. So the dispatcher asked my driver, said, "Do you have General Cooper?" My driver said, "Yes, I have General Cooper. He's right here in the back seat." The dispatcher said, "Which one?" The driver said, "The dark green Marine."

The line stuck, invariably humorous to Cooper—he was the dark green Marine. But he was also mindful of the racial progress the Corps had made. On January 15, 1985, he spoke to more than five hundred Marines at a Camp Pendleton service marking the birthday of the slain civil rights leader, the Reverend Dr. Martin Luther King Jr. Cooper recalled the obstacles young black Marine officers had faced earlier and their determination to succeed and open doors. Addressing a mostly black audience, he said King's birthday should not be celebrated only as a black holiday:

The commemoration can be a way to honor the achievements of
black Americans. But Martin Luther King wanted complete racial integration to free the people of the moral burden of racial segregation.
His dream was a global model for social, racial and economic justice."[297]

Speaking later to reporter Dan Weikel of the *San Diego Union*, he
said conditions for minorities in the Marines had greatly improved since
the first blacks were recruited and sent to Montford Point during World
War II: "Today we are getting Marines, both white and black, who grew
up while King was alive. They are coming in without the preconceptions
and the prejudices. It has helped."[298]

In his fitness report, Lieutenant General Gray had said Cooper should
be given "the broadest possible and most demanding responsibilities
possible." To this end, Cooper initially was tapped to work as deputy
commander at Parris Island, the Marine recruit training base famed for
its tough drill instructors.

Every Marine who lives or has lived knows about Parris Island. It is
different from the Basic School in some ways, and then there are some
similarities. What they do is, the drill instructors that worked at Parris
Island, they get assigned to officers' school. So they bring some of the same
discipline to the young officers when they're attempting to train them.

After Parris Island, Cooper became assistant division commander of
the New Orleans-based 4th Marine Division, and a year later, in 1986, he
was named commanding general of the largest U.S. Marine Corps Reserve
unit commanded by a Reserve officer, the seven thousand-member 4th
Force Service Support Group, based in Atlanta.[299]

The assignment was Reserve duty, but the 4th Force oversaw Reserve
units in more than fifty cities and provided logistical support to one-
fourth of all Marine Corps combat forces. That was a posting that took
lots and lots of time. It also connected him with his old friend from the
Birmingham artillery battalion, Joe Wilson. He had been the 4th Force
readiness officer for about a year when Cooper became its commanding
general. As in Birmingham, Cooper had plans for Wilson.[300]

"Next month I'm going to meet with my commanders at Camp Lejeune in North Carolina, and I'd like for you to go with me," Cooper told him.

"Yes, sir. That would be great."

"I want you to go as readiness officer."

"Yes, sir. And how about the chief of staff?"

"No. Just you."

"Yes, sir."

Wilson: "We got there and we met in this conference room with about eight battalion commanders. Gary said, 'I want us to go around and have each of you introduce yourself. Tell a little about your background, what you're commanding. Take a couple of minutes, each of you, and go around the room.

"Then he added: 'And by the way, I don't think we need any introduction for Colonel Wilson. He's my chief of staff.' That was the first news I got of that! No warning. Nothing. Not until he announced it to the battalion commanders that day. Bingo! I was the new chief of staff."

Not all of Cooper's surprises went as Wilson anticipated.

Having reached the rank of colonel, Wilson had enjoyed a great Marine Corps career despite a busy private life as an entrepreneur and university professor. His wife was a dean and he was a department chair at the University of North Alabama, but the couple had also been in private business since 1965. Now they had a new venture, which required more of his attention—all of it impinging on the time he wanted to spend with his wife and children. Service in the Marine Reserves had come to seem one obligation too many.

"It was not an easy decision for me," Wilson said, "but I decided I was going to retire from the Marine Corps. I went to drill weekend in Atlanta. I was chief of staff and he was commanding general. I wanted to go ahead and see him early on Saturday morning and tell him, but I didn't quite have the courage. So I waited until Saturday afternoon, and the moment I went in he wanted to talk about something—I don't know what, but he screwed me up. I couldn't make my speech.

"So I wanted to do it on Sunday morning, but that didn't seem to work either. Late Sunday evening I decided it's time. I've got to get this done. I'm doing it this weekend. So I walked in. As chief of staff, you have a close

relationship. . . . Usually you just knock on the door and walk in, and he'll
say, 'Sit down.' You just sit down and you start talking about whatever you
want to talk about. Or you can stand at ease and talk about it.

"Anyway, I had tried and I couldn't get out what I wanted to get out.
So I knocked on the door and said, 'Colonel Wilson, sir.'

"'Come in.'

"So I walked in, like I was marching. Not route step, but a march step. I
walked directly in and stopped two paces in front of his desk and snapped
to attention. I said, 'Sir, I have a very, very important matter, which I've
given great thought to. I've discussed it with my daughters and I would
like to relate to you my thoughts at this time.'

"He said, 'Continue, Marine.' He was just as formal as you could be.

"I said, 'Sir, as you know, I've been in business for a long time. I have
a career at the University of North Alabama. My wife has a career there.
We have a business.'

"He said, 'Yes, I understand it's doing all right.'

"I said, 'Yes, sir, we've discussed that. I'm very pleased with it. I don't
think I can share the time for my responsibilities. I've got to work there.
I've got to continue my work at the university. And I just basically had to
make a decision about what I'm going to do, and I just wanted to share
with you—and you're the first individual I'm sharing this with—I'm retiring from the Marine Corps. I've served you for a long time in different
ways. I've been your chief of staff. You wanted me to be your chief of staff.
I know we'll have time to get another. There are many people who want to
be your chief of staff, who would like to work for you. I thought I would
just like to tell you today, sir, and I won't be back next month. That's it.'

"Then I was expecting him to stand up and shake my hand and say,
'I understand. You've given a lot to the Marine Corps. I wish you well in
retirement.' So I stand there at attention after I've given my little speech
and he doesn't say anything for about ten seconds. He wasn't making
eye contact with me. He was sort of staring straight at my body. Then he
looked up and made eye contact.

"He said, 'You asshole. You're going to be coming in the zone for
general. You're not going to retire now. You're going to stick around.

You're either going to make general or you're not going to make general and you're going to be passed over. Get your ass out of here! AH-BOUT . . . FACE! . . . MARCH!'

"That was it."

Wilson turned and left. He put off retirement.

"I was selected brigadier general about five months later," Wilson said. "I was just very blessed."[301]

> *I was serving on a promotion board when they were picking one person to become a Reserve brigadier general. Joe Wilson's name was among several. I supported him for the promotion—and I wouldn't budge.*
>
> *Joe got promoted.*
>
> *Wilson told me: "If my daddy knew a black man had helped me become a general, he'd turn over in his grave."*

Shawn

As the youngest of Gary's children, Shawn was not just trying to live up to the expectations of a successful, demanding father. That was a motivating force, but family competition was tough, beginning with her older brother and sister. Shawn at one point decided she must be dyslexic because she was a slow reader, at least compared to Patrick and Joli. "I think there is a bit of sibling rivalry," Shawn said. "That was very hard, because they were so academically overachievers, and I wasn't, at all."[302]

Shawn opted to forge a different plan. It wasn't laid out very clearly at first.

"Shawn was the live wire," recalled James Harrell. "Gary once told me that when she was a senior in high school, he had given her a big old car that he had. A Catholic father, one of the teachers at McGill-Toolen High School, stopped him one day and said, 'Gary, I'm glad to see you. I'm having problems with Shawn. At least tell her to stop letting the empty beer cans fall to the ground once she opens the door of the car!'"

Partying aside, Shawn was an engaging personality with an abundance of people skills and energy. Early on, her only certainty was that she wanted to explore outside the boundaries of Alabama and liked the idea of the foreign service, seeing many parts of the world. She also threatened to do something to trump both her siblings in her father's eyes: join the Marines.

Patrick and Joli were gone from the house. Shawn was not getting along with her stepmother, Gloria, so she was basically alone with her father.

"And it was a challenge," she said. "When he pissed me off, I'd go, 'I'm not going to college, I'm going to join the Marine Corps.' And he would say, 'Let me tell you something, your ass is going to college. I don't care what the hell you do after that, just don't think that you're going to come back home because I'm not taking care of you.'"

But where should she go to college? Joli had picked Notre Dame. Patrick had picked Yale. So Shawn headed west for—why not?— USC.

"If you are the daughter of a Notre Dame grad, and they piss you off, and your older sister goes to Notre Dame, and you just want to piss them off—you go to the University of Southern California. I wish I could say, 'Oh, USC had the most amazing international relations program.'"

But that wasn't it. "Literally it was the fact that I loved football," she said. "Growing up we would watch football and there was nothing more fun than watching the USC versus Notre Dame rivalry in the house. As a bonus, those USC guys were so handsome, *and* USC did have a great international relations program. But I was like, 'I'm just getting out of here.' Again, I think it was a subconscious effort to piss Dad off."

At Southern Cal, Shawn scouted out the best route to the foreign service.

"I knew the foreign service exam was a killer," she said. "My freshman year, my RA [resident assistant] took the exam and came back with clumps of hair out of her head. When I read the prerequisites to be chosen for the foreign service, it said 'living abroad experience, military experience, and foreign language, second language.' So my thought was, *Damn, what do I do?* I figured if I graduated, lived abroad, studied a foreign language, joined the Marines. . . . If I do all these things, and I'm black, they just got to take me in the foreign service! Mind you I was not studying too hard at USC. I was partying. I mean I graduated in four years as expected. But there was no Rhodes scholarship. I just did what I had to do and kept moving."

Her father recalled that, in fact, she moved back to Mobile—without a job and with her fingernails painted purple.[303] Her best friend, Judy Schultz, was from a well-to-do family and had done a semester at sea. That sounded good to Shawn.

"So I came home and said, 'Daddy, can I do a semester at sea?' He said, 'Let me tell you something: Little colored girls from Alabama do not go study on cruise ships. You better be happy your black ass has a desk!'

"That took care of that. But Judy devised a plan for us to go to Paris and be au pairs. So we went to Paris together and we worked as au pairs."[304]

15

Washington Calls

In 1988, Cooper received his second star, and with his promotion to major general, he returned to active duty as director of personnel at Marine Corps Headquarters in Washington, D.C. Part of his new mission covered recruiting—long a point of contention for Cooper—and changing the recruiting playbook was a priority. At that time, the Corps was doing no serious recruiting at historically black colleges and universities.[305]

An earlier attempt to start ROTC programs in these colleges in the late 1960s and early 1970s had barely moved the needle. In a USMC oral history, Brigadier General George Walls said:

> That first effort that we had at minority officer recruiting, I don't think was very successful. We didn't make the kind of numbers we needed to make to have an influence on the Marine Corps as a whole. If you look at the way you build an organization, it's kind of like a pyramid. You've got to put in a whole lot of second lieutenants down here at the bottom to get a bunch of majors up here in the middle and eventually get to the general officers at the top of the pyramid. Along the way, for a number of reasons, we either didn't bring in those numbers, or the ones we brought in just didn't succeed or chose not to stay. So the numbers rocked along for a long time.[306]

General Frank Petersen, who followed Lieutenant Colonel Ken Berthoud as the head of minority recruitment efforts, said there was a problem from the get-go. He was to lead a USMC program called "Negro officer procurement." He knew the title had to be ditched.[307]

"In my view, it connoted some sort of body purchase," Petersen said in the USMC oral history. ". . . No single Negro goes into the black community (even if he represents the Marine Corps) and attempts to recruit by calling himself a 'Negro procurer.' My God, that's reminiscent of slavery days."

Nearly twenty years later, Cooper felt that reaching out to historically black colleges was essential to minority officer recruitment.

That was always an excuse the Marine Corps had. You know: "We can't find them. We can't find the minority candidates." So I said, "The Army and the Air Force finds them. They go to historically black schools and they look for them."

I got the Marine Corps for the first time to recruit in the historically black schools. They started slowly getting some officers. Of the [African American] generals that we have now, I think the majority have come from historically black schools.

Now, is that good or bad? Right now, I don't think it's good. Because these schools—people would kill me if I say it, but I would say it anyway—these schools don't produce the number of academic achievers that a Harvard or Yale or Duke or a Princeton produce. They don't have the same entry standards. But because it became easier to find and get these folks, our recruiting service started going to the historically black schools and not looking at the Harvards and Yales and the Princetons and the Notre Dames.

That's a real challenge that they have now. One of the recruiters told me, what they're doing each year is they raise the standards for officers. He tells me a few years ago he had thirty-five to forty young minority officers ready to come in that year and the year after that. The next thing he knows the Marine Corps announces they want officers with an SAT score that is higher than the score previously targeted. They had moved it up, and that wiped out half his pool.

During this period overseeing Marine recruiting, Cooper had occasion to raise his concerns at the very highest levels.

I went to a leadership seminar, where the commandant called all of his generals to Washington. I was determined to bring this subject up before a general officers symposium, and I was given some time to speak. These were almost all the generals in the Marine Corps. I asked them to help me. Did they think we had racism in our Marine Corps? Let me see your hands if you think we don't. And of course all the hands went up, and they were saying, "No. No. We don't."

I said, "Well, if we don't have racism, how is it that I am the only black general in this room? Help me understand how this can happen."

Some of them grumbled, and some of them were really pissed. But one came to me and said, "Cooper, you hit the nail right on the head."

Being a major general was thrilling. That really gave you the chance to express yourself. You didn't have to worry about another fitness report in your life. But you want to set the example—I did; I still do—to make sure that the generals know that being a black Marine officer is a special challenge.

Not that long ago I went to a conference of Reserve generals in Chicago. People were saying, "What are you doing now? Why are you here? Why did you come?"

I said the reason I'm here is to remind you gentlemen that we live in a changing America, and a group of all-white generals like I see here is not going to be able to lead a strong Marine Corps.

LOSS & CELEBRATION

A year after Gary received his second star, the Cooper family experienced heartache: in the spring of 1989, Gladys Mouton Cooper died at a hospital in Washington, the city where many of her children and grandchildren then lived.

Mama went up from Mobile to have her knees replaced. My sister Peggy wanted her to come up to George Washington University Hospital for the surgery. She didn't want her to get it done in Mobile. So Mama had it in Washington, and she got a staph infection and died in the hospital.

Four days of mourning, reflection, and a celebration of the matriarch's life followed in Mobile, April 7–10, with the extended family on hand—some forty of her children, grandchildren, Mouton relatives, and relations rode in seven limousines to the funeral mass at Prince of Peace

Catholic Church and interment at Pine Crest Cemetery.[308]

"People really looked up to her," said her daughter, Dominic. Local television stations even sent camera crews to record the funeral.[309]

A brunch was held at her home, 603 Delaware Street, and a family photo was taken. It was a historically memorable picture. As the four-day printed schedule noted, those who would gather for the photo included most of the direct descendants of Gladys Cooper's parents—the children, grandchildren, and great-grandchildren of Agnes and Clarence Mouton, the proud couple from the Creole world of Lafayette, Louisiana, who had "the four beautiful Mouton sisters."

New Opportunities

With his second star as a Marine general, Cooper's service in the American military was about to change. But first, he gained national recognition of another sort—he was honored in July 1989 with the Roy Wilkins Meritorious Service Award from the NAACP.

Presenting the award at the Armed Forces Dinner in Detroit, NAACP President Dr. Benjamin Hooks said Cooper was selected "in recognition and appreciation of meritorious service for his contribution in the field of civil rights and defense of this nation. With a few more like General Cooper, this country would be able to reach one of its highest ideals—social equality and justice for all."[310]

While the NAACP was taking note of Cooper, so were Alabama Republicans. He had spoken with Jimmy Faulkner about a possible post in the new administration of President George H. W. Bush.

Faulkner wrote Montgomery Mayor Emory Folmar, state chairman of the Alabama Republican Party, who was involved in the Bush transition: "It has occurred to me that the new administration will need to appoint some blacks, and Gary, with many achievements, would do well in a worthy position."[311]

In reply, Folmar was upbeat about Cooper's chances:

> He and I have been friends a long time and I think highly of him.
> He has an outstanding record and would bring many credentials to

any job that he undertook. You are correct—there will be some new opportunities in the new administration for blacks and Gary certainly should be considered. I think I will have some input to the transition team and it will certainly be my pleasure to recommend Gary for a position in the new administration.[312]

It wasn't certain what that position might be. An April 1989 letter from U.S. Senator Howell Heflin, an Alabama Democrat, had informed the White House that Gary had an interest in the post of assistant secretary of the Department of the Navy for Manpower and Reserve Affairs.[313] But the job that came available in November was assistant secretary of the Air Force, a civilian post with presidential appointment that flies a flag with four stars. It didn't hurt that the Air Force secretary at the time, Donald Rice, was a Notre Dame graduate. When the offer came, Cooper was happy to accept.[314]

A whirlwind series of events followed. Word of the president's decision to nominate him reached Cooper in Mobile on a Sunday. Flying out of Mobile at 6 a.m. the next morning, he was promptly briefed by Air Force personnel when he arrived in Washington, appeared before the Senate Armed Services Committee that same afternoon, got the panel's recommendation later that evening, and was confirmed by the full Senate at 2:57 a.m. Tuesday.[315]

Cooper was now assistant secretary of the Air Force for manpower, reserve affairs, installations, and the environment. His job description?

Really a huge range. All of the personnel issues, for Guard, Reserve and active duty. We also had all the schools in the Air Force under us, all the bases in the world under us, and the environmental challenges. And I probably knew 3 percent of what was going on!

Beverly

The job in Washington had many attractions for Cooper. He had been single for a decade after his divorce from Gloria, and in D.C. he had met a bright, ambitious young woman, Beverly Amanda Martin, who had been a racial pioneer in her own right. She was a politically active Democrat, had a master's degree in business, and was at ease with an on-the-move lifestyle.

They met when Beverly moved back to Washington after serving as a Blue Cross Blue Shield vice president in New Jersey. It was an exhilarating time for both. While Gary was moving into government service at the highest level, Beverly was keen to run her own consulting enterprise, resume work with the Democratic National Committee, and play a role in political circles.[316]

"I didn't like being in New Jersey," Beverly said. "I had been there about three years, and I missed everything I was doing in Washington. Politics. The Democratic National Committee. All kinds of things. So I decided to leave the job in New Jersey and come back.

"I did work for the DNC before I went to New Jersey. Working with politics in Washington, when you're a young person, you tend to think that the end-all and be-all is right there in Washington, D.C. At that point, you really don't care—as unrealistic as it is—about any other life. It's as if there's no other life outside of Washington, particularly when it's politics. That's everything in the world it could possibly be.

"So I moved back and met Gary. I didn't know it, but I already knew his brother Mario and sister Peggy. I even had met Jay.

"The first time I actually went out with Gary, we had been put in touch and he called. 'I'm busy, I have an engagement,' I said. 'I'm going to a political fundraiser.'

"'Oh, where?'

"'At the home of a woman here who is very involved in politics. Her name is Peggy Cooper Cafritz.'

"'Who did you say?'

"'Peggy Cooper Cafritz.'

"'That's my sister.'

"'You're kidding me.'

"'When you get there, be sure to tell her that I said thanks for inviting me to her party.'"

"So when I got there, I said, 'Peggy, you're not going to believe this. Do you have a brother named Gary?'

"'Yes, that's my older brother.'

"'He was calling to ask me out and I told him I couldn't go because I was coming here.' The look on her face was like, *Where did you find Gary?*

"I knew Peggy through being involved in a lot of Democratic Party activity. I didn't know her, not like friends, but you knew who she was. And of course Mario was involved in Democratic politics at that time, too. Mario. I was completely caught off guard that he was Gary's brother. And I knew Jay. I used to see Jay on these trips when I was doing consulting. My consulting business was in health care. I was taking all that I had learned at Blue Cross Blue Shield and individually working with companies and nonprofits to help them establish their own health care program. So I was at a conference for car dealers. And here's Jay, who is a lawyer for the car dealers association.

"It was like I had run into the Coopers in a variety of ways but had never made the connection to Gary."

And there was the Mobile link.

"I did community work and consulted with Upward Bound. The director for the Howard University program was Joseph Bell. I dated him. And guess where he's from? Mobile. For a while it seemed that my life was circling Mobile, and I didn't have a clue what that was all about. In fact Muriel, a childhood friend, put Gary and me in touch. Muriel had been a playmate in Richmond. Her dad and mom were my parents' buddies. And it turns out she married Dr. Oliver Gumbs from Mobile, a black physician."

In an added twist, Beverly was something of a matchmaker for Muriel. Dr. Gumbs was the top national officer of the Kappa Alpha Psi fraternity and was coming to an event in Richmond. He needed an escort. Beverly suggested Muriel.

"She became the escort for that evening, and before you know it, a few years later, they're getting married, and she's moving to Mobile. And believe it or not, Oliver had been a good friend of Gary's dad."

Dr. Gumbs, whom Muriel married late in his life, was described by the Mobile historian Shawn Bivens as a "social, economic, cultural, civic, educational leader and humanitarian." He had come to Mobile from the Caribbean island of St. Eustatius and was listed as one of *Ebony* magazine's "100 Most Influential African Americans" while he was the national president of the Kappa Alpha Psi fraternity, 1979–1983.[317]

"Oliver died and Muriel moved back to D.C.," Beverly said. "I actually hired her. She came to work for me and there she is in Washington. And Gary called her—they knew each other from Mobile. By now he had the job with President Bush as assistant secretary of the Air Force. He called her and said, 'Muriel, I need an escort. Do you know a lady with a dress?'

"She said, 'Do I know a lady with a dress? Yeah, I know a lady with a dress.'"

Lady with a Dress

The lady with a dress was Beverly, and in fact her having several dresses proved essential to the numerous Air Force-related functions that were part of Gary's routine. It wasn't long before Beverly was the lady on his arm at these parties and receptions.

"The way Don Rice did these gatherings of his staff, you were always together," Beverly said. "It was this gathering or that gathering, and the guys wore black tie, and the ladies wore dresses. We all felt compelled to wear something different. I joked with Gary about having to have a dress. It's not like an endless group of dresses, but the cost of them—this is getting really expensive!"

Soon she made her first trip to Mobile.

"I met a bunch of his friends. We drove up to Montgomery and saw James Harrell and his wife. We drove up to Birmingham for the Magic City Classic football game. Had a nice time. I flew back to D.C.

"And of course, when I got back to D.C., it was business again. Gary kind of realized how it worked. He was always inviting me to Mobile—I could go there and just disconnect, it was so wonderful—but when I was in D.C., I was *on*."

As they saw each other more and more, the unspoken subject was due to come up.

"We had gone out to dinner one night, and he said to me, 'Beverly, have you ever thought about getting married again?'

"I said, Not really. You know I've done that, and now I'm at an age, I'm past the age of being able to have kids. If I were younger, that would be a reason I would get married. I said I really never thought about it. I was fortunate the first time I married. We parted good friends. We remained good friends."

"I've done this a couple of times," Gary said. "It's the kind of thing you really do need to focus on, or really think about."

They came up with a plan.

Beverly had an apartment not far from Georgetown, and I moved in. We were not married, but we lived together with the agreement that we would live together for a year, and then if we were going to get married, we'd get married, and if not, I'd move out.

There had been other social opportunities for Cooper. His old friend and legislative colleague from Mobile, Sonny Callahan, was now a congressman who lived on a spacious, custom-built yacht that berthed on the Potomac at the wickedly named Gangplank Marina. A short drive to the Capitol if a vote was needed, it was a favorite spot for politicos to unwind.[318]

"We stayed in touch while he was there," Callahan recalled. "Gary would come down and have dinner on the boat occasionally, and we'd talk about old times and good times."

Army General Colin Powell, the chairman of the Joint Chiefs of Staff, also became a Cooper friend.

When I first heard of him, after Vietnam, I saw an announcement that there was an opening for a White House Fellow. I thought that would really be good to help you get promoted, and I applied to be a White House Fellow. I did not make it, but later I read that a guy named Colin Powell did. . . .

The times as assistant Air Force secretary that I met him—I still recognized that he's senior to me, but in those days we were the same rank—I said to him: "I don't understand, we're the same age, we graduated from college the same year, we got commissioned the same year, how can you be a damn four-star general and I just have two?"

He said, "You joined the fucking Marines!"

On one occasion Powell offered to line Cooper up with a date for a party.

"Well," I said, "I really can't do that. I'm really tied up."

"You'll really like this lady. She speaks seven languages."

I laughed. "Don't no damn Marine want a lady who speaks seven languages!"

Powell laughed, too. Cooper missed out on the date—it was to be with future Secretary of State Condoleezza Rice, the first female African American to hold that post.

THE FAMILY DNA

Along with having an MBA and experience as the first black woman with a direct commission in the Virginia Army National Guard, Beverly came from a family, like Cooper's, determined not to let racial segregation hold it back.

"My mom and dad were high school sweethearts. They met at a little school in Summerton, South Carolina, called Scott's Branch High School. My mother comes from a large family—twelve children. Her parents sent her off to Girls High in Philadelphia to finish school. My dad, meanwhile, by the time he graduated from high school in South Carolina, joined what was then the Army Air Corps. He goes and gets my mom, and the next thing you know they're getting married."

The couple moved to Richmond, Virginia, where his father lived and where operating family enterprises was part of the Martin DNA.

"You know, it's in my family. My dad comes from entrepreneurs. His grandparents, Hampton and Amanda Martin, owned a grocery store, a garage, and a barber shop. Growing up, my dad worked in the store.

"In South Carolina, my mother's family was from a big farm outside the little town of Summerton, in an area called Pinewood. We spent summers there. I would pick cotton, string tobacco, chase the cow and the pig through the pastures."

Among the Martin family businesses in Richmond, one was of particular note in those segregated times: her dad's father obtained a Good Humor ice cream franchise, one of the first in Richmond run by an African American.

Briggs v. Board & AFTER

Beverly's family in South Carolina, like Gary's in Mobile, opposed the segregated school systems of the 1950s.

In Summerton, the issue at first was simply to get a school bus for blacks who had to walk two hours, in some cases, to reach an all-black school. Later it became a wider court fight against segregated schools and eventually, as a federal court lawsuit, *Briggs v. Elliott*, it would be consolidated with the historic *Brown v. Board* case out of Kansas.[319]

But it took its toll on Summerton blacks who joined in a protest.

"There had been several incidents in Summerton," Beverly said, "and my dad's family, specifically my aunt, Annie Martin Gibson, and my dad's mother, Mary Martin, were going to help organize this protest, a boycott that was launched by the NAACP. As they got involved in it, that little town of Summerton really did feel the impact. It hit the black community really hard. The boycott was started and suddenly any black males in the community who had jobs working in any white organization or for any of the power structure found themselves without jobs. The only persons who were bringing any money into the households were the women who either worked as maids or on house staffs to the wealthy white families who lived in Summerton.

"What was interesting was when the NAACP was looking for a test case around school desegregation, initially they were going to use this case—*Briggs v. Board of Education*—in Summerton, South Carolina. Briggs was a cousin. My aunt was one of the ones who collected all of the names for a petition to be a part of it."

The *Briggs* case, Beverly said, "had certain elements that helped create a lot of the depth in what became *Brown versus Board of Education*, but they decided to go with *Brown*."

While the Kansas case went down in history as the game-changer for black Americans, *Briggs v. Elliott* included a famous dissent in 1951 in which U.S. District Judge Waties Waring, a white Southerner on the federal bench in Charleston, South Carolina, declared for the first time that segregated public schools were unconstitutional and had not been equal since "separate but equal" became the law in America in 1896.[320]

Beverly also played a part as the court action led to school system changes.

"In Richmond, Virginia, many years later, my brother Freddie and I integrated Huguenot High School. This was in 1964 and 1965. We were the first two blacks to go to this school."

They attended under a "freedom of choice" program that allowed blacks to begin attending previously all-white schools. Studious and with good grades, Beverly and her brother Freddie became two of the blacks asked to be a part of "freedom of choice" in the Richmond schools.[321]

Because they spent a lot of time in South Carolina growing up, Beverly and her brother were well-versed already in the rules of segregated society. Even as a child, she learned not to walk in the front door of certain stores run by whites.

"But you know, you're in a very protected environment," Beverly said. "Families just made sure those were not things that you misunderstood. Families were very protective about what kinds of experiences you had."

PULLING RANK

For college, Beverly attended Virginia Commonwealth University, graduating with a major in sociology and a minor in accounting, but sampling a number of other fields, and getting married to boot. Her husband, Floyd Coleman, was a student who worked with the police.[322]

"I was in my junior year," Beverly said. "We were very involved in things in school and he was very well liked. He ended up working in the Intelligence Division for the Richmond Police Department. Kind of the undercover stuff, political stuff. And here I am, on the convocation committee, the committee that brings different speakers to the school. This was a time when schools brought in members of the Black Panther Party to speak, and there was a Black Panther organization on campus. So the Richmond Police Department asked Floyd if he would ask me to record events undercover. Well, no, I wasn't going to be involved in that kind of thing.

"But he was a student and also on the police department, and Alabama Governor George Wallace comes to Richmond, Virginia. This was around 1972 when Wallace was running for president. My husband ended up being one of the police officers assigned to protect him. I think I still have an autographed picture of George Wallace! Now who would have guessed I would end up coming to Alabama?"

Turning to postgraduate studies, Beverly earned a double masters— in social work and business—from VCU and added the Virginia Army National Guard to her resume. Along the way she and Floyd divorced but remained friends. He went to law school while she opted for a career in business.

Her path to the Guard began when she was still an undergraduate and taking on a series of part-time posts with then-Governor Linwood Holton's administration. One item that landed on her desk: how to get more women into the Guard and Reserves, which had become short of manpower because of Vietnam.

"The issue for me was: What are the areas we can identify that would make sense for women in the Guard and Reserve?"

A warrant officer felt Beverly could learn the ropes best by joining the Guard. She said she didn't want to be in the National Guard, but he upped the ante by suggesting that with her two master's degrees she could probably get a direct commission. So she became the first female and first African American direct commission in the Virginia Army National Guard. She served with the Guard for a decade, putting together its first curriculum on race relations at the Defense Race Relations Institute at Cocoa Beach, Florida.

"All the military was there. This was for the Virginia National Guard, but the Defense Race Relations Institute was doing this for all of the military back then. I became the race relations officer for the Virginia Army Guard and would do all of the race relations training. We did management training, we did sensitivity training. I would do the weekend drills with all of the enlisted. The Army Guard and the Air were together, so a lot of this was for both of them."

While Beverly eventually left the Guard, the experience came in handy after she met Major General Gary Cooper.

"Gary liked to tell that story of my Army National Guard experience. He used it in his speeches. He would be introduced and would say, 'Thank you for being here. My wife Beverly is here.' Then he would tell about me being in the Guard, and give the kicker: 'Just so you know the kind of person that she is, for the longest time, and even to this day, I still have trouble convincing her that a first lieutenant doesn't outrank a major general.'"

Test Time

Gary and Beverly had given themselves a test.

"The test was going to be, we will move in with each other for a year, to see if we like each other well enough to go further," Beverly said. "I always joke about it—we never defined the 'go further' part."

Gary moved from his executive quarters in Crystal City, joining Beverly in her condo near Georgetown.

"The year went by so fast," she said. "I think we did really well with our little test. We even took a trip to Amsterdam. We had so much fun on the trip that we missed the plane coming back!"

"It worked out," she said. "I had met the kids by then. Shawn had become my best buddy. She was the one the other two had sent to check me out. I had met Gary's friends. He was great with my friends. My family loved him. All of the pieces about bringing someone into your life when you're in your mid-forties, it all came together."

A March wedding was planned before a justice of the peace, a friend of Beverly's. The timing coincided with Gary needing knee surgery. He hobbled in for the vows.

"It was small. My sister Sonja stood up for me. Gary's college buddy Corky was his best man. We invited a couple of friends. Shawn was there. Then we all went to dinner."

16

Air Force Missions

From his position in the Air Force, Cooper was able to orchestrate a gathering without precedent in the U.S. military. He invited three African American living legends—Air Force Lieutenant General Benjamin O. Davis Jr., Navy Vice Admiral Samuel L. Gravely Jr., and Cooper's friend of thirty years, Marine Lieutenant General Frank Emmanuel Petersen Jr.—to appear together and share their experiences with about thirty young black Marine officers.[323]

It dawned on me that these three men had never been in the same room together.

That changed on Sunday, May 5, 1991, when the three who had broken racial barriers time and again in their military careers sat together and shared their experiences with a new generation of black Marine officers. The occasion, a professional development session that included Sunday brunch, was held in the officers' club at Bolling Air Force Base in Washington, D.C. The session was designed to provide the junior officers with accounts of the personal military experiences of Davis, Gravely and Petersen, covering issues such as career progression, education and leadership.

Davis, the first black to earn the rank of general in the Air Force, had commanded the Tuskegee Airmen, the all-black unit of fighter pilots who gained fame for their achievements in World War II. Gravely was the first of his race to become a Navy admiral after being the first black officer to command a fighting ship—Cooper had memorably sent him a flag message at sea while serving as Officer of the Deck Underway on the USS *Chicago*. And Petersen, the trail-blazing Marine aviator who met Cooper at Kaneohe in 1960, became the first black Marine general in 1979.[324]

"It was historic," said Petersen, who had met Davis only briefly once before. "He had two stars and I happened to run into him at Andrews Air Force Base. I was then a lieutenant colonel. I approached him rather timidly and I introduced myself and he was extremely gracious. Very much a gentleman. I spent about fifteen minutes in discussion and that was it. We just met in passing."[325]

Davis was the elder statesman—Gravely, Petersen, and Cooper were from the next generation. On this day in 1991, however, they all shared at length their experiences in defying stereotypes and overcoming the obstacles of racial segregation inside the military and out. Petersen, recalling the event, liked Cooper's way of offering advice.

"Whereas I would voice concern with anger, Gary would voice it with a slow Southern drawl and very diplomatic," said Petersen. "I always admired Gary for that. He still has that trait. When Gary talks, you may think, 'Oh, here's another mush-mouth from Alabama.' But Gary has a statesmanship that many others I've met do not have. Gary is very, very polished."[326]

The event also honored another longtime Cooper friend who was being promoted to flag rank—USMC Brigadier General George Walls Jr. Walls, who also spoke to the young Marine officers, had met Cooper in Vietnam and became the only black Marine general officer on active duty when he received his star in June 1991.

"The big thing was having the first generals together," Walls recalled. "It was a great gathering. I had known those three—General Petersen, Admiral Gravely and B. O. Davis—for a long time, but had never been in the same place with all three of them at the same time. It was really an exciting thing for me to be at."[327]

The young officers in attendance included a number who would lead the next wave of high-ranking African American Marine officers. Among them were three who became flag officers: Lieutenant General Willie J. Williams, an Alabama native who became director of Marine Corps Staff; Major General Ronald L. Bailey, the first African American to be made commanding general of the 1st Marine Division; and Major

General C. L. Stanley, who became commanding general of Marine Corps Base Quantico.[328]

Williams, shortly before retiring after nearly forty years in the Corps, fondly remembered the 1991 event.

"I was a young officer, starting out, beginning to find my way around the Corps," Williams said. "What impressed upon me most was that these three very accomplished individuals would take time to spend mentoring and talking to us. There was something about these individuals—they wanted to help others succeed, to pass on anything that may have influenced their careers to make sure we had the advantage of that as we tried to make our way."

For Cooper to have seen the need—and the potential benefits—of that historic event was not lost on Williams.

"I think it was obvious during that time that all of us were still struggling somewhat with the numbers of African American officers making their way up the ranks to achieve senior level positions," Williams said. "I think General Cooper and others realized that we all should be about doing everything we could to insure that there were equal opportunities across the board. That's kind of what I took away."

The Marine Corps would offer opportunities to pursue your dreams, Williams said, and the African American flag officers speaking to them that day were "in their own way trying to help prepare us, so when those opportunities present themselves we would be ready to take advantage. Whether we do or don't, that would be left to us. But they would have done what they could do in that short span."[329]

A SPECIAL GENERAL

Another highlight for Cooper was a trip he arranged for Davis. The aging Air Force general had not seen the Tuskegee Airmen statue that had been unveiled at the Air Force Academy in Colorado in 1988. Cooper flew to the site with him.[330]

> *After I met him and found out he was in the D.C. area, I would invite him to my Pentagon office Christmas party, or a little reception—I would invite General Davis and he would come.*

It seems I had a trip planned. I had been invited to speak to the cadets at the Air Force Academy, and I asked the general had he seen the statue of the Tuskegee Airmen? He said he had not. So I arranged for him to join me. I told him when we were leaving and I went by to pick him up in the limousine.

We get out to the academy, and we go to see the statue. What a moment! He looks at it with tears in his eyes.

I can only remember saying once, "Those must have been some days."

"Oh, yeah," he said, "those were."

We talk. By then the word is out that General Benjamin O. Davis Jr. is there. So the Air Force Academy commandant asked if the general would speak. Of course. So we went to this auditorium—it was a totally impromptu speech—and there were kids all over the floor, under the tables. He thanked them all for coming out and how proud he was to be a member of the Air Force. He said, "Today I'm going to tell you what it was like being a black officer fifty years ago." He spoke—he was so well-received.

And what you have to realize, at that time he was a retired three-star general. Later he would be honored with a fourth star. But at that time he was three-star. By my position I had four stars, and he deferred to me! Here he is, a West Point graduate, he is eighty-something years old, and he was opening the door for me! It was ingrained in his character. He would follow protocol. I said, "Well, General, let me." But he said, "No, sir, Mr. Secretary."

"He was so respectful of Gary," Beverly recalled. "His attitude was: 'You have moved some place where I never could have, and the respect is due. Forget that you may be younger than I am or any of that kind of thing.' It was just so incredible. Gary could barely be around him without his eyes getting full just because of his respect for General Davis. And Agatha, his wife, was the same as her husband. So respectful of others. You could just see this wonderful partner he had for everything he had done in his life."

His strength of character. It made the difference. It's why he played such an essential role. Younger officers, like Chappie James maybe, they may have wanted to just raise hell over segregation in the military. But

Benjamin Davis determined that the Tuskegee Airmen, this World War II experiment, would never work if they raised a lot of hell about racism. But if they endured, if they proved they could in fact fight, that would have long-term value.

Benjamin Davis. He's one of those people you get a special feeling in their presence.

E-CORRIDOR CHITLINS

The side of Cooper that enjoyed a good laugh was also in play in his Pentagon post, even when the occasion was serious.

To raise awareness, Cooper arranged for a Black History Month celebration in his office on the E corridor in the Pentagon. The E-Ring, the outer corridor of the building, is where the senior officers work, and, at least by Cooper's reckoning, there had never been a special event in the E corridor as part of the annual Black History Month observance. This one was particularly memorable—Cooper arranged for guests to be served chitlins. All through the corridor, the Pentagon brass could pick up a whiff of that venerable Southern cuisine: cooked pig intestines.

Cooper's administrative assistant, Ruth Thornton, remembered the occasion well: "When Beverly arrived, you placed her fine mink coat next to the wonderful smelling treat!" Thornton still got a kick out of the memory years later. Cooper, too.[331]

We don't remember where they came from, but I brought them in— and you could smell them all the way down the hall. People ate them up. We of course also had other great food on the table, but the chitlins were the delicacy no one forgot.

I had eaten them a few times as a youngster. Pretty good stuff.

"TOTAL QUALITY"

Cooper came to the Air Force job with a Marine's spit-and-polish sense of decorum. He did not feel it was fully shared in this wing of the military services.

I'd see Air Force generals, below me in rank, and I would say, "General, would you mind taking your hands out of your goddam pockets?"

One aide to Cooper was so flustered about this that, to make sure Cooper did not catch him again, he sewed his pockets closed.[332]

Once a top Air National Guard general arrived for a meeting in Cooper's conference room without wearing military dress shoes.

"General, how are you?"

"These are the notes we're going over, Mister Secretary."

"General, are those civilian shoes?"

"You know, we were rushing this morning."

"You know what I'd like for you to do for me?"

"What?"

"Get the fuck out of my office! Setting such a bad example!"

For Cooper, the issue rose even higher.

One day I went to see the chief of staff for the Air Force, General Merrill McPeak. Prior to that I had written him a letter. The reason I wrote him is the Air Force had decided they wanted to embrace something called "Total Quality." This was a way to improve your management. Joseph Juran and another professor, Edwards Deming, came up with the concept of total quality management, and it became well-known after World War Two.

I had met Dr. Juran. He had the idea of how to make American companies more efficient by getting their employees involved and everybody working toward the concept of total quality. But the United States industrial complex had rejected Dr. Juran right after the Second World War. So guess where Juran and Deming went? They went to Japan and the Japanese endorsed it and became industrial leaders in the post-war world.

So the head of the Air Force, General McPeak, decides he wants to start total quality in the Air Force because it is renowned to be successful. In fact they sent a plane to Japan and flew Dr. Juran back. Many American businesses were supposed to start it, and General McPeak asked me what did I think about the Air Force starting "Total Quality." The letter was sent July 24, 1991.

Dear General McPeak,

I have always thought it a serious responsibility as a military leader to set a good example for my juniors, not only in the performance of my duties, but in my personal appearance. I became convinced of the requirement to write you on this subject when an Air Force general officer visited me in my office in uniform—but wearing civilian shoes—a few weeks ago.

It is NOT unusual, on any given day, to see Air Force general officers and other officers of senior grade who are overweight, in need of a haircut or shoe shine, or have their hands buried in their pockets. Some of these violations of uniform regulation and military bearing are so blatant that an observer would conclude that military bearing is of little importance in our Air Force.

Standards must be set and our leaders must be positive role models!

It will take your personal leadership to point us in the direction of a truly professional force. Total quality need not be attempted in the work place by those who fail to achieve personal quality. I recommend strongly that we should make every effort to aggressively encourage those officers who feel no need to strive for total professionalism to become part of the reduction in our forces rather than part of those we retain.

I stand ready to assist you in any way you deem necessary.

Very Sincerely,

Gary[333]

He didn't answer.

So I go pay him a visit. I go see General McPeak and tell him that I really thought the Air Force was not ready for total quality. I say, "Before you can embrace total quality, you have to have quality leaders"—and you should have seen his face!

Then I say, "General McPeak, we've got a big problem. You guys have almost no black generals and you're talking about total quality and diversity?"

General McPeak says, "I tell you what. I know one is coming up for promotion. He's a Thunderbird pilot and he's not too smart. But we're going to make him a general."

Perhaps Cooper had misunderstood McPeak's meaning. McPeak had been a Thunderbird pilot himself at one point over his long career. But Cooper took offense.

I got up and walked out. The guy he was talking about was Lloyd Newton. His nickname was "Fig"—Fig Newton. He was a small black guy, a Thunderbird pilot. Fig was a colonel when I met him. He ended up a four-star general. He ran the whole education command in the Air Force.

And Newton did not forget Cooper.

After Newton received his first star, he sent a letter to Cooper, who was near the end of his tenure as assistant AF secretary. Newton wrote:

> Your leadership in ensuring equal opportunity in jobs, promotions and overall upward mobility is well known and is deeply appreciated. This has been a long-time goal of many Air Force leaders. However, you have brought us closer to the true reality of this than anyone.
>
> I am personally grateful for your guidance and counsel to myself and hundreds of other minority officers. You demonstrated how one can work within the system and get the job done.[334]

APPEARANCES

Cooper also was involved in personnel decisions and the work of promotion boards of the Air Force. In this role, he was dismayed to see generals interfering on behalf of their friends.

No one is to interfere. To interfere is a fatal blow. Yet at meetings of Air Force promotion boards there were generals going down, calling people out, talking to them, interfering with the results of a promotion board for their friends and such.

Despite such experiences, overall Cooper came away from his Air Force years feeling its officers were top-notch.[335] Even though he had a disagreement with General McPeak over total quality and diversity, he was a beneficiary of McPeak's generosity when he and Beverly were invited to join the Air Force chief of staff on a trip to Paris and Germany.[336] McPeak's airplane—known as the "Speckled Trout"—came with amenities.

"The plane had sleeping quarters," Beverly said, "so we got in our bunk and went to sleep. We awoke a few hours out from Paris, got dressed and had breakfast. But even then, you would get off the plane and they would take your things, they never wanted your hands encumbered. So I never had my purse when we were there, because when you get off the plane you're meeting people, greeting and shaking hands."

As for Air Force officers' deficiencies in attire—civilian shoes, rumpled shirts, hands in pockets—Cooper could laugh at himself for his own lack of attention to footwear on an occasion when he and Beverly attended a top-level reception.

I had my dress uniform on, and as we were getting off the elevator Beverly said, "Gary, what is that behind you?" And there, behind me, the patent leather on my shoe had started coming off in little chunks. My whole shoe was falling apart! By the time I got through the reception line, I found a place to stand for the entire rest of the event. I stood in one place, standing up straight with my foot under a chair. For the whole reception—the whole reception—I stood in one place, straight up!

FRIENDS IN DEED

Gary did not change his spots when picked for high rank in the Air Force. He was still the man James Harrell knew as a friend from their early days at the Alabama Statehouse.

"When he was in Washington," Harrell said, "he would make trips back to Montgomery. He would come out to my house. One time, he had flown in and had about twenty or thirty generals fly in to Maxwell to hear from him. But he had gotten his car broken into in Washington and one of the items stolen was his Rolex. He had a little rubber jogger's watch on. He was at my house. I had just gotten a new Rolex and he looked at it. I said, 'Why don't you take this? I don't want you going before these generals with that little jogger's watch on.'"

Harrell laughs. "That's been fifteen years ago and I've yet to get my Rolex back!"

I don't recall the Rolex gift from James. But you know, I do have a

Rolex—and I don't know where the hell I got it!

But I do remember a loan. I lent James $10,000 and he hadn't paid me. He'd do five dollars, ten dollars. Finally I told him—he had this little bitty pistol—I said give me the damn pistol and forget the loan. So I got a little bitty pistol—for $10,000!

DESERT STORM

Cooper's service in the George H. W. Bush administration included duties during the 1991 Gulf War. He had played no role in the planning of Desert Storm, which successfully ran Saddam Hussein's Iraqi forces out of Kuwait, but the war's logistics kept him busy.[337]

This was a different form of combat altogether from his time in Vietnam in the mid-1960s.

In Vietnam, we had something called walkie-talkies. You'd say, "Move to the right." And if there were two trees between you, nobody could hear you over the walkie-talkie. They were horrible. If a unit was spread out a mile or two, you'd have to lay wire. You couldn't talk to them on the walkie-talkies.

What I found so amazing at the Pentagon during the gulf war were the loudspeakers. The communications. You could actually hear people on the ground talking, and they're talking from the war end, and you're in the Pentagon.

While at a distance from the fighting, he felt its anguish personally. His childhood friend from Mobile, Harold Jackson, had a son, Kevin, who worked for General Motors but was a Marine called up to serve in the gulf war.

Harold was in the same Cub Scout den that Joaquin and I were in as kids. He grew up on Weinacker Avenue, near Ladd Stadium. We went through high school together.

His son Kevin always wanted to be a Marine. He asked me to perform his re-enlistment. Then Desert Storm broke out, and Kevin was in motor transport, maybe a staff sergeant, and he was helping some people change a tire on one of these huge combat vehicles. It exploded and blinded him.

*His mama and daddy called me and said they'd got this message that
Kevin had been seriously injured, and that they didn't know where he
was. I was able to find out and to help get him out of the country and
transported to a hospital.*

"Gary was instrumental in giving us information on a daily basis how
Kevin was," Harold Jackson said. "They had flown him to the hospital in
Germany. My mother and my wife and his wife flew to Germany to see
about him. And we flew back to Bethesda Naval Hospital with him. He
had about thirteen or fourteen operations."[338]

Kevin Jackson didn't forget the role Cooper played in his life. He kept
in touch and, years later, expressed his gratitude in a letter: "You have
one hell of a story to tell," he said. "You can really motivate many young,
middle aged and older people to get out there and do the best they can
as there is nothing holding them back but themselves."[339]

Pentagon Visitor

Cooper was having a particularly busy day with multiple meetings and
appointments when an aide told him of the arrival of a Pentagon visitor.

"Mr. Secretary," the aide said, "I've gotten a call from Security. There's
someone there with his wife. He doesn't have an appointment, but he says
it's important that they see you. And his name is Fob."[340]

I immediately knew who that was.

Fob James. The former Alabama governor who had made Cooper the
first black to lead a sprawling state agency with Cabinet rank, then ousted
him in a political entanglement that cast James in a not-so-flattering light.

But James was unfailingly friendly and, like Cooper, had left their
1981 dustup in the past. Besides, James was with his wife, Bobbie. Her
presence indicated it was a non-political visit.

The purpose was soon apparent. With the start of the gulf war, they
came to the Pentagon for Bobbie to express her personal concerns, drawn
from her religious faith.

*So they came up and sat on the sofa in my office. He said the reason
he was there was that Bobbie had some information that the Lord had
told her to share with someone senior. He said he knew that I knew*

Colin Powell, and that's why they were in Washington."

Cooper tried to digest this. He turned to Bobbie.

"Well, Gary, sir," she said, and then she proceeded to explain to me that the Lord had given her insights and she wanted to caution us that there were certain areas in the Middle East region where we should never put troops on the ground. She just wanted to make sure that if anyone was interested in finding out those details, she would be available. So I got all the information.

And, no, I did not give it to Colin Powell. He'd have said, "Cooper, are you crazy?"

Cooper found this encounter strange, to say the least, but over the years he has kept in mind James's genuine friendliness and the times when they shared a desire to bring change—a "new beginning"—to Alabama: *I liked Fob. He and Bobbie, we got along fine.*

James also remained invariably upbeat and did not lose his political drive. With Bobbie at his side, he switched parties and won a second term as governor in 1994, becoming the only person elected governor of Alabama once as a Democrat and once as a Republican.

USS *Alabama* BATTLESHIP

From his Air Force post, Cooper was able to settle a score with powers-that-be in Mobile.

The battleship USS *Alabama*, a huge tourist attraction at the Mobile harbor, featured in one of its rooms pictures of Alabama natives who had reached flag rank in the military. After Gary got his first star, it was assumed his picture would join those of the others who had distinguished themselves in military service. But it didn't.

Now they've got pictures in the wardroom on the ship, where the officers eat, and at the battleship Alabama *they had pictures of generals from Alabama, the flag officers, the admirals and generals. But they didn't have my picture. A friend of mine noticed this and wrote them a letter.*

And they respond that only officers who were born in Alabama could have their picture in the wardroom. They say General Cooper might be from a fine, prominent Mobile family, but he was not born in Alabama, so consequently they could not hang my picture.

When I was born, of course, the Mobile hospitals wouldn't let blacks be born there, and there was no black maternity clinic. My parents wanted me to be born in a proper place, so they went to my mother's home in Lafayette, Louisiana. So I wasn't born in Alabama and they didn't do anything about my picture at the battleship.

But then, years later, I was assistant secretary of the Air Force. In addition to having all these people, all the reserves, all these bases, I also was in charge of museums. And I had five museum-quality Blackbird aircraft, the spy planes, to give away.

Guess who found out that Cooper made the decision on where they would go? The Battleship Alabama! The battleship folks said, "General Cooper, we have decided to hang your picture in the battleship!"

The Mentor

During Cooper's Air Force service, he took an early retirement from the Marine Corps: *I was taking up space. Better to hold the rank as a retiree and give someone else the opportunity to become a general officer in the active service.*

Navy Secretary Henry Garrett III wrote a send-off in July 1991:

> Your regard for the Marines whom you led is commendable and your deep concern of the quality of life for them has inspired the trust, confidence, and loyalty afforded to few. . . . May you always be blessed with "Fair winds and following seas."[341]

A year and a half later, Cooper also was coming to the end of his service with the Air Force, and black USAF officers took notice of his efforts on their behalf, much as General Lloyd "Fig" Newton had done earlier. In the April 1993 issue of a newsletter, the *Mentor*, an editor's note spelled out their gratitude.

> This issue of the *Mentor* is dedicated to Mr. J. Gary Cooper and his service to the Marine Corps, Air Force and America. He is a giant of

a man, both in stature and as a leader, who has dramatically reshaped the consciousness of the military. A major force in bringing social issues to the forefront of military consciousness, Mr. Cooper has made a significant and profound contribution toward equal opportunity in today's military—a contribution from which all military personnel will benefit for years to come.[342]

Some of the steps Cooper took were spelled out by Major David Fax in an article titled "Secretary Cooper—A Legacy to Remember." Fax pointed out Cooper's work targeting "possible past prejudicial treatment" when promotion boards review minorities for advancement:

> The intent was to bring to board members' attention that there may be institutionalized problems affecting performance ratings of minority officers and enlisted members.
>
> The results of Mr. Cooper's influence speak for themselves. Recent promotion statistics indicate that, for the first time in the history of the United States Air Force, promotion percentage rates for minorities either matched or outpaced those for line personnel as a whole.... His efforts not only helped minority service members, but served to strengthen the very fabric of our American heritage.[343]

With little fanfare, Cooper also played a role in raising the stature of the Tuskegee Airmen in Air Force eyes. This accomplishment took place a few years before the 1995 HBO movie, *The Tuskegee Airmen*, and a subsequent cascade of books gave the all-black unit a new measure of national fame and accolades they had not received previously.

As a Marine, Cooper had viewed Montford Pointers as deserving of a high place on history's pedestal. In the Air Force, while getting to know General Benjamin O. Davis Jr. as a friend, he helped put a spotlight on the courageous black pilots who trained at a remote Alabama air base and then fought with skill and success in World War II.

As Cooper's service in the Air Force was coming to an end, the *Mentor* ran a piece about members of the Tuskegee Airmen joining USAF

officials to thank Cooper for his actions on their behalf. The event, the
article said, was "an intimate ceremony in Secretary Cooper's office on the
Pentagon's prestigious 4th floor E-ring." Cooper and others stood before
"a backdrop of a historic portrait of the Tuskegee Airmen, clad in flight
suits with helmets in hand."[344]

One of the dignitaries, Major General Albert J. Edmonds, a prominent African American officer who would earn a third star with the Air
Force, said Cooper has "made the jobs of our senior Air Force leaders a
lot easier by dealing with issues that most people don't want to deal with."

He also spoke of "the superb support Secretary Cooper provided the
Tuskegee Airmen by opening doors to help us all better interface with the
Air Force senior leadership. . . . Secretary Cooper brought the Tuskegee
Airmen into the mainstream of Air Force and Department of Defense
thought, by recognizing that the Tuskegee Airmen is not a 'black' thing.
It's an 'Air Force' thing!"[345]

The comment echoed the words and beliefs of General Davis, whose
biography was published by Smithsonian Institution Press in 1991, mid-
way into Cooper's Air Force tenure. The book's title: *Benjamin O. Davis
Jr.: American*.

"As the title suggests, General Davis wanted people to think of him as
an American, not as a hyphenated American," said Daniel L. Haulman,
an Air Force historian and chronicler of the Tuskegee Airmen's story.[346]

At the ceremony with the Tuskegee Airmen, Cooper also spoke:

> When I was a young Marine captain, I really had no hero. Then I
> saw a picture of General Davis in *Jet* magazine, when he had made his
> second star. I wrote him a letter telling him I was a young officer who
> wanted to be a career military person. He wrote me back and sent me
> an autographed photograph of himself; a picture I still have to this day.
> So, you see, my first real hero was an Air Force officer.[347]

17

Fights on Many Fronts

E ven while working in a top Air Force post, Cooper's concerns for greater diversity in the Marine Corps remained a priority. It had been nearly fifty years since the Corps opened its doors to black recruits, but little was happening to get black officers moving up in the ranks to significant leadership positions. At one point the three black generals—Cooper, Petersen, and Walls—met with Marine General Carl E. Mundy Jr., the commandant of the Marine Corps, to discuss the issue.[348]

Mundy, whose Alabama connections included graduating from Sidney Lanier High School in Montgomery and Auburn University, was a tough, square-jawed Marine who got along well with Cooper. He was agreeable to the session. He had concerns about diversity, too.

He has always been a charming, wonderful guy. What was so interesting during the course of our conversation, where we were asking them to get more officers, he says, "You know, gentlemen, I'm going to share this with you. You don't know it but I have just had a study completed, and I find the results rather shocking."

We said, "What study? And what's shocking?"

Mundy said, "I've had a study done on how minority officers are rated on their fitness reports. You know, gentlemen, this is something I don't understand. In almost every case, the minority officers are rated lower than other officers. It didn't matter if you went to Yale, Harvard, the Naval Academy—it didn't matter. I don't understand it."

I said, "General, let me help explain it to you. It's something we call racism."

He didn't answer. But with me personally he has been a great supporter.

In fact, Mundy earlier appeared to feel strongly enough about countering any racial obstacles faced by black officer candidates that on July 1, 1991, the day he became commandant of the Marine Corps, he wrote a letter seeking Cooper's recommendations.[349]

Cooper sent a detailed response, including a cover note underlining his main points:

> Our officer Corps in each rank must reflect the ethnic diversity of our Corps and our Nation. The minority officers, Active and Reserve, and the senior civilian force must perceive that they are treated fairly in each facet of their career.
>
> Some of the recommendations may require nontraditional action. We must accept the fact that minority officers are a special asset who are needed in our Corps. When we need officers with specific MOS's [Military Occupational Specialties] we take special steps to reach and maintain the desired inventory.
>
> I do not consider it an overstatement when I state that the future of our Corps will depend on your personal and consistent attention to this challenge.[350]

Cooper's recommendations focused on thirteen areas of concern, beginning with "Sensitivity of Leadership." This went right to the top. He argued that generals and other senior officers in the Marine Corps were not adequately aware of the challenge or the benefit of a culturally diverse USMC. At a recent high-ranking change of command, he wrote,

> there were more than 200 invited guests from Beaufort (S.C.) in attendance. From an area that is 40 percent black, I was the only minority at the reception.

Almost twenty years after the National Naval Officers Association was formed to enhance diversity among officers in the Navy, Coast Guard and

Marine Corps, no USMC commandant had attended an association func-
tion, he said, while the Chief of Naval Operations and the Coast Guard
Commandant had accepted invitations on many occasions.

Cooper was concerned over high rates of attrition among minorities
at Officer Candidate School.

> This must be stopped. These youngsters return to their communi-
> ties and relate experiences that severely damage our recruiting efforts.

Cooper suggested a review of how Brigadier General Gail Reals
had reduced attrition rates for females at OCS by 50 percent when she
served as director of manpower plans and speculated that a thinking and
creative commander could do the same with minority attrition without
sacrificing quality.

Another area of concern was drawn from Cooper's own personal
experience—serving as a Marine officer in Infantry.

> A disproportionate number of minority officers choose noncombat
> arms. This results in the number being in career fields that normally
> do not produce the general officers of the future. . . . Somebody might
> say, "Oh, I like Supply. I work in the office. I won't have to go out in the
> rain and snow, won't have to march in time over the hills." But there
> was nobody on the staffs who would say, "Hey, young man, or young
> woman, that's NOT what you need to do."[351]

Role models was a crucial point. As Cooper would describe it years
later, the lack of role models from combat specialties at the Basic School
invariably allowed black officers to drift off course.

There also was a perception among minority officers that the deck
was stacked against them in getting picked for professional schools and
desirable command assignments—"That the perception exists is a problem
in itself which hurts retention," Cooper wrote to Mundy. To eliminate it,
he said, those minority officers with strong growth potential should be
identified and kept on a fast track. Quarterly reports should be provided

to the Commandant on the progress of those picked for advancement. He wrote:

> The numbers are so small they could easily be tracked. . . . Some will be quick to say "Why this special treatment?" The answer is simple. We need these young officers to stay on active duty to build a stronger Marine Corps."[352]

He felt black Marines should be seen—by other Marines and by the public—as much as possible. His suggestion: bolster the racial composition of units like the Marine Corps Band, the Drum and Bugle Corps, ceremonial units, security staff at Camp David, high performance aircraft pilots, and the staff at the Marine Corps Museum.

Also, for civilian posts, the commandant himself must be visible in communicating his vision of the Marine Corps as an Equal Opportunity Employer.

> Written statements on bulletin boards have limited impact on improving this situation. The CMC could make a video in which he states his feelings about leadership, particularly with regard to equal opportunity for all of the Marine Corps' civilian work force.[353]

The commandant and Cooper were not entirely on the same page, but Mundy was responsive. When the national conference of the NNOA rolled around in the summer of 1992, Mundy became the first Marine Corps commandant to accept an invitation to participate.[354]

In his speech, he saluted Montford Point:

> The approximately 20,000 black Marines who passed through Montford Point from 1942–1949 were acutely aware of their uniqueness and possessed that "esprit de corps" which is instilled in all U.S. Marines. . . .
> In the words of our former Commandant, General Leonard F. Chapman Jr. . . . "The footprints of Montford Point Marines were left on the beaches of Roi-Namur, Saipan, Guam, Peleliu and Iwo Jima. Tide and

wind have, long ago, washed them out into the seas of history. But, the 'Chosen Few,' in field shoes and leggings, also left their mark in the firm concrete of Marine Corps spirit. And, as new Marines learn to match those footprints, their cadence assumes the proud stride of the men from Montford Point."

As your Association prepares for its next twenty years of service, I ask that you remember the patriotism of those who paved the way before you.[355]

Despite the resolve in his remarks, the path forward was hardly smooth.

At one point when General Mundy was commandant, he made a comment on the CBS show 60 Minutes *that kind of shocked some of us. He seemed to say he really didn't think diversity was the best thing for the Marine Corps. It was more like: "You take the top people, regardless. This is going to make you a better fighting force than attempting to have diversity. Who cares if the Marine Corps officers corps looks like America if you've got people who can win wars?"*

We were kind of shocked. The meeting that Petersen, Walls, and I had with Mundy should have given me a clue to the comment he made on 60 Minutes. *But I will tell you, I have found him to be a super person, helpful in any way he could, and he was a great leader. He evidently was not thinking when he spoke with* 60 Minutes *and probably wouldn't do it again.*

In the October 1993 *60 Minutes* program on the lack of minority promotions in the USMC, Mundy stated:

> In the military skills, we find that the minority officers do not shoot as well as the non-minorities. They don't swim as well. And when you give them a compass and send them across the terrain at night in a land navigation exercise, they don't do as well at that sort of thing.[356]

Mundy soon apologized, and at a November 1993 ceremony honoring the USMC's 218th birthday, he said: "My words on another occasion have given the impression that I believe that some Marines, because of their color, are not as capable as others. Those were not the thoughts in my mind, nor are they or have they ever been, the thoughts of my heart."[357]

In any event, among the ranks of African Americans holding top Marine officer posts, Mundy had his defenders.

Major General Charles Bolden Jr. said that in the 1990s the Marine Corps leadership did undertake positive action "when people like General [Charles] Krulak, General Mundy and others went to the secretary of the Navy and got him to put in the precepts for promotions, the selection boards for general officers, 'If there are black or minority officers who are otherwise fully qualified, pick them.' The board was told, 'You have to pick them.' Up until that time, it was optional. . . ."[358]

And Colonel Alphonse G. Davis was summoned to Headquarters for a new posting in the wake of the CBS program.

"It was about becoming an advisor on equal opportunity matters to General Mundy, because of this *60 Minutes* interview. General Cooper had recommended me: 'Hey, this needs to happen, and Al Davis is the guy.' So I get up there and things were buzzing. I worked personally for General Mundy, interfaced personally with him. When General Mundy's talking points were prepared, he would have benefited from the diversity of folks who are in those staff officer positions to be able to look at that and say, 'That doesn't sound right.'"[359]

Mundy's remarks on the CBS program prompted Navy Secretary John Dalton to order a "complete review on the recruitment, retention and promotion of minorities."[360] But it would be years later before the suggestions Cooper wrote out for Mundy would draw the interest—and bring action—from another commandant.

A COUNTRY OF GIRAFFES

After his term as assistant secretary of the Air Force ended, Cooper expressed in July 1993 his displeasure over the lack of progress in officer corps diversity across the military services, not just the USMC. In an interview, he elaborated on his feelings, including a story called "A Country of Giraffes" that he used in speeches:

We are woefully lacking in minority representation in our officer corps. The percentages are much too low in most of the critical fields.

What's happening? When I talk to some people who don't understand, they say, "Well, Cooper, what do you expect? The military is a meritocracy." They mean that you survive based on merit, your ability, so if these people have not gotten promoted, it must mean that they are not meriting the promotion.

What I explain to them is that at the Atlanta University Center there is the American Institute for Managing Diversity. It is headed by Roosevelt Thomas, a Harvard Ph.D. who became well-known for his work in corporate diversity. His studies say there are many meritocracies in addition to the military—IBM, Exxon, all these major corporations.

In order to survive in a meritocracy you must have three things. First, you must perform in an outstanding manner to reach the top. Secondly, you must be very welcome. And third, you must have a mentor, a sponsor. Very seldom do you get to be great in any of these organizations unless someone likes you and sponsors you.

The minority officer is very capable of doing a good job, but we don't live in a culture that is accepting us. To that people will say, "Well, what do you mean?" And I say, it's like the house that the giraffe built.

In a country of giraffes, the giraffes prospered for years. They owned everything. They were very wealthy, had the biggest houses. Then gradually people started moving into the neighborhoods that were different from the giraffes. This one very wealthy giraffe had had a house designed just for himself—beautiful high ceilings and high commodes, just for the giraffe.

But this giraffe leader noticed these other people moving in. Being a nice guy, he invited the head of one of the families over to have a drink one evening. And the head of this other household got there and barely could get in the door, because his name was rhinoceros.

Finally, rhinoceros got in, but no matter how much rhinoceros moved around that house, he could never be comfortable because he was living in a house that was built for a giraffe.

That's what the military is today. We are living, blacks and Hispanics and Asians and women, we are living in a house that was built for the white man. And we have not yet made the effort to really change this house.

We make little spurts at it. We've got change in the hair care and the PX's, the music on the boxes, all those are little changes. But we have not yet changed the attitudes that would really make the difference in this house that was built for the giraffe.

The other one is the need for a sponsor. These youngsters don't have sponsors. They don't see the black generals and the colonels in enough numbers. Nor do they find the white leaders who will come forward and help them. Not many are trusted.

So we don't have the three factors available to make a meritocracy work, and that's why we must go about doing this cultural change, which we've got to accomplish if we are really to solve the lack of diversity in our officer corps.[361]

"A BEAUTIFUL PLACE"

Cooper's time in Washington took a somber turn with the death of his longtime friend and fellow Marine, Alden Lawson Jr. They had met during Cooper's student days at Notre Dame when Cooper visited Chicago along with his roommate, Corky Parker. Lawson was a bit younger than Cooper and Parker, but after meeting at a dance, the threesome became close. The friendship grew over the years, as Lawson joined the Marines after attending the University of Illinois.[362]

It was renewed a last time in Washington, where Alden lived with his wife and young daughter, Layne.

Alden was one of the first disc jockeys at Howard University. Howard had a radio station, WHUR, and Alden was one of their first DJ's. They called him "A. J. Squared Away."

Then they started laying people off at Howard. I was then assistant secretary of the Air Force. I go to the top civilian in the Pentagon and tell him about Alden. The federal government ran a program called Voice of America, which included radio broadcasts. They hired Alden to work at the radio station in the Pentagon.

One day I get a call from Alden's wife. This is after Alden had been working in the Pentagon three or four months.

She said, "Gary, you've got to help me. Alden is so sick that he cannot even put his pants on in the morning. But he gets up and makes me put his pants on so he can go to work. He doesn't want to miss a day at work because you got him that job. Will you please get ahold of him and make him go to the doctor?"

So I called the people at the radio station and had Alden sent up to see me. To make a long story short, we sent Alden to the doctor and he had a brain tumor. He died not long thereafter.

At Alden's memorial service in Washington, Gary remembered his and Corky's friend:

Between Corky and me, not many weeks over these thirty years have passed without one of us sharing our life experiences with our brother, and he with us. He became a Marine, and what a Marine he was! Immaculate in his uniform, true to his duties.

He loved his Corps. Not many weeks ago, in fact only ten weeks ago, Alden and I rode to Quantico to watch the young Marines train. We took a few pictures and he wanted to see the National Cemetery. We found the cemetery and rode through. It was a beautiful afternoon. The grass was green, the flags fluttering. Alden said to me, "This is a beautiful place. This is where a Marine should be."

He looked at me with a few small tears flickering in his eyes, and he said, "Now if I get buried here, will you and Corky come down here too?"

I said to Alden: "Maybe—but I hope not real soon!"

Alden loved his friends. He wanted us with him.

He loved his family—and Alden did love Lil' Layne. Layne was Alden's joy. She was his life's accomplishment.[363]

Although Alden was gone, Gary remained friends with his wife as her child, Layne Lawson, grew up. It touched Gary that the college Layne chose, Hampton University, was where his mother and father had met in the early 1930s.[364]

NETTIE STEWART

Moving back to Mobile in 1993, without Air Force duties to command his attention, Gary had more time to devote to his businesses, including Commonwealth National Bank. It had been a bumpy road for the bank, and for Cooper, one of its founders.

> *The challenge was we spent about fifteen years not knowing what we were doing, and fighting each other. Finally I had a group on the board, and those with different ideas had a group. All of them were great, but some were businessmen and some weren't.*

> *But I could never win in an election. They would count the votes in a room. I don't care how many votes, I would lose. One day I got off the board and put Nettie Stewart on it. Everything changed.*

Stewart is from Lower Peach Tree, a poor Alabama community in the backwoods of Wilcox County about ninety miles north of Mobile. This did not hold her back. Valedictorian of her high school class, she had opportunities to attend Harvard or Yale, but her mother wanted her closer to home and eventually she earned a degree from the University of South Alabama, majoring in business. A small person, she soon rose in stature in the eyes of both Jay and Gary Cooper.[365]

"When I graduated from South Alabama, my first job was with the Prichard Housing Authority, as administrative assistant," she said. "But I only worked there for about three months. That's when Mayor A. J. Cooper decided he wanted me in his office.

"Do you know he sent the chief of police over to the Prichard Housing Authority to pick me up and bring me to his office? The director had told him about my skills, he kept bragging about the type of work I did, the quality of work I did. So Gary's brother, Jay, decided he wanted me to work with him, and he had the chief of police come over to the Prichard Housing Authority and export me, deliver me to his office.

"Jay said that was the only way he could get me moved."

She worked for Mayor Cooper from around 1977 to 1980, when he wrapped up his second term in office.

"Jay made a decision to move to Washington, D.C., and go into law practice there, and he really wanted me to relocate, too. But my husband at the time did not want to move. So Jay recommended me to Gary, to work with Christian Benevolent. I accepted and that's where it all started."³⁶⁶

The first time I met her, Nettie was working for my brother. When Jay left, he recommended that Nettie come and work for the insurance company. I said, "Nettie's so short, Jay, how is she going to get around?" He said, "Don't worry about it. She can stand on boxes. She'll do ten times more than anybody else in the office."

"With the insurance company, I was Mr. Cooper's executive secretary and also the corporate secretary for the corporation," Stewart said. "He traveled a lot, but he still served as the chief executive officer. I worked closely with him and really learned the business. But I can't say I was running the insurance company. No."

She helped keep the insurance company on its upward financial path until it was sold in 1985. By then Cooper was a busy Marine general as well as an executive well-acquainted with Stewart's business skills. She became president of Christian Benevolent Funeral Home.

"I served as president until 1994. I was the first non-family member, and the second lady, other than Mrs. Pearl Madison, the founder, to serve as president and run the funeral home.

"I really, really enjoyed it. A lot of people say, 'How do you enjoy running a funeral home?' But it's about the customers and people, so I got a lot of satisfaction from that job."

Cooper was the one who gained satisfaction when Stewart took a seat on the board of Commonwealth National Bank, at his request.

"I took his place on the board. He was having his differences with some of the factions. With Cooper, he's a businessman. Most of the other board members were educators. Their philosophies about running the bank were totally different. The educators, they perceived the mission or purpose as being more of a social organization, a social service organization. Mister Cooper, his outlook for the bank was to make money, to turn a profit, and the only way you could do that, as with any business, you've got to take in more money than you spend, and hold on to a certain percentage of it, and that's your profit.

"Now I served on the board for a number of years, and during that

time I got to know the other board members and was able to work well
with them. After, I guess about three years on the board, they decided to
appoint me as a proxy for the annual shareholders meeting. In the past,
Mr. Cooper had a lot of problems with them actually counting the votes
properly. He never could really prove the votes weren't correct because
he didn't have anybody there who was actually part of the voting. But
when I was appointed proxy, then my job was just seeing if they count
the votes right."[367]

Competing slates of board members were up for a vote at the annual
meeting.

> *They had taken a vote to elect the board members. They finished
> counting the votes about eight o'clock at night. The CPA says Cooper's
> slate has won. But then they say, "No. That was a test vote."*

> *So they send out to find more proxies for a second vote, and we
> hire Palmer Hamilton, a banking law expert, to take the case to court.
> We've got Stewart on our side. Palmer's our lawyer. The judge rules for
> us. Our slate won.*

Palmer Hamilton, an elegant and energetic political operator and
lawyer with Old Mobile connections, had been Cooper's neighbor in the
Oakleigh Garden District and counted Commonwealth National among
his clients. Unlike Cooper's bank, Hamilton's law firm was an extremely
tony outfit.

> *Palmer would do work for us, and they'd charge us, and I'd say,
> "Remember, we're a small goddam bank!"*

> *Then I'm in Washington, I'm the assistant secretary of the Air
> Force, I'm in my office and there's some people Palmer wants to know
> something about, in some section, maybe banking. So Palmer calls me,
> I call somebody else, I get some research done, Palmer calls and gets
> the information.*

> *Then Palmer sends me a damn bill for two hours!*

> *I called him up. I said, "Palmer. I've got one question. Just one: Have
> you lost your fucking mind?"*

Cooper's experience in the Marines helped shape his sense of how to
operate a bank. Rodney Lee, who rose to vice president and compliance

officer, was a perfect example of Cooper's approach.

I was out at the PX at the Coast Guard base and I saw this fine-looking guy. He looked like a Marine, and I started talking to him. Turns out he was a Marine. He was telling me he was a senior recruiter for the Marines in Alabama and that he was getting out.

I asked, "What are you going to do? Where are you going to work?" He said he didn't have firm plans.

"Do you know anything about banking?"

"I don't know anything about banking."

"That's good. We won't have to retrain you."

Lee was hired.

It was a gospel that Cooper would spread:

I convinced my people at the bank that you can teach someone to be a banker a lot faster than you can to be a leader. It didn't matter that Rodney came to us without a background in banking. He knew how to lead others.

When you teach leadership, though, it's not just honor, courage and commitment, what most people think of military officers, but also tact, dependability, and bearing.

GETHSEMANE CEMETERY

Nettie Stewart also helped Cooper clear a business hurdle in the acquisition and development of a cemetery in Mobile. He saw adding a cemetery to his business portfolio as a natural progression.

I'm in the funeral business, I've got family members buried here, and the cemeteries are all owned by someone else, maybe old white families. There was an obvious need to open a cemetery owned by blacks.

But there were some problems. One was that the city no longer approved permits to put a cemetery inside the city limits. Another was that the old black graveyards already in the city limits were in disarray: Nobody has records. They don't know who is buried where. There is no money for perpetual care. Grass is overgrown.

With Stewart's help, Cooper put his hopes on a large piece of vacant and apparently abandoned property in northwest Mobile where ten or twelve slaves were buried. A group led by a black historian, Henry Williams, had been sweeping, raking and tending to those graves for years.[368]

Williams knew Stewart, and when he learned of Cooper's interest in operating a black-owned cemetery, he went to see her.

"He told me, 'I have a piece of property that you-all can have.'

"'You do, Mr. Williams?' I was kind of skeptical.

"'I certainly do,' he said. 'All I want you to do is to create something that our community will be proud of. And you can have it.'"

Cooper and Stewart were concerned that Williams had no deed for the land. But Williams persisted.

"He said, 'I have squatter's rights. I meet all the requirements of the law,'" Stewart recalled.

Attorneys for Cooper then researched the issue of "adverse possession."

"And indeed they thought Mr. Williams and his group—it was named the Progressive League of Prichard, Plateau and Magazine Point—had met all the requirements of the law," Stewart said

A court ruled in favor of the Progressive League, and the property eventually was conveyed, with Cooper paying a nominal fee for the land.

"It took us about two or three years to get the deed," Stewart said, "but we prevailed, and there indeed were graves of slaves on that property."[369]

According to Williams's research, the land was part of an old cemetery called Lincoln Graveyard, with the graves of slaves on about twenty-five acres. Stewart said that Williams posted this property with "Private Property, No Trespassing" signs and maintained the graves for many years, validating the "adverse possession" claim.[370]

"We had a contest to name the cemetery. I think it was my idea along with Mr. Bobby Brown, down at the Christian Benevolent Funeral Home. We asked all the black churches in Mobile to suggest a name, and a committee that received the recommendations made the selection—Gethsemane.

"This promoted the cemetery, which was the purpose of the contest, to get all the churches involved, get the community involved."

I went to David Volkert & Associates, the architectural firm, and for the first time in our community we have a cemetery that is professionally designed. It is based on the design at the National Cemetery

at Quantico, where there is one building for the funeral services. By having one place for services, tents don't have to be erected over graves here and there across the cemetery.

The theory was that rather than going to the side of the grave and burying people, you would have your ceremony at the permanent site. Then, after the ceremony, you would leave and cemetery staff would bury people like they do at many of the national cemeteries.

In naming the cemetery, we sent letters to all the black churches and told them about this challenge to select a name. The church that won would get $1,000. So when we opened, every church in the city knew about this cemetery.

Naming the cemetery Gethsemane was a stroke of genius—I wish it had been my genius.

FUNDRAISING FIASCO

Along with tending to his Mobile businesses, Cooper remained on the board of trustees of Talladega College. In 1992, Cooper found himself at odds with the school's president, Joseph B. Johnson, over questionable use of funds by the administration, including more than $100,000 for a Las Vegas fundraiser which had not been approved by the trustees.[371]

I was chairman of the finance committee when this president was hired in 1991. He came from Grambling. Of course, finance committees weren't new to me, and in the course of serving as its chairman I find out Talladega College is going to have a fundraiser in Las Vegas.

In a meeting, I said, "Mr. President, we of course have a budget. Would you like us to make a motion to approve anything from the budget?"

He says, "No worry, General. You don't understand. This is FOR Talladega, not BY Talladega."

But listen, I've been the finance chairman and I know the people in the office. They tell me they've been writing travel checks and stuff. Then I find out that they're spending Title III money for something that is not authorized.

To make matters worse, the 1992 fundraiser turned out to be a bust, and Cooper began demanding an accounting. Johnson pushed back, denying that any rules were violated and asserting that the fundraiser had been undermined by events beyond his control. A majority of the board sided with Johnson.

> *I got together with the board in executive session. I said, "This is very clear to me, this is real simple, we've got to discipline the president. It would satisfy me if you give him a letter of reprimand. When I have knowledge of a violation, I have no choice but to report it. But if in fact you folks take some rapid action, write him a letter of reprimand and instruct him not to do this any more, then I think I could live with this. If we do not, I would have no choice but to report it."*
>
> *They didn't, and I reported it—and they voted me off that board.*

After investigating, the federal agency that oversees Title III grants spelled out in September 1994 a number of steps Talladega College's administration needed to take to fix problems with the funding program. By then, Cooper had been removed from the board.[372]

Cooper still pressed his point. He and two other former Talladega College trustees filed suit. Part of it questioned expenditures at the 1992 fundraiser in Las Vegas.[373]

Johnson contended the fundraiser had been knocked out by riots and violence in Las Vegas in the aftermath of the April 29, 1992, acquittal of four white police officers in Los Angeles for the videotaped beating of Rodney King, an unarmed black man, after a high-speed chase. Johnson wrote to Cooper:

> Violence in Las Vegas on this weekend was a continuation of reaction in Los Angeles and other western cities. There is no doubt our event was affected. One incident is plainly illustrative of the uneasiness felt by citizens and officials. On the evening of the first performance, members of the Las Vegas police appeared and demanded a fee of more than $1,100 or they would "close the show down." This is only one example of the many problems we experienced in attempting to put on this event. The receipts were unpredictably low for a star packed line-up like ours.[374]

A separate part of the suit claimed Cooper was improperly removed from the board. The college's bylaws required a majority of the full board to remove a trustee, the suit said, and with nineteen members the board was one short when it voted 9–5 to remove Cooper.

"Anyone, even with less education than a Talladega College graduate, knows that nine is not more than half of 19," the suit said.[375]

Dr. Jewell Plummer Cobb, a Talladega College graduate who became president of California State University-Fullerton, told the *Anniston Star* the former trustees were trying to make mischief with the suit. "I think there's mountains being made out of a molehill, frankly," she said.[376]

The suit eventually was dropped.[377] And in any event, Cooper already had bigger challenges on his hands.

18

Jamaica

Befor returning to Mobile after his service as assistant Air Force secretary ended, Gary had felt it necessary to stick around Washington a little longer. He had been getting calls from the new administration indicating he was being considered for secretary of the Navy or secretary of the Army. Further service, for incoming President Bill Clinton, might be in the works.

But no nomination materialized, nor any firm word on whether he was still a candidate, and in any event Cooper had some concerns about the new president from the military perspective.[378]

So I just said to hell with them and we came back to Alabama.

Gary and Beverly had been in the Mobile home for more than a year when, in the fall of 1994, he got a late-night call. It was about 11 p.m. The caller was Alexis Herman, the old family friend from Mobile—Gary and Alexis had dated when he was single in the 1970s—who had become a big-time political player with the national Democratic Party.[379] Under the Clinton administration, she would become the first African American to serve as U.S. labor secretary.[380]

Prior to the call, Alexis had been brainstorming with Clinton officials late at night in Washington.

"Gary, we really need your help," she said.

"What can I do?"

"There is a country where we have not yet sent an ambassador, and they are very unhappy with us. We need an ambassador, and we need one who would not need months to be confirmed. I thought of you. Would you consider being an ambassador?"

Gary was initially skeptical. She had not identified the country needing an ambassador.

"Alexis," he said, "I'm not going to Uganda. I'm not going to Rwanda.
I'm not going to Haiti."

"What about . . . Jamaica?"

"Ahhhh! Jamaica Mon!"

He had vacationed in Jamaica and knew the island's charms.

*I was impressed by the beauty of Jamaica and the personalities and
beauty of the Jamaican people. I once even visited a famous resort called
Hedonism. A very beautiful place known for partying and having a
good time. It's known for its nude beaches, so not many people go there
who don't have a good time.*

More to the point, an ambassadorship to Jamaica would be a new
experience, a test of his leadership skills across a range of new challenges. And an ambassadorship carried with it four stars. These stars
might not be the exact equivalent of those received as a general officer
in the military or assistant Air Force secretary, but they were part of the
diplomatic trappings.[381]

*As ambassador, you have a flag flying in your office, on a stand, with
the State Department seal on it and four stars.*

Cooper again was happy to accept a new president's call to service,
and his Mobile connections again had made a difference.

He soon learned how he had been picked. Jamaica was a Caribbean
island nation that had never had a black U.S. ambassador. President
Clinton wanted to change that. His first choice was Shirley Chisholm,
the former New York congresswoman. But the once-feisty Chisholm
was said to be in poor health and her nomination had to be declined.
Now it was the fall of 1994 and the ambassadorship had been left vacant
for months. Time—along with Jamaican patience—was running short.
The Clinton administration needed a nominee who could be quickly
confirmed.

Cooper fit the bill. He already had been vetted and confirmed by the
Senate three times—twice to be a Marine general and once to be assistant
Air Force secretary. When the Clinton team started looking around for a

candidate who could be promptly confirmed, Alexis Herman spoke up: "I know somebody."[382]

It was only a week or so after the call and I was flying to Washington. They sent a plane down to get me. I got confirmed almost immediately by the Senate, in less than three weeks.

"Just at the moment we were back in Mobile, getting settled, it all turned around for us," Beverly said. "Gary played well on both sides and it went boom boom boom boom boom. Before Thanksgiving, we were in Jamaica."

Gary's friend James Harrell told him in jest that through all the Senate confirmations, no investigator ever contacted him: *"And they never will,"* Gary replied.

Gary indeed played well on both sides. With Republican friends in Congress and fresh off service for President Bush, Gary also had the support of Democrats close to their party's new president and first lady. Being a Marine general above the partisan fray didn't hurt, either.

On October 21, 1994, wearing glasses and with a trim mustache, Cooper signed the official papers in the Ben Franklin Room of the State Department to become U.S. ambassador to Jamaica—filling a post that had been vacant since March 1993.[383] A letter to Cooper arrived not long before his investiture, recalling the day nearly thirty years earlier when he had to "Request Mast" to get command of a rifle company in Vietnam. The letter was from Marine Brigadier General E. H. Simmons, who in the spring of 1966 had cleared the way for Cooper to command Mike Company.

Simmons had not forgotten:

Since those early days together in Vietnam, I have watched each step of your climb up the career ladder with pride and pleasure.[384]

THE BIGGEST SHOW IN TOWN

Despite their past familiarity with Jamaica, the ambassadorship cast the island in a different light for the Coopers.

"Gary and I both had spent times down there, but just vacationing, being tourists," Beverly said. "So here we were in a real different situation. He's now ambassador, and they had never had an African American ambassador before. So this was pretty significant for them, and for us. Jamaicans would often ask Gary, 'Why do you call yourself black? Or why do you call yourself an African American?' When they looked at him, he looked like any other light-skinned Jamaican, a white Jamaican. They would call me 'Brownie.'"

The racial background of the new ambassador and his wife was not overlooked by the island press. In a story in the *Gleaner*, Beverly's childhood in the segregated South was noted:

> Born in Summerton, South Carolina and raised in Richmond, Virginia, Beverly Cooper could not forget her father's entrepreneurial spirit when he became the first African-American to operate a "Good Humor" ice cream franchise. She also remembers vividly that he could not sell ice cream after certain hours nor in certain areas because of the segregation laws that existed in those days.
>
> Still, she says, her father had his pride—a pride that she sees in Jamaicans and which is something she and her husband relate to.[385]

The Coopers began to get a feel for the diplomatic side, how they would connect with the embassy operation and, beyond it, the island people.

"That quickly falls on you," Beverly said, "to be the representative of the president of the United States. That was a big deal. Someone said to Gary early on, 'You realize you're the biggest show in town, and Mrs. Cooper is the second biggest show.' So the respect that they had for the United State and the president of the United States—you got all of that."

With the new ambassador expected to be on the go with myriad meetings and greetings, Beverly was happily agreeable to spending part of her time back in Mobile taking care of the businesses. While in Jamaica, her marching orders were a bit different.

"On one level, we were able to talk about important matters, issues important in Jamaica," she said. "But then you would not discuss them as thoroughly as you'd like because you need to be careful you're not making a statement that could be misconstrued or misinterpreted."

Gary, of course, tended to be outspoken. A Marine general and an ambassador work different arenas.

Being an ambassador was very difficult for me because, you know, when you're an ambassador and somebody really tees you off, you need to sit down and talk about it. You know what I wanted to do. So it took me awhile. We tend to be a little more authoritarian in our leadership style in the military. Then as an ambassador you're taught to work things out.

As ambassador, Gary was diplomatic when required, certainly—but saying what he liked and didn't like was part of his constitutional makeup.

"He was outspoken," said Beverly, "but as he settled in, he was very respectful and mindful. You could see he was feeling his way in, learning this, learning that. He was very much aware of, 'Let me get the lay of the land first.'

"What he didn't have patience for was the double-speak you so often get in politics and certainly in the diplomatic corps. People would say one thing to you simply because there was another agenda.

"Gary started to move around the country. He knew how poor it was anyway, but when he saw how poor it was—the general air of neglect on the part of the politicians, the wealthy, all of that, then he took it on: 'Anything I can do to try to change this, I'm going to do it.'"

I was at a party one evening and a Jamaican parliamentarian was having a little too much to drink. He was saying unkind things about my country. This is one thing about not being a diplomat by nature. I tend to do this sometimes. I called him aside and said, "Look, Mister Minister. If you don't like my country, tell me why you've got a thousand of your people out in front of my office wanting visas every day to get the hell out of Jamaica."

You should have seen him stutter and turn red. I didn't have that many people around us, and I probably shouldn't have told him that. But I didn't put up with too much bullshit from them.

Beverly: "He became so outspoken that at one point the Jamaican prime minister, P. J. Patterson, commented when I left the island while flying back and forth to Mobile: 'Civility has left the ambassador's residence.'

"Then when I'd come back, he or the newspaper or Muddy Perkins, one of these talk radio show kind of people, they'd say, 'Mrs. Cooper has returned. Civility has returned.'"

Hush-Hush

The State Department had a week or a week and a-half orientation session for new ambassadors. There were seven or eight in the class. Some were going to Africa, some were going to other places.

In this class I met a couple of black guys who were career diplomats and they were getting briefed to go to another assignment in Africa. They said, "General Cooper, when you get to your post, you should be very, very careful." They said very often the CIA will spy on you and report your actions just like they do other people. If you ask the CIA officer if they are doing this, they are required to tell you, but if you don't ask them, they're not. Also, they can get people in the community to give them information, like undercover agents, and they're not required to tell you who they are. But they are required to say, yes or no, we do have information.

After being in Jamaica a month or two, I had not met my CIA chief, the guy who was the station head. I kept inquiring about where this guy was. It turned out he was undercover in Haiti. He was evidently a black guy who had grown up in a Haitian family or speaking Haitian Creole in New York City.

Finally, this guy comes back to the embassy and I want to see him. He comes up, he's got a beard, he looks real scraggly. I said, "Listen, you and I need to talk. I understand that if you are reporting anything on me, you don't have to tell me, but if I ask you, you're required to.

He said, "That's right, Mr. Ambassador."

I said, "Look, can't we make an agreement? So that if there's something that concerns you, as your boss, can't you just come sit down with me?"

He said, "No, sir. If you don't ask me, then I can't tell you."

And I said, "Good. I will see you here in this office every morning at six o'clock to ask you that goddam question. You understand?"

"Yes, sir."

So the next morning, he wasn't there, and I sent my Marines—I had a small detachment for security—I sent them out to his house, and they brought his ass in. The next day, again he wasn't there. I sent my Marines out again. He damn near had his pajamas on.

After that, the next Monday, he was there at six in the morning. I said, "Let me ask you, sir, is there anything you're reporting on me that I should know about?"

He said, "No sir."

So Tuesday morning he came in, said the same thing. Wednesday morning, he said, "Mister Ambassador, can you and I have a talk?"

I said, "Yeah, we can have a talk."

He agreed that maybe he could talk to me. The early morning meetings weren't necessary. And that was the end of that.

Except that a few years after I finished serving as ambassador, I'm going through the airport in Miami. I look in the corner and I see what looks like some Cuban guys, Hispanics, and they're all sitting in the corner around this black guy. I look—and it's the same guy! My CIA officer in Jamaica!

He looks at me and puts his fingers to his lips. Hush-hush.

HOUSEKEEPING

In learning the lay of the land, Cooper discovered early-on that the embassy staff took a casual approach to their assignments.

"Jamaicans and Americans were very laid-back about their jobs. There was no urgency really about doing anything, and that drove Gary crazy," Beverly said.

During the State Department orientation, listening to the two career diplomats alerted me to some of the things a new ambassador might find. I think what I found more interesting than anything was the condition of the embassy in Jamaica.

I was really disappointed in the quality of leadership that the State Department provided, because they gave no leadership training. I'd go to places in the embassy that were filthy. The place was just scroungy. I'd go to places where we stored furniture, they were filthy. The inside of refrigerators, they were filthy. I was really disappointed.

So I started leadership classes. As far as I knew, we were the only embassy, maybe in the world, that had regular leadership classes. In fact, we were written up in the State Department magazine. I had these leadership classes not only for my American leaders but for the Jamaicans, too—they were called FSNs, for Foreign Service Nationals.

The Jamaicans were thrilled because we had a large number of nationals, and we started giving them leadership classes and it was like an eye-opener.

When I visit Jamaica now and see one of them, they still remember those leadership classes.

The classes would be for fifteen or twenty people. Our total number of employees in the embassy mission was somewhere around three hundred or four hundred. We had several dozen Peace Corps volunteers, a hundred or more USAID staff, with a PhD woman from Harvard who led that. A fairly sizable staff at the embassy. We had what we called a Marine Security Detachment. They were responsible for internal security. There were only seven or eight of them.

I conducted some of the classes, but luckily I had military aides. I had an Army colonel or lieutenant colonel, maybe a Navy officer. So along with them, we conducted the leadership training. And we got the embassy cleaned up. We started having regular inspections and we started looking good. It kind of reminded me of when I was commissioner of human resources in Alabama and I used to come in and inspect—even the top of the Coke machine!"

"Gary was a stickler for all of that," Beverly said. "It was an old building, they were in an old office building, no one had cared or paid any attention."

Beverly recalled that General Colin Powell, whose parents were from Jamaica and who enjoyed star power on his visits to the island, had an amusing view of Gary's military-minded modus operandi at the embassy: "Even Colin Powell told him: 'Stop going into the office so early! You're ruining it for everybody else!'"

They were good, hard-working folks at the embassy. On the personal staff, I had a chef, two housekeepers, three gardeners. Plus a Jamaican policeman as my bodyguard and an armed Jamaican driver. In those days, I had an armored limousine. Bullet-proof tires. Bullet-proof windows. The whole bit.

When I first got there, if I went and stayed at a hotel, they'd have Army people on the outside, guarding. That's how protective they were. If I wanted to go to the grocery store or the laundry, they had a Jeep behind me with four armed Jamaican Army people. I felt so self-conscious I had them stop doing that because the places I went in Jamaica weren't too much different than the ghetto in Mobile, Alabama. I felt pretty much at home.

"A Cat Among the Pigeons"

Cooper's typically plain-spoken nature made news—and at times set off island-wide controversy—but he was never called on the carpet by Washington.

I never got a call from the State Department. No one said, "Being ambassador, you shouldn't say this. Or be careful." Not one time.

His candor first stirred up significant media heat about a year after his arrival, when he gave a speech to the Jamaica Council of Churches. His subject—using gambling revenue to better educate Jamaican children—set off a round of righteous indignation from the church, but the speech also drew praise for its frankness.

He had invited several members of the council to drop by to discuss the topic of the speech he was to give.

So they came to my office at the embassy, about five or six of them. I went on to express to them that nothing disturbed me more since I had been in Jamaica than traveling the area and seeing the horrible conditions of schools. When I say horrible, that's exactly what I mean. Blackboards that you couldn't read what was on them, the covering was falling off. Raggedy chairs. Horrible.

I asked them had they ever considered authorizing gambling? Not in the Jamaican neighborhoods, but in the tourist capitals where people from outside the country would spend their money. They said, "We would never do that. That would be using tainted money to educate our children."

I said, "Where should the money come front?"'

They told me: "We think it should come from U.S. aid."

"My taxpayers should help educate your children because you don't want to use tainted money?"

Their eyes were getting big then. They said, "Yes, yes."'

I said, "Thank you so much, and I will give my speech."

The speech to the council pulled no punches:

When I was a little boy in Alabama, I attended a small school and many of the youngsters were very poor. Our priest every week held a bingo game and with the proceeds from that bingo he bought books, paper, shoes for the children and helped educate a group of young black children who may never have been educated without this priest and the money he raised from bingo.

Could he have done it another way without those funds? Could be, but he didn't know another way. And he was not willing to see the young kids in our community miss going to school while he was trying to figure out another way.

I make no judgment on whether or not gambling should be further legalized in Jamaica. However, I share that story with you because in my research for this speech I have determined that in Jamaica as we speak there are over seven hundred betting shops in operation. There is a legal lottery. There is an illegal lottery. There are slot machines in almost every hotel and rum shop. There are blackjack machines in most of your tourist hotels. You have horse racing week at Caymanas. And you have private casinos operating in homes. So as I speak to you tonight, millions of Jamaican dollars are changing hands and almost none of this money is being used to benefit your children who are growing up illiterate and need it so much.

I know many of you disagree. You will say to accept this money to educate our children will legitimize gambling. I submit to you, better to legitimize gambling than to continue having a nation raising children who are illiterate, irresponsible and lawless.[386]

The ambassador had struck a nerve, but the Jamaica Council of Churches struck back. At a meeting called to discuss Cooper's proposal, the JCC refused to yield, sticking with its stand against all forms of gambling.

Gambling erodes the family structure, the JCC said, and many "have gambled the household income away in search of the promise of easy riches."[387]

Cooper's remarks were scorned as "a breach of protocol" by the Reverend Ralston B. Nembhard in commentary in the *Jamaica Observer*.[388] But some found Cooper's forthrightness admirable. Dr. Leachim Semaj, in a *Sunday Herald* opinion column, wrote that the US ambassador "put the cat among the pigeons. His remarks did not go down very well with the churchmen and I am happy that he has not withdrawn what in my opinion are valid observations."[389]

> As I understand it, people still quote what I said.
> Now they've got gambling in Jamaica. It's legalized in many places.
> But I think the politicians did exactly what I expected them to do. That is, give the money to their buddies and political cronies. I still don't think the tax money is going to help the children, and it's really sad.

THE *Silver Dollar*

The back-and-forth over Cooper's remarks on using gambling revenues to improve education was joined by other flare-ups—most notably a presumed breach of Jamaican sovereignty at sea by a U.S. Coast Guard detachment on a British ship.

The ship, HMS *Liverpool*, was operating in support of the regional anti-narcotics drive named "Operation Summer Storm." On the night of June 23, 1997, the HMS *Liverpool* encountered a Jamaican fishing boat, the *Silver Dollar*. Accounts differed, but the key issue was whether the *Silver Dollar* had been improperly confronted in Jamaican territorial waters or in international waters.[390]

A diplomatic contretemps ensued, with indignant reports by Jamaican officials claiming two powerful nations had "flouted" the authority of a sovereign Caribbean country by stopping and searching the *Silver Dollar*.[391]

At the time, the U.S. and Jamaica were at odds over what was known as the Shiprider Agreement. It was designed to let American ships operate anti-drug efforts in Jamaican waters. Unlike some other Caribbean nations, however, Jamaica refused to give up much of its authority over waters within the 12-mile territorial limit. The *Silver Dollar* case was the first since Jamaica had balked at the U.S.'s initial model agreement.[392]

After the *Silver Dollar* episode occurred, Jamaican Foreign Minister Seymour Mullings insisted on an apology and compensation for the fishermen. The Jamaican government also said that Cooper and British High Commissioner Richard Thomas had been "called in" by Mullings within days after the incident to hear Kingston's protest.[393]

The controversy was that the Jamaican foreign minister made the statement that he had called the U.S. ambassador in and had a serious discussion with him. They were lying. They hadn't called me in at all. Needless to say, I expressed that.

Cooper said it was not until July 8—more than two weeks after the incident at sea—that he met with Mullings and other senior Jamaican officials to discuss the *Silver Dollar*. A statement by the U.S. Embassy also blasted "provocative" claims by Jamaican officials that were full of "factual errors."

By the U.S. Embassy's account, the *Silver Dollar* "stopped of its own accord, showing no lights," and that a U.S. Coast Guard detachment sent from the HMS *Liverpool* on a boat asked the customary "right of approach" questions about the Jamaican ship's flag and if it was carrying arms. There was no attempt to board, and after determining that the *Silver Dollar* was a fishing boat requiring no assistance, the Coast Guardsmen returned to the HMS *Liverpool*.

"The entire sequence of events ... took less than 20 minutes," the embassy statement said.[394]

This was hardly the view from Kingston, and the sizzle of denunciations led to a pro-Jamaica report from the Council on Hemispheric Affairs titled "The '*Silver Dollar*' Incident: U.S.-Jamaican Relations at New Low."

It accused Cooper of being "little more than a fall guy in a complicated game being played by the U.S." to get Jamaica "to step-up its anti-drug role and cut back its growing friendship with Castro's Cuba."[395]

Despite the bluster back and forth, there was an eventual return to more normal diplomacy, although the dispute over the Shiprider Agreement was ongoing at the time.

"TAKE ME BACK TO PARADISE!"

While U.S. ambassador to Jamaica, Cooper received a visit from his old friend from Mobile, U.S. Representative Sonny Callahan, who was now chairman of the House Foreign Appropriations Subcommittee. Callahan had arrived in Kingston with a delegation and was to meet the next day in Haiti with President René Préval.[396]

The Haiti trip was one of many political path-crossings by Callahan and Cooper. It was not lost on Callahan that he and Cooper had made an interesting journey in their political life from Mobile to Montgomery to Washington and then to see each other in the Caribbean.

Callahan, who did not get a scholarship to a university like Notre Dame but took courses at the Mobile extension center of the University of Alabama, enjoyed the irony of their divergent beginnings.

"I used to kid Gary, when he was ambassador to Jamaica and I was chairman of the House Appropriations Subcommittee on Foreign Operations. I remember making a speech in Kingston, saying that Gary and I sort of grew up together in Mobile. I said we grew up in the same neighborhood, but I was a little older than he was, and we were separated and segregated, not because of race but because of wealth—his family was rich and mine was poor."[397]

On this trip, Callahan asked Cooper to ride with him to Haiti.

Callahan recalled, "From the time we got on the plane until the time we landed, he kept telling me all the problems in Jamaica, and how they needed money to fight crime and to fight drugs, all the poverty and illness."

On the ground at Port-au-Prince, Cooper got an eyeful of human destitution. Seeing Haiti up-close, his view of Jamaica changed: *I was always complaining about Jamaica but Haiti proved worse.*

"When we left Haiti," Callahan said, "we got back on the airplane and Gary said, 'Take me back to paradise!'"[398]

MICHAEL MANLEY & BARCLAY EWART

I had a chance to meet the former Jamaican prime minister, Michael Manley. He is famous for many reasons, but one is that he attempted to take Jamaica in a communist direction. He became a friend of Fidel Castro. Many people feel he set Jamaica's economy so far back that it could never recover.

Manley was the charismatic heir to the leadership of the People's National Party, which was founded by his father, Norman Manley, the island's premier when it gained independence in 1962. A democratic socialist who won two terms, Michael Manley was widely popular for his efforts to improve the lives and health of Jamaica's poor but was decried by critics as an anti-capitalist wrecker of the economy.[399]

One of his supporters, however, was a successful Jamaican businessman, Barclay Ewart, who had been Gary's classmate at Notre Dame. Ewart and Manley may have agreed on political matters, but a conflict occurred on the personal side.[400]

Michael Manley was quite a schemer—and a lover. They said you better not let him near your wife.

It happened that Ewart used to hide Michael Manley from the police. He would hide him at his house—and then Michael Manley had an affair with Barclay's wife! As it turned out, Barclay's wife divorced him and married Michael Manley.

But Barclay remarried and we were great friends.

One evening two of Barclay's girls—they were the daughters of his former wife, the one who married Manley—they were over at my house visiting when my son Patrick was there. The girls were saying what a wonderful week they had, that they had been in Cuba as guests of Fidel Castro, and they had just landed back in Jamaica a few hours ago in Fidel Castro's plane, which had flown them back from Cuba. So while Patrick was entertaining them downstairs, Beverly and I were getting dressed to go to a dinner at UWI, the University of the West Indies. Its

president had invited the U.S. ambassador and his wife to a dinner, so
Beverly and I get our driver and we go to dinner.

We sit around the table. I'm sitting next to Michael Manley, who at
that point was a former prime minister. I say, "How are you, Mister
Prime Minister?"

He says, "Oh, I'm good, Mister Ambassador. It's so good to see you."

I whisper, "Mister Prime Minister, how was your trip to Cuba?"

He said, "I never go to Cuba. I don't know what you're talking about."

And I had just talked to his wife's children who were saying they had
just gotten back on Castro's plane!

Whether he had made a trip to Cuba or not, Manley remained a friend
of Castro, close enough that Castro attended Manley's funeral in 1997.

"When Michael Manley died, we were able to see Castro up close,"
Beverly said. "There had been all this news at the time that Castro was
near death. But here he was in Jamaica for the funeral, this strong, very
erect person walking in the street. Nothing suggested that this man was
near death. He was in for the long haul."

Gary, meanwhile, remained a friend of Barclay Ewart.

Barclay was a famous track star from Jamaica. He was a sprinter
who excelled in the 100 and 200 meters and went to Notre Dame on a
track scholarship when I was there. He majored in business administra-
tion, became an engineer. When he went home to Jamaica, he became
a senator in the government. He also was a businessman who sold the
chemicals that purify water all over the Caribbean.

Barclay became a very wealthy man, and a great friend. When I was
ambassador, he would call me and say, "Be careful of this." I would call
him and get his opinion. We were great buddies.

They remained close long after Gary's tenure as ambassador had ended.
Making frequent trips to Jamaica for business and pleasure, Gary would
see Barclay often—the last time on an evening in 2012.

I took Barclay and his wife, Diedre, to dinner. This was a Friday. I
leave Saturday. His wife calls the next week and Barclay is dead. He
had gone jogging in the morning at a golf course in Saint Andrew, had
a heart attack, and died.

He stayed in shape, ran every day.

MANY RETURNS

For years after his ambassadorship, Gary returned to Jamaica regularly. This was partly to contribute to charitable causes as a member of American Friends of Jamaica. It also was partly for business—he served for a time on the board of directors of a Jamaican company, Paymaster, which was formed near the end of his term.

> *While I was ambassador, a very sharp young lady, Audrey Marks, came to see me. She had a master's degree in business from the University of the West Indies, and she was an entrepreneur. She was wondering, What was a business that would really work in Jamaica? What could a young entrepreneur do?*

> *We came up with the idea that they needed a place where they could pay their bills. The postal service was very inefficient. You could mail something and they would never see it again.*

> *So we came up with a business by the name Paymaster. It now has 150 locations in Jamaica where people go and pay all their bills, and they can send money back and forth to the United States.*

Although Cooper stepped down from the company's board, he noted his role in giving Paymaster its name.

> *The reason we used "Paymaster" is that when I was a young lieutenant, before credit cards and direct deposits, when payday came in the Marine Corps they took the youngest lieutenant and assigned him to be the "paymaster." You would go to disbursing, get a suitcase full of money, go back to your unit—you'd have a couple of guards with you—and everybody would line up and you would pay them cash.*

The company Marks founded became successful, but it also was involved in a long-running legal case after it filed a breach of contract and copyright infringement suit in 2001. At issue was whether a rival company improperly used Paymaster's business plan and software.[401]

Marks's star, meanwhile, rose in Jamaican government circles and in 2010 she was named the country's ambassador to the United States—the first female ever to hold the post.[402]

Another reason for Cooper's continuing visits to Jamaica has been for relaxation, including the pleasures of scuba diving in the incredibly clear, aquamarine waters at Port Antonio—the dive shop there was named Lady G'diver.

Finally, the island simply was a special place for him, even when that fondness was not always apparent to some Jamaicans. As Cooper's term as ambassador began winding down, he had given an interview to the *Press-Register* on a trip home to Mobile. Among his remarks, he said, "When we think of poverty and malnutrition and violence, we don't understand what it really is. There is poverty in Jamaica that would shake the toughest Americans, simply by seeing it."[403]

In Jamaica, the reaction was swift. Headlines fumed: "Ambassador's Outburst," "Think Again, Mr Cooper!" and "Gary Cooper has gone too far!"[404]

· Later at a news conference, Cooper said his comments had been taken out of context and that relations between Kingston and Washington were "warm and getting warmer."

"What I said was this island does have its problems, but I thought that everyone knew of my love for Jamaica: the beautiful island, the wonderful culture and the warm people, and particularly the children."[405]

19

Rounding Out

Cooper's children, in different ways, tracked their father's path: Shawn served in the Marines before entering business, Joli graduated from the University of Notre Dame before turning to finance, and Patrick tried his hand at politics when he returned to Alabama to practice law.

"I told Gary, 'You know, what most people don't know about you is your family," Beverly said. "That's the part people really like finding out about. All of these things about you are a little bit one-dimensional. But by the time we put all of the pieces around you, what's going on with the kids and the grandkids, that's the part that rounds you out."

PATRICK

When Patrick moved to Birmingham in 1994, with an eye toward entering the political arena, much had changed in the two decades since his Uncle Jay and father had won elections and helped lead a new era of Alabama politics.

The state's most populous city, beset by rigid segregation, officially sanctioned police brutality, and Ku Klux Klan violence in the 1950s and 1960s, had transformed into a majority-black municipality (mostly because of white flight to suburbs). It elected its first black mayor, Richard Arrington, in 1979.

The politically astute Arrington dominated city hall for twenty years. But the power of his political coalition frayed over time, and when Patrick made his first run for mayor, in 2007, he was a candidate with appeal to white voters as well as blacks.

He also had fundraising acumen and a glittering resume. After graduating from Yale Law School, he clerked in Birmingham for Judge Sam Pointer Jr., the chief federal judge for the Northern District of Alabama. He married Julia Boaz, a fellow law student at Yale who had been No. 1 in her class as an undergraduate at Columbia. Stints with two prestigious law firms followed—New York City-based Cravath, Swaine & Moore, and later McCutchen, Doyle in San Francisco.[406]

When he returned to Birmingham, he became a partner with Maynard, Cooper & Gale, a large and politically connected legal powerhouse—the Cooper in the firm's name was Lee Cooper, no relation to Patrick but soon to be president of the American Bar Association. It was at Maynard, Cooper that Patrick's interests turned increasingly to Birmingham's biggest job, the mayor's office.

Larry Hallett, a Mobile lawyer and friend of Patrick's father, saw the upside of his candidacy: "He is handsome, bright, personable and charming," Hallett told Chip Drago of *Mobile Bay Times*. "He will be able to raise a great deal of money for his campaign and will obviously have the support of the big law firms and their clients, and their clients' money. He is Alabama's answer to Obama."

But Hallett was puzzled.

"Why in the world would Patrick want to be mayor of Birmingham?"[407]

Patrick's uncle, Jay Cooper, told Drago he asked the same question.

"His response," Jay said, "was to the effect that Birmingham had been good to his children and to him and that Birmingham needed fresh energetic leadership not hidebound to the past."[408]

"I made a conscious decision to come to my home state in 1994—specifically Birmingham," Patrick told the *Birmingham News*. "Having watched the death spiral that the city has been in the last eight to 10 years, it really breaks my heart. At some point you ought to do something or shut up, so I decided to do something."[409]

By 2007 Patrick, now with three children—Sophie, Celia, and Sam—was amicably divorced from Julia, who remained a top supporter of his campaign. "He cares about this city's future and what its citizens struggle with on a daily basis," Julia told the *News*.[410]

Patrick had been active in civic affairs, serving on the city crime commission formed by Arrington in 1998, coaching and helping finance Alabama Roadrunners, a girls' basketball travel team, and founding Birmingham Vision, a nonprofit which put young people to work cleaning up neighborhoods and helping the elderly.[411]

He even tried to teach chess to community youth.

"I decided to have a program that teaches just chess to kids who live in the projects," he said. "So I go to one of the projects and have a conference room with all the chess boards and pieces set up, but there are no kids in there. They're all playing basketball. I come out a second week, none of them are in there. I can't persuade them. They want to play basketball.

"So the third week, I bring a hundred-dollar bill. I tell the kids, 'Look, here's a hundred dollar bill. If y'all can beat me in basketball—choose any four kids—if y'all can beat me in basketball, y'all can have this hundred-dollar bill and split it up however you want. But if you lose, you got to come in here and we'll play some chess.'

"They're all excited. They're all about seventh or eighth or ninth graders. I'm taller than them and I wound up beating them. They're moaning and groaning and I bring them to the chess room. Over the course of a month, I probably have fifty kids who come in every week. They had their little brothers and sisters and cousins, their little nieces. That was fun."

But the end game of the mayor's race was not as he had hoped. Despite a strong showing for a new political face, he lost to a flashy, well-known Birmingham-area personality and politician, Larry Langford.[412]

Patrick, finishing second among nine candidates with nearly 30 percent of the vote, narrowly missed forcing Langford into a runoff. But a second shot at the mayor's office opened just two years later, when Langford was convicted in a bribery and corruption case stemming from his time as president of the Jefferson County Commission.

Patrick was a candidate again: "I'm a risk taker. I said, 'Let's roll the dice and see what happens.'"

This time, Patrick emerged as the front-runner in the 2009 special election, leading with about 40 percent of the vote to second-place William Bell's 25 percent.[413] But Bell, a protege of Arrington and a political figure in Birmingham for thirty years, wasn't done. The number of voters casting ballots in the runoff surged well beyond the first vote, and Bell won with 54 percent to Patrick's 46 percent.[414]

Patrick did not get the endorsements of the major black political organizations, which can help greatly with turnout, but in retrospect he did not see that as a key.

"The reason I lost was because the white corporate community was terrified about me winning," he said. "I wasn't the type of black political official they'd ever dealt with."

Funds to pay for negative ads, he said, "didn't come from anybody black."

"They put a picture of my ex-wife on TV. Blond hair and blue eyes . . . I mean, it was a different dynamic."

With the loss, Patrick returned to his law practice and eventually moved to New Mexico, where his ex-wife had moved, and where Sam, the youngest of their children, was in school. Daughters Celia and Sophie had already gone off to college and graduate school.

Active once again in his law practice, Patrick is amused when asked what kind of law he enjoys most: "I'm suing Birmingham corporations!"

Patrick's father was supportive of his bids for mayor, but the city has not been kind to past mayors—Arrington was charged with taking a kickback, though federal authorities dropped the case, and Langford was basically sentenced to life in prison—and the ills of inner cities are as acute in Birmingham as in many other majority-black urban centers.

I tell Patrick that maybe the Lord blessed him by not winning. You never know.

JOLI

After returning to complete graduate work in business and finance at the Wharton School of the University of Pennsylvania, Joli envisioned a future in the corporate world. "My exposure to folks coming on Wharton's campus—I didn't know what brand management was, I didn't know what investment banking was, I had no idea about consulting. Going back to Wharton really broadened my horizons and professional opportunities."

At Wharton, she became president of the entrepreneurial club and received an award for her service work in the community.[415]

"Great exposure at Wharton. From a career perspective, I could not have asked for more. When I think where I am professionally now, it's definitely directly related to the guys I went to Wharton with."

Joli worked on the New York trading floor for Shearson Lehman Brothers between her first and second year at Wharton, then went to Bankers Trust when she graduated in 1988. But she was not enamored of Wall Street.

"I had worked there for a year. I said, Oh my god, there's got to be more to life than this," she recalled. "There was a bunch of elite white guys, yucking it up all day. It was just not for me. I think you have to have a passion for that industry, and I was just bored out of my gourd. I didn't particularly like the people I was working with. I didn't dislike anybody, but I just didn't feel fulfilled at all. Now my dad loved it. He loved the fact that I was on the Street. He used to call me and talk about the markets. But professionally it was just not fulfilling."

At Wharton, Joli had met her first husband, Ashley Cooke Jr., the father of her oldest child, Ashley Cooke III. The marriage didn't last, and for a time she was a single parent, raising her son while advancing as a successful corporate executive.

Her bonds with Wharton remained strong. In 2002, she received the Kathleen McDonald Distinguished Alumna Award, presented annually by the Wharton Women in Business organization.[416]

With some of her Wharton colleagues, she was a founding partner of Cordova, Smart & Williams, LLC, a New York-based private equity investment firm. Joli's base remained in Tampa, Florida, near where she had settled and where she met her second husband, Anthony Nelson.[417]

Nelson, with whom she has two children, Alana and Anthony, is from Pawley's Island, South Carolina, where family ties are close.

"Such a strong foundation," Joli said. "His people are there. Family reunions. My father's family was always very well-traveled, with the children in boarding schools. My grandmother was always traveling. It was not like we never had family reunions, but it was different."

Outside her professional career, Joli also became active in philanthropic work, including service with Jack and Jill of America, Inc. Eventually she became national president of the organization, which is dedicated to nurturing the development of African American children, with the goal of creating strong leaders of the future.

Joli's son, Ashley Cooke III, furthered the Cooper family's unique connection to Notre Dame, Gary and Joli's alma mater. When Ashley graduated in 2011, the Coopers became the first black alumni family with three generations of Notre Dame graduates.[418]

Gary, with a number of Cooper family members on hand, was beaming.

"My father thinks about it the most," Joli said, "and it was a wonderful weekend because they always have a specific ceremony for African American graduates. My dad went and, during it, unexpected by him, they acknowledged him as one of the trailblazers and asked him to stand up. He was so honored and excited. To be there for that was wonderful. The weather was great. Being back on campus, the three of us—we knew that this was kind of it. We spent time at the grotto. Notre Dame is a place you appreciate more as you get older and get away from the campus. It's hard for a twenty-one-year-old, who is just trying to get the heck on out of there, to appreciate it like someone who was there thirty years ago or fifty years ago like my father and I."

Notre Dame by then was much different racially.

"I think for the younger generation the biggest challenge is really staying in touch with your cultural center," Jolie said. "We used to have parties just for African American students. I asked my son, 'Hey, do you guys have frat parties?' And he looks at me like I have two heads. 'What are you talking about? Are you asking if we have parties based on race? No! We don't have parties based on race.'

"So times have changed. His friendships and core friends, they're just like his high school friends, they're white, they're international, their decisions are definitely not made on race."

She said that at Ashley's graduation, "we were just reveling in the serenity, the beauty, the meaning of the institution to our family in general.

"Having been a single parent for a number of years before I met my second husband, I have to say my dad did a phenomenal job in raising us. When I think of all his accomplishments, be it his success in the military or in the Legislature or as an ambassador, the differences he has made in his lifetime is the legacy he has left us and that we leave with our children. I truly believe that."

SHAWN

After her short stay in Paris as an au pair—and a month and a half in Nagoya, Japan, to stay with a friend and consider a teaching job—Shawn returned to Mobile with thoughts of joining the Marines.[419]

She liked the idea of being an airline flight attendant, too, but the Marine Corps held a special appeal. If it would be the Marines, she definitely wanted the officer route, not enlisted. At a football game with her father, upon viewing the honor guard present the colors, her dad explained that Marine officers are leaders and give orders, while enlisted Marines follow orders.

"I knew I didn't want to take orders," Shawn said. "Once he explained that to me, the officer route was the only way I wanted to go."

She was oblivious to the physical challenge that was elemental to Marine life. "I had no clue," she said. "Ignorance is bliss. I was truly Private Benjamin."

James Harrell bet her $500 that she wouldn't cut it.[420]

"What do you mean?" she said. "Dad did it. What's the big deal?"

Once again, she didn't have a clue. But at a five-year high school reunion, she learned that one of the guys in her class, Matt Sullivan, had become a Marine pilot. And here she was thinking of being a flight attendant.

"Huh?" she thought. "A pilot? For free? They taught you for free?"

Soon she made her trip to the Marine recruiting station in Mobile.

"Hey, I want to fly," she told the gunnery sergeant.

"Honey, women can't fly in my Corps," he replied.

"Because I'm a woman?" With that, she took on some of her father's attitude. "Let me tell you something, honey, " she said. "I'm going to share some knowledge with you. Let me enlighten you. What you just said, that's called sexual discrimination, and I recommend you not use that term. My dad's a Marine, and I like you. But I would just watch that."

The exchange prompted her to go next door and check out the Air Force recruiting station. But the Air Force wanted a recruit with a bachelor of science. Shawn held a bachelor of arts degree.

"The Navy's uniform contained way too much polyester," she said, "and the Army—every person in America was joining the Army, so I didn't want to do that."

Eventually she decided on the Marines, which offered public affairs as a career field. She broke the news to her father while driving him on a business trip: "'Dad, what would you think if I told you I was going to join the Marine Corps?' I swear he almost fell out of the car. I could tell he was trying to be cool about it, because he knew I wanted to be a flight attendant, too. He said, 'You know, being a Marine officer, I think that would be an outstanding career decision for you. What I can tell you is, it takes outstanding leadership skills and that no day will be the same.'"

She was soon headed to Quantico.

"They gave me a big going away party," she said. "Everybody came. So I knew damn well that whatever happened, I could not come back not being a Marine. My ego was just too big."

She made it. Commissioned at Quantico and trained at the Basic School, she earned the public affairs designation—and learned to shoot as well or better than her father.

When you go through the Basic School, you have to qualify on the firing range to wear a badge. So everybody wants to be an expert. It's quite a task. I didn't have much shooting experience, but I just worked hard and reached the "expert" level.

Shawn didn't have shooting experience from her youth, either. But at Quantico, she worked hard, too.

She tore me up. We were both experts, which is the highest level, but she was higher than I was. I shot like 221, which barely makes it—220 qualifies for expert—but she shot something like 232. She outshot her dad.

She reached the rank of captain in six years of active duty.

"It was everything Dad told me, and I would say about twenty-five times more. I feel like I am part of the largest fraternity in the world. You know, I didn't pledge anything in college, and I'm not an organized group girl, but I absolutely loved the Corps. Sometimes I look back and I go, 'Damn, I didn't realize how good I had it.' That was my first real job. If I knew what I know now, I probably would have stayed in even longer."

Her challenge was more that she was a woman in the Marines than that she was a minority. Her light brown complexion helped put a check on racial issues, but gender was another matter.

"One time we were on an exercise at Twentynine Palms [California Marine base]. They had something at the O Club and I happened to be the only woman in the club. A group of the pilots 'stack me.' Before I knew it, they had me pinned to the ground and were all piled on top of me. Needless to say, I was cussing and biting and kicking. But the bottom line was that it was inappropriate. I'm not one who is overly sensitive—I'll tell you to kiss my ass and go screw yourself in a minute."

But after being "stacked," she did invoke her father, noting that he was a Marine general, and with that, she said, "They all got up, and they were very uncomfortable. 'She's a general's daughter! She's a general's daughter!'

"Later, I told Dad. His initial response was, 'Well, you shouldn't have been in the O Club.'"

"What?" she said. "Hold on!"

It did not go well with Shawn that her father thought the Officers Club was off-limits to women officers.

"It took about a week or so," she said "and he called me back. He said, 'Shawn, you know what? I'm sorry. That was not the right response. That was inappropriate behavior by the guys.'"

In Shawn's view, the Marine Corps hierarchy tends to agree with her father's first response, that there is a double standard—women cannot do things that are allowed for men, and women can be hammered if fraternization is suspected, while superiors look the other way if a man is the aggressor.

"Of course," she said, "I didn't have that occur, and I don't know how much was because folks knew my father is a general. I don't know—my godfather is General Petersen. I like to think it's because I was a very good Marine. That's what I want to keep saying, but who knows?"

Accepted into the foreign service, Shawn left the Marines for a posting at the American embassy in Mexico City in 1992. But her Marine Corps experience had left an indelible imprint; she later became a member of the board of trustees of the Marine Corps University Foundation, a post once also held by her father.

She was with the foreign service almost three years.

"I was getting ready to pick another duty station," she said, "when I realized I needed to come back to the states to get a graduate degree—only because Patrick, Joli, and my cousin Casey Cooper had one. What more reason would you go to graduate school?"

She chose to go to Kellogg, Northwestern University's business school, in Evanston, on Chicago's North Shore. Armed with an MBA from Kellogg, diplomatic service in Mexico, and public relations work in the Marines, she became highly sought after in the equities market on Wall Street.

"When I went through my Wall Street interviews, I had more job offers because of idiots saying stupid things like, 'Oh my god you're a woman and a Marine, now all we need is a black.' 'Well, damn it, here's your lucky day. I'm the black one.' And then someone would say, 'Oh my god, what a great tan.' 'Well, it's not a tan, really I'm black.'"

She ended up with J. P. Morgan, first as a sales trader in New York, then with its equity office in Boston. But after being transferred back to New York, Shawn hit a wall.

"While I'm aggressive and have the type of attitude that fits New York, I just wasn't happy. It wasn't a fit for me. At heart, I'm a Southern girl. I like to say hello to people. I like to smile and not have folks look at you like you're crazy."

But where to go?

"I had lived in all the major cities—L.A., New York City, Boston, D.C., Chicago. Where hadn't I lived? I hadn't lived in Atlanta, and it's just a one-hour flight to Mobile."

So the choice was Atlanta.

"And I do like the South. I like the warmth, I like the fact that people smile and say, 'Hey.'"

20

Home Again

Making Mobile his home again after three years in Jamaica, Gary
began raising funds for local causes—the Franklin Primary
Health Center, a nonprofit serving the indigent in a mostly
black part of Mobile, the Boys & Girls Club, and the Dearborn Street
YMCA. He now had added leverage to raise funds: as he had anticipated,
he began serving on major corporate boards.

Service on the boards of these companies—U.S. Steel, PNC Bank,
GenCorp Inc., Protective Life—connected him with John W. Rogers Jr.,
the founder of the Chicago-based Ariel Investments mutual fund, one
of the largest minority-owned investment firms in the country.[421] Rogers
was instrumental in establishing the annual Black Corporate Directors
Conference to advance diversity in corporate America. Cooper was among
those participating.

*Rogers would bring in successful African Americans who served on
corporate boards to discuss leadership and ways to be effective in the
corporate and financial worlds. This event has really grown over about
a dozen years. In 2014, there were more than two hundred attending
the one at Laguna Beach.*

Among those on hand at Laguna Beach was *Star Wars* filmmaker
George Lucas—he is married to Mellody Hobson, the president and
board chairman of Ariel Investments. Lucas had produced the film *Red
Tails* about the Tuskegee Airmen. Rogers's father was among those WWII
fighter pilots.[422]

*I saw Lucas at the Ariel Investments event at Laguna Beach and
kidded him about* Red Tails. *I told him that he made a movie about*

those guys in air-conditioned planes, while it was the black Marines from Montford Point who were in the damn mud!

While serving on the U.S. Steel board, Cooper met Neil Armstrong. The former astronaut thought highly enough of Cooper to come to Mobile, stay at Cooper's home, and take part in a 2001 weekend fundraiser for the Franklin Primary Health Center.[423]

Armstrong preferred to keep a low profile and limit his public exposure.

I noticed that he didn't sign his notes. I asked him about it and he said that he can't sign anything anymore. As soon as he signs a note, he turns around and it's for sale on eBay.

Cooper arranged for other celebrities to be involved so the focus of the charity weekend would not be entirely on the famous astronaut.

"I have received letters from the Governor and the Mayor," Armstrong wrote Cooper in advance of the visit. "That is already plenty of exposure for me."[424]

In a later email, Armstrong firmed up his plans for a busy three-day weekend of charity events: "It looks like that will give us the opportunity of creating as many major problems as the community can stand. All the best, Neil."[425]

During the fundraising weekend, the Coopers put up Armstrong in their Palmetto Street home. Indeed, when a young grandson was visiting later and spending the night, Cooper had a treat in store for him.

"You're going to get to sleep in Neil Armstrong's bed," Gary said.

The boy was thrilled at getting to sleep in the very same bed as the great American astronaut. He was all smiles when bedtime arrived. But the next morning, when he came out of the bedroom for breakfast, he was crying uncontrollably.

"What's the matter?" Gary asked.

Amid tears, the boy replied in a stricken voice: "I peed in Neil Armstrong's bed!"[426]

ANOTHER DOOR OPENED

Cooper also became a director of the Alabama State Port Authority and continued to open doors for African Americans. One door had been firmly shut for more than a century by Mobile's Old South mindset: in 2002 he became the first black member of the venerable Country Club of Mobile,[427] which was founded in 1899 and once did not allow Gary's daughter Shawn to swim in its pool because of her color.

With Cooper's encouragement in 2005, Commonwealth Vice President Rodney Lee helped form a Mobile chapter of the Montford Point Marines and became its president.[428] To celebrate the annual Marine Corps Birthday, what better place to hold the Mobile chapter's ball than the Country Club of Mobile?

That was an event. They had never had more than three black folks out there at one time.

The national president of the Montford Point Marine Association, retired Master Gunnery Sergeant Joe Geeter, flew in to attend the event, as did Lieutenant General Frank Petersen, who was the guest speaker. Geeter presented the Mobile Chapter charter to Lee—with five original Montford Pointers on hand.[429] The august old country club had never experienced anything like it.

Cooper and Lee also worked with the mostly white P. L. Wilson Detachment of the Marine Corps League to foster racial unity among Marines in the Mobile area. Vietnam veteran Joe Fell, a white Marine who sought more black participation in the Wilson Detachment, also attended meetings of Lee's Montford Point Marine chapter.

"I'm encouraged about the future of the two groups," Lee told *Press-Register* reporter George Werneth. "Mobile and Baldwin counties have the largest concentration of former Marines in the state of Alabama. Because of these two organizations, both former and active-duty Marines will always have a place to call home."[430]

"Someone Who Speaks Our Language"

Long after his service as ambassador to Jamaica, getting calls and communications about military and diplomatic matters was not unusual for Cooper. But a call he received from Jim McGee was decidedly different.

When I was ambassador to Jamaica, McGee was a career State Department guy who worked with the embassy. Years later I got an invitation from him to come to Washington because he had been appointed the U.S. ambassador to Zimbabwe.

So I got a call from Jim one day in 2008. He's now the ambassador. He says, "Sir, I've been talking to the staff here in Zimbabwe and we need your help. We think that with your military background you may be able to help us out of this international crisis."

Tensions had been rising in the country. Robert Mugabe, the strongman who had been president since Zimbabwe gained independence from Britain in 1980, seemed to be losing his grip on power as new elections approached. McGee, a decorated Vietnam War veteran, was outspoken in criticizing political violence by the Mugabe regime against its opponents. The ambassador's convoy had been stopped by police and threatened.[431]

Jim says that as a Marine general I might have some influence. I ask, "What do you want me to do?"

He says, "The only reason Mugabe is still in office is because he has the support of his army. We'd like you to come to Zimbabwe and talk to the generals."

"You send me an email," I say, "but in the email I want to see how you're going to guarantee that I get my ass back home."

In an email to Cooper in July, McGee said he had been in Washington the past two weeks for consultations. Those meetings had included talks with Secretary of State Condoleezza Rice and Assistant Secretary Jendayi Frazer, who specialized in African affairs.

In those talks, McGee said, it was felt that the situation in Zimbabwe would be well served if a senior military person from the U.S. could meet with major players on the political scene in the African country. McGee said these officials asked for "someone who speaks our language" and that Rice had approved "my approaching you to find if you would be interested in helping in this time sensitive issue. I know how busy you are, but I could think of no better person to deliver our message to these people than you. I hope we can work something out."[432]

The email did not provide any details on Cooper's overriding personal concern—"how you're going to guarantee that I get my ass back home."

I told Jim, "You will not see me in Zimbabwe."

SMART FIGHTS

As a young Marine officer, Cooper had laid out keys for a successful future career. Most remained unchanged in his later years. One of them, spelled out for the magazine of the National Naval Officers Association, had long been part of his personal protocol: "Keep Up Appearances."

Even at 69 I strive to visit the gym daily. It's a struggle because of my travel schedule, but it's a worthwhile one. A sharp physical appearance is a much-overlooked key to success. People downplay this, but it's important whether you're serving as a military or a corporate officer. And nothing bothers me more than seeing an officer look anything less than sharp while in uniform.[433]

Also, Cooper said, learn from the best, those who have been successes.

I knew early that I wanted to be a general, so I set about early doing what I needed to become one. Many people think that African Americans didn't have many role models back then. In many respects that was true, but if you think about it, we really did have a lot of role models. I made a habit to read the bios of generals, and I read the chest of any general I came in contact with. That way I could see what jobs they had done and where they had been. I knew, for instance, that if I wanted to be a general I would have to serve in combat. That's why I pushed so hard for command while I was in Vietnam."[434]

Another key, expressed in an interview, was to pick "smart fights." For blacks, this has long been a dilemma when faced with injustices—when do you hit back?

One thing that is clear to me is that you're going to make a lot more progress if you pick smart fights. If I saw a fight, that might be a wonderful fight, the cause might be the best in the world, but if I couldn't win, or even make a big dent, why make people pissed off at you by fighting?

In the Marine Corps, I started off as a deputy commanding general at Parris Island. The general—he was a nice guy, didn't mean a harm in the world—but he said to me one day, "You know, Cooper, you're not like most black folks. You're really different."

Now ordinarily that would piss you off. But this is the general who

*would write my goddam fitness report next month. Why be stupid and
say, "I don't like that."*

I said, "Thank you, sir."

*Like I always tell the youngsters, "Don't bitch when you're a captain.
Wait till you're a major or a colonel, because otherwise you'll never get
to be one."*[435]

AT ODDS WITH USA

One fight he picked got mixed results.

In 2007, he resigned from the University of South Alabama's capital
fundraising campaign, making front-page news. Among several deficiencies at USA, he said, was a dearth of tenured black professors and
upper-level administrators.[436]

University officials countered that any underrepresentation of blacks
mirrored a nationwide problem. They also noted that Cooper's resignation letter was sent two months after the university withdrew a $1 million
certificate of deposit it had kept at Commonwealth National Bank for
several years before investing it elsewhere.[437]

*I go to the first meeting of the fundraising committee and here's a
roomful of folks. Probably fifty or sixty and they've got three black folks.
At the same time—and I've got to admit this is one of my motivations—
they had closed an account with Commonwealth Bank.*

*They had like a million-dollar CD. I thought it was time for me to
raise some hell. At that time they did not have one tenured black professor, not one. Any other way you measured, they had fallen.*

*So I had a press conference and I resigned. Of course they say I
resigned because they canceled their account.*

University officials said the $1 million was placed in a commercial
paper investment that provided a 5.3 percent return, higher than Commonwealth's best offer of 4.5 percent.[438] Cooper didn't make the issue
public at the time, but he said later the university had moved the money
to a Mississippi bank, an added blow to local and Alabama financial
interests.[439]

The *Press-Register*, in an editorial, took the position that "both parties have erred in this matter." The paper said that by virtue of his stature in the community, Cooper's allegations could be damaging to the university's important first fundraising campaign. But it also said the school should have continued its goodwill gesture with the minority bank, since USA stood to gain only about $8,000 by pulling the CD.[440]

Cooper was just as outspoken over the failure of blacks to support their own economic best interests: *I have lived in developing countries that looked better than what I see when I drive down St. Stephens Road, but we have gotten so used to seeing it, it looks normal to us.*

He deplored the reluctance of blacks to spend money in black-owned businesses or save it in banks like Commonwealth, driving past its branches to leave their money with huge regional banks run mostly by whites.

I hope as we go along we can get our consumer educated to say, "Why don't you bank where your child can be president one day?" For now, though, the problem persists. I think it's a lack of trust, believing that their ice is colder than ours.[441]

EQUITY IN AMERICA

Cooper, after service as ambassador, began receiving a string of honors, including the Port City's "Patriot of the Year" award in 1999. Two years later, Birmingham chose him for its prestigious annual Veterans Day award—past winners included Army General Omar Bradley, Navy Admiral Hyman Rickover, Marine Commandant General Carl Mundy and—as Cooper noted on the occasion—"my friend Neil Armstrong."[442]

But when Mayor Bernard Kincade failed to show at the Veterans Day Dinner, Cooper's short thank-you note for receiving the key to the city concluded:

Like many veterans in your City, I was disappointed that you were unable to attend this affair for the second straight year. Hopefully, next year your schedule will permit you to join us and pay tribute to those who sacrificed so much to ensure that you and I enjoy the benefits and freedoms of this great Democracy.[443]

His speech on the day of the award closed with poignance:

> Lastly, we must remind our young people that freedom is like a bank
> account. You cannot continue to draw on it without making a deposit.
> The veterans that we honor today have made their deposits. They have
> purchased equity in America.[444]

MOONWALK MELODIES

Eventually Gary's service on major corporate boards came to an end,
but the friendships remained. These included Neil Armstrong. Gary
and Beverly had put on a birthday party for Armstrong on his visit to
Mobile for the charity fundraiser, when he stayed at their house. It had
been memorable.

"The police officers who knew he was at our house could not stop
coming by to make sure he was okay," Beverly said.

A neighborhood child wanted to come by, too.

*A young kid down the street, little black kid, wanted Neil Armstrong's
autograph, because he knew he was staying at my house. I told him Neil
did not do autographs, but if the boy was there at about three o'clock
on Sunday, we'd be walking out to go to the airport and the kid could
take a picture.*

*So he got there a few minutes late. Beverly, Neil and I were in the
living room, and the kid stuck his head in the room and said, "General
Cooper. Is 'Louie' Armstrong still here?"*

*Beverly and I went to Neil's eightieth birthday party in Cincinnati and
he told that story. People literally fell out of their chairs. "Louie" Armstrong!*

"We got the invitation to the birthday party," Beverly said, "and Carol,
Neil's wife, was making sure we knew all the people who were coming and
how special it was. We weren't going to miss it. We got there and checked
into the hotel and went over to the country club that they belonged to.
Neil comes in and he's walking around. When he saw me—I told Gary
this is a picture you should have had—Neil just walked over and grabbed
my head and we just kissed, he was so pleased that we were there and a
part of the group.

"All of these folks were coming in and you would hear someone say, 'Oh, that's Buzz Aldrin.' 'Oh, that's John Glenn.' Pick any of that group, the pioneers of space, these guys were there. They told great stories. They were joking. John Glenn was joking about Neil being the first man to walk on the moon. He said it was because Neil made sure he was sitting nearest the door. "

Gary gave some remarks, too.

I told them the story of the little boy asking Neil, "Did you fly your spaceship to Alabama?" And then the kid said, "Show us how you walked on the moon." And Neil walked around, doing, I guess, a moonwalk.

I also told them the story about the grandson who cried over peeing in Neil Armstrong's bed.

But the point I made was, speaking to his character, Neil Armstrong gave to others selflessly. On that visit to Mobile, when time came I took him to the airport, and I said, "Neil, listen, I promised that I would reimburse you for first class. How much is it?" He said, "Gary, listen to me. Just seeing the faces of those beautiful children was worth it all. I will accept no reimbursement. "

"I was loving every bit of it," Beverly said. "We had met Neil's children and they all told stories about growing up. Neil apparently had always been very much there for his family, but a very private individual. He was always very private, so what does he decide to do at his birthday party that was put together by his wife? He played the piano. Broadway tunes. It was something he loved dearly, and apparently he had done this in school, too. So Neil gets up and goes to the piano. Apparently the little orchestra combo at the party was ready for this, and he starts singing love songs to Carol. You name it. Pick any Broadway show tune, Jerome Kern, any of those. He did this. And she's sitting there just, 'Oh, no, I do not believe he's doing this.' She blushes like crazy.

"Then other people started singing. It was wonderful. He got up and everybody just clapped. I think for a lot of them, like us, we didn't know he was a piano player. And singing—pretty respectable, too. That night was really something."

21

Capital Times

Mobile had been the Cooper family's home base from the start and remained Gary's address of choice over the years. But the children of A. J. and Gladys in adulthood began gravitating to Washington, D.C. The nation's capital seemed for some—Peggy, Mario, Jay—the most natural and suitable setting for their large ambitions and talents.

Gary's service in the Marine Corps and as assistant Air Force secretary had also made D.C. a site he frequented and the locale where he met Beverly. And while the second-oldest brother, Billy, had died, his son, Casey, found the capital to be a natural fit for his law career.

Even Dominic, after graduating from Saint Mary's, followed her sister Peggy to George Washington University. But she did not share her siblings' feel for the capital's political allure. "For Peggy, Mario and Jay—Washington really became their city. I was different. Jay and Peggy knew what they wanted to be and they were like lawyers when they were ten years old. They had a lot of determination. They were like that. I wasn't. Everywhere I went, I was Gary's sister, or A. J.'s daughter, or Peggy's sister, or Jay's sister. You know, a pain in the butt!" she laughed. [445]

But Dominic, who majored in dance and enjoys artistic pursuits such as felting, has affection and gratitude for those who put her family on its determined, eventful course. The affection flows both ways. Her brother Jay, in a short profile for a lawyer's association, noted the remarkable achievements of Gary, Mario, and Peggy, and added that Dominic of all the siblings at that time had "the most important, rewarding and difficult job; she teaches kindergarten students." [446]

Dominic includes her parents and Great Aunt Pearl Madison among the sources of her generation's sense of mission. "Part of Shug being so serious, I think she was modeling, showing us by example that we need to be serious and do good things. That's what my dad did. He didn't just live life and go party. You had to give back. You could do something for other people and for yourself. You had to do well—my mother encouraged us, too—this was a serious thing."

TO REMEDY RACISM

After leaving Prichard, Jay spent a busy two decades in Washington in the practice of law. He was on the staff of Housing and Urban Development Secretary Moon Landrieu and chief of staff and tax counsel to U.S. Rep. Harold Ford Sr. of Tennessee, among several posts, before he left the Hill in 1988 to became a partner in the well-connected law firm of Ginsburg, Feldman and Bress. Meanwhile, he was the father of three—Lauren, Jay III and Benjamin—and a mentor to others.[447]

Eventually Jay returned to the Mobile area, settling across the bay in Fairhope. He married BJ Cooper, an artist active in environmental protection and community projects, as well as the local arts scene that flourishes along the Eastern Shore of Mobile Bay.

Once back in Alabama, Jay rekindled his enthusiasm for campaign politics, running in 2007 for a state senate seat as a Democrat in a heavily Republican district. He was defeated by the Republican, but it was clear the causes he championed as a young man remained close to his heart.[448]

As founder of the Black American Law Students Association at NYU in 1968, Jay had seen it grow impressively over the decades into a truly national organization. In time it was renamed the National Black Law Students Association, with some two hundred chapters and several thousand members in the law schools of forty-eight states and Puerto Rico.[449] At its fortieth anniversary convention, in Detroit, Jay reflected on its formation and its future:

> We organized at NYU during the halcyon days of the late '60s, in the midst of riots, and our mission was contemplated, debated, discussed,

agreed upon, refined and re-refined as only law students can do. But finally we decided that our mission was to articulate and promote professional needs and goals of African American law students . . . to initiate a change within the legal system that would make it more responsive to the needs of the African American community.

Those promises, he said, still await fulfillment.

We would not have the people we have here tonight if there wasn't a need. If BALSA wasn't a bridge over troubled waters for black law students, they would not be here. We have more black mayors than we have black partners in law firms. BALSA was founded in large measure to remedy racism, and the reasons are as compelling today as they were then."[450]

"A Legacy and a Purpose"

As the Duke Ellington School grew in its first decades, Peggy's role in the nation's capital and in its cultural life grew as well. This included regular appearances as an arts critic on WETA-TV's "Around Town," a program for which she won another Emmy award.[451]

Her knowledge in the arts and cultural worlds was so highly regarded that she was chosen to serve on boards with national impact, including the Pratt Institute in New York, PEN/Faulkner, the W. E. B. Du Bois Institute at Harvard, the Whitney Museum Painting and Sculpture Committee, and the American Association of Museums' national advisory committee on education.[452]

President Bill Clinton appointed her vice chairperson of the President's Committee on the Arts and Humanities. She also began service that year on a Smithsonian Institution panel seeking to bring more cultural diversity to the museum.[453]

Peggy had married prominent real estate developer Conrad Cafritz, whose father, Morris Cafritz, had built a far-flung empire of properties across the Washington landscape, and whose mother, Gwen, had reached social royalty of the first order. Conrad and Peggy shared an affinity for the capital's political and social culture.[454] Within a few years, the two built a spacious and architecturally appealing mansion in the leafy Kent neighborhood of northwest Washington. The home served partly as an A-list political salon, but it was an elegant venue for a range of events, and its door was open to young people, no matter their status in life.[455]

Peggy continued to extend her hand to those at the lower end of the economic and social ladder, from foster children to Duke Ellington students and artists struggling to make a name and a career. Peggy, as Rachel L. Swarns wrote in the *New York Times*, "has long considered herself a bridge between the haves and have-notes in a city still polarized by race and class."[456]

Peggy also had begun seriously collecting the works of African and African American artists. The pieces she chose—paintings, assemblages, sculpture, photographs, mixed-media—reflected an eclectic vision, but invariably they were created by artists whose reputations would grow. "Her collection of some three hundred works, one of the largest of its kind, comprised a lengthy roster of many of today's most compelling artists," wrote Stephanie Cash for *Art in America*.[457]

The collection added visual splendor to the broad comfort of the grand house. "It was fabulous without being ostentatious," said Pam Horowitz, wife of civil rights leader Julian Bond, a couple invited to events in the home.[458]

Peggy had two sons with Cafritz—Zachary and Cooper—and became guardian, foster parent, godmother, mentor or simply life-saver for scores of others.[459]

While Peggy's marriage to Conrad came to an end with a divorce in 1998, she increased her focus on civic affairs and the education of children. She won election as president of the District of Columbia's board of education in 2000 and was re-elected in 2002.[460] In winning her first term, she pledged to tackle the district's many problems "by focusing on what I call the '3 A's': Academics for every child's mind; Athletics for every child's body; and the Arts for every child's soul."[461]

When Ellington School co-founder Mike Malone died in 2006, as Peggy was finishing her tenure as D.C. school board president, she reflected on his—their—singular achievement with the Ellington project:

> He left a school with a legacy and a purpose to continually fill the
> ranks of America's artists with highly trained African American artists.
> I don't think that goal exists anywhere else in high schools or colleges.[462]

Cathleen Medwick, who visited Peggy's home in 2009 for an article
in O, *The Oprah Magazine*, found her demeanor still one with a no-
nonsense edge:

> She is a handsome, some would say formidable, silver-haired woman
> whose manner is slightly formal, though in an offbeat way. . . . Some-
> thing in her face suggests a sense of humor, but also limited patience
> with foolishness.

Medwick was there to write a piece, "Art House: Supporting Talented
Young Artists of Color," that paid homage to Peggy's role as a virtual godmother to a new generation of African American artists. It also focused
on the home's display of 19th and 20th century African and African
American art. The article included an on-line version with a sumptuous
tour of rooms filled with eye-catching works.[463]

Not long after, Medwick's article became a valediction to a lost world.
On July 29, 2009, a raging fire consumed the huge house on a verdant hill
and all of its contents, not least the truly priceless collection that Peggy
had acquired and displayed as a testament to the achievements of artists
of color.

David Montgomery and DeNeen L. Brown reported in the *Washington
Post* on the fire:

> A neighborhood lost its signature architectural landmark, styled like
> a summer manse with its gables, columns and big, welcoming porch. A
> city lost one of its more memorable artistic, political and social salons—a
> vital interracial crossroads where problem-solvers and creators could
> mingle and brainstorm.[464]

"It was her dream home," said her nephew, Casey Cooper, then a lawyer in Washington, later a federal judge. "It was a real gathering place for her large and close circle of friends."[465]

Peggy was away at the time, vacationing on Martha's Vineyard, and no one was in the house when it was engulfed in flames.[466]

That was a miracle. The house was always full of young people. I would go up, I would take a couple of kids from Mobile and stay in Peggy's house, and every room in the house would be filled with young teenagers.

Investigators determined that the fire began accidentally, possibly set off by oil rags in a trash bag on the porch. That small fire grew into a spectacular blaze when arriving firefighters were unable to get sufficient water pressure from hydrants to put out the flames.[467]

With many millions of dollars of property at issue, litigation sought to recover Peggy's losses financially—Gary's son Patrick helped oversee his aunt's legal case—but there would be no offset to her losses emotionally, at least not through courts.[468]

Early on, she realized there was no way to replicate the collection.

"I will continue to collect," she said a few months after the fire. "I'll just have to start looking for new, younger artists."[469]

During Medwick's visit to the home, Peggy made a comment that echoed poignantly afterward:

I feel guilty if I'm not civically engaged. I was always taught that each generation has a responsibility to bring people along who are not as favored by virtue of birth. I don't know what my next phase is, but I can assure you my bond with art will never be severed.[470]

It wasn't.

With impressive resilience, she began creating a new collection in a very different setting. Instead of the spaciousness of the sprawling mansion set back on a wooded hill, she chose a tighter, more vertical urban space at Dupont Circle. Purchased in 2011, she soon turned its rooms and rising walls into modern salons of arresting contemporary art. Featured in a *New*

York Times piece four years after the fire, the home and collection were described by Penelope Green as "eye-popping, lovely and provocative."[471]

Thelma Golden, director of the Studio Museum in Harlem, told Green that Peggy had admirably not tried to duplicate the invaluable work lost in the fire. Instead, Golden said, Peggy had continued in her original spirit: "collecting work that she loves, championing young artists and embracing the pioneering work being made by diverse artists from around the world."[472]

AN UNASSUMING HERO

The youngest Cooper, Mario began to put his roots down in Washington after he graduated from Middlebury College and took a post with the Jimmy Carter team, working as an advance man for the new president. It was mostly a diversion before he set about to get a law degree, from Georgetown Law School. Unlike Jay and Gary, he had no interest in being a political candidate himself.

"I think I was probably reacting to my older brothers' influence, their almost graphic need to assume power and be the focus. That was just not me," he said.[473]

Armed with a law degree, the job he got was not in law, strictly speaking, but as a lobbyist with a huge corporate law powerhouse—Finley, Kumble, Wagner, for short—which got so big it imploded into bankruptcy. The job was a money-maker but also an eye-opener for Mario: It showed ways to work on issues close to his heart rather than to work just for candidates.[474]

And he connected with Ron Brown through his childhood friend from Mobile, Alexis Herman. "Her mother taught me reading," Mario said. "I was always in touch with her one way or the other, as if I were her little brother."[475]

Herman and Brown had been active in Democratic Party politics in the 1980s, and they were keen to find ways for their party to rebound after the GOP rise under Ronald Reagan. Mario was brought aboard at the DNC in advance of the 1992 convention. Brown needed a cool, competent assistant. "So I quit my law job and became his deputy chief of staff," Mario said. "The focus was on putting the whole convention together."[476]

"Mario was well-spoken and comfortable in the fraternal culture of national Democratic politics," author Jacob Levenson wrote. "And he was that rare political junkie who wasn't driven by ego or a thirst for fame."[477]

He did gain notice, however. A December 1991 profile in *New York* magazine by Michele Willens was titled "The Other Mario."

As opposed to New York Governor Mario Cuomo, she wrote, this Mario "may be the city's most important Democrat through July 1992"—when he would oversee the Democratic National Convention at Madison Square Garden. Cooper was "37, handsome and serene," and he helped make the nominating convention of William Jefferson Clinton a smooth, upbeat occasion for the party, delegates, and the viewing public.[478]

Mario, along with DNC Chairman Brown, and Deputy Chairwoman Herman, formed what Levenson called "the first black team to orchestrate a presidential convention."[479]

It was heady stuff. After the convention, however, Mario did not join the Clinton campaign or seek out a post in the new administration. His interest had increasingly focused on AIDS and the HIV crisis that had emerged in the 1980s as a health catastrophe in the gay community. As a gay man, he had experienced its impact personally. "I thought something was up because I had buried two friends," he said. "And I found out what was up was up, and that was enough to change behaviors."[480]

Mario's personal struggle with the disease and his fight to get HIV/AIDS care and information to black America is detailed in Levenson's indispensable book, *The Secret Epidemic: The Story of AIDS and Black America*, which is the chief source of information on this phase of Mario's life. For Mario, the objective was to stop a devastating health epidemic that was hitting African Americans far harder than other ethnic groups.

Mario was HIV-negative when he joined Ron Brown's staff to prepare for the 1992 convention. But in the summer of 1993, he was struck with fever and agonizing sweats over a period of days. Tested for HIV, the lab results came back positive. He did not try to hide his condition. He told his family and members of the AIDS Action Council board, which in December elected him chairman—the first black and first openly HIV-positive person to serve in that position. [481]

But from the start, Mario saw an uphill battle for African Americans.

"I remember the tension in the room when I disclosed my own HIV-positive status to leaders I had respected and worked with," he wrote years later for *The Body* online magazine. "I left more than one meeting with tears in my eyes. It was a reality check about what African Americans with HIV were up against."[482]

As the impact of the epidemic took an increasingly disproportionate toll on blacks, Cooper urged that funding formulas to fight the disease and help the infected be changed. It turned into a political battle full of frustrations and disappointments for Mario.[483]

In one instance, he lost the support of a key member of the AIDS Action Council Board who argued that his funding formula would hurt those it was designed to help, including people of color. Mario shot back, saying that "as an African American, HIV-positive person, who grew up in the South, and whose family spent decades in the battle for civil rights, I know racism when I see it. Your attempt to inject that issue into this debate is both mistaken and misguided."[484]

He did not seek reelection as chair of the council, and he felt distress when President Clinton—heading into a reelection campaign year—avoided talk about a needle-exchange program that had been shown to reduce HIV transmission rates among drug users and addicts. "How can they have an AIDS policy with any integrity without advocating and implementing needle exchange?" Cooper told *POZ* magazine, a resource for those affected by HIV/AIDS.[485]

In that atmosphere, Mario sought to bring black leadership to the crisis by founding the Leading for Life organization. Its objective was to increase black political involvement on AIDS issues, including roles for prominent civil rights figures.

A board member of the Harvard AIDS Institute, Mario contacted black author and Harvard professor Henry Louis Gates Jr., who arranged for the conference to be cosponsored through Harvard's W. E. B. Du Bois Institute for Afro-American Research.

Through his DNC work and organizational skills, Mario had an impressive stable of contacts. When the conference was held at Harvard on October 22, 1996, about fifty people attended, including Dr. David Satcher, the black director of the Centers for Disease Control, and Dr. Eric Goosby, the black physician in charge of HIV/AIDS with Health and Human Services. Gates's address was to the point: "In part because of the traditional homophobic tendency in our culture, in part because of ignorant stereotypes of HIV and AIDS, our people, our leaders, our culture have long been in denial about AIDS in the black community."[486]

Mario reflected years later on the moment: "The tears in my eyes *that* day were tears of hope."[487]

The next year, however, Mario's bid to gain traction with the black political leadership seemed to go off the rails. He drew the ire of key leaders of the Black Congressional Caucus. But while Mario had perhaps hurt himself with an ally, he persisted. At his behest, NAACP Chairman Julian Bond told the organization's July assembly that AIDS had clearly become "a black epidemic."[488] And due to the work of many black leaders and officials, wheels also were turning in the Clinton administration.

Mario already had become upbeat over news that antiviral drugs, including protease inhibitors, were shown to reduce HIV. Instead of easing his workload to preserve his health, Mario now felt he might resume his professional career "to accommodate what may be an extended life."[489]

More good news came from Washington as President Clinton, in his second term, committed to providing $156 million for programs to fight the spread of AIDS among blacks and other minorities. But Mario's feelings were mixed and complex, as Levenson noted. Mario told the *Washington Post* that the money will help but is "really only chump change for what is going to be needed for this horrible disease."[490]

As years passed, Mario remained watchful. When the numbers still were grim for those of color, he urged a new, more aggressive approach, something like ACT UP, the acronym for AIDS Coalition To Unleash Power. In 2006, Mario wrote a piece for the *Body* magazine with the title: "Get Your Black Up!"

"Forget money, meds and media," he wrote. "What we need most is an African American ACT UP."

He had been hopeful, he said, when Leading for Life kicked off in

1996. "But I look at where we are in 2006 compared to where we were a decade ago, and it's as if we're in the same place—and that is heartbreaking. It's not that we haven't made progress. It's that the virus has made so much more."[491]

Looking back on his fight with the system years later, Mario found the experience positive, even his conflicted time with the AIDS Action Council.

"I have a great sense of accomplishment," he said. "Although my major initiatives didn't pass the council's board, it was enlightening, seeing positions you take that later become absolute fact. I was certainly being part of the elite intellectually and on policy, the important issues."[492]

Suffering from severe depression and a long fight against HIV-related health crises, Mario died on May 29, 2015. He was 61, and by then he was mostly off the radar of younger HIV activists. But among those who had known him and joined him in the fight when the AIDS epidemic first drew alarm, he was remembered as an unassuming hero.

"He was innately modest and humble, preferring the behind-the-scenes role he played so perfectly," his friend Sean Strub, executive director of the Sero Project, wrote in remembrance. "But in the 1980s and 1990s, Mario was an extremely important link between grassroots AIDS activists and both the Democratic political establishment and many of the most important African American leaders in the U.S."[493]

That was evident as Alexis Herman gave remarks at a memorial service Peggy arranged for Mario's friends at her Dupont Circle home, and Presidents Jimmy Carter and Bill Clinton wrote letters of condolence.[494]

A GIFT

As Matt Metcalfe had said, William Madison Cooper was "reserved and carried himself well," displaying "the countenance and the stature and class that they all showed. Billy seemed to have that, too."

Metcalfe's description of Billy is echoed by many others, often with the added note that he was tall, handsome, gifted, the kind of man who would attract the lovely, accomplished Paulette Reid of Selma.

Billy had been a dutiful son. He was the first of the Cooper children to be sent out of state as a teenager after the family was rocked by his expulsion from all-white McGill High by the Catholic bishop. He followed Gary and graduated from the University of Notre Dame. He came home to take up the family business with his dad, to marry Paulette, and to have a son—Christopher Reid "Casey" Cooper.[495]

"Billy was so brilliant and so talented," said Dominic.

But his life, like those of his siblings, was changed with his father's death, and in time he and Paulette divorced. He died in Florida in 1987.

At the time, it was already clear that his son, Casey, was on a trajectory toward a life of accomplishment. He was a standout student at Yale, where he would graduate summa cum laude the next year and become a member of the national honor society, Phi Beta Kappa.[496]

"I think with everybody there is tragedy, but out of that tragedy came Casey," Dominic said. "So that's really a gift. Out of everything there comes a gift."

Casey was elected president of the Stanford Law Review and was busy with many extracurricular pursuits, including a summer internship with the NAACP Legal Defense and Education Fund in Washington. He also was political chair for the law school's Black Law Students Association— a part of the organization founded by his uncle, Jay Cooper, at NYU a quarter-century earlier.[497]

With a law degree from Stanford, Casey landed a coveted clerkship with Abner Mikva, chief judge of the U.S. Circuit Court of Appeals in Washington, D.C. Then he worked in the Justice Department before joining the D.C. law firm Miller Cassidy.[498] In 1999, he married Amy Jeffress, a Justice Department prosecutor who had earned a law degree at Yale after graduating magna cum laude from Williams College and being elected, like Casey, to Phi Beta Kappa.[499] Her father, William Jeffress, was well known as a top white-collar defense attorney and a partner at Miller Cassidy.[500]

At the time of the marriage, Casey's mother, Paulette Cooper, had returned to Mobile from Florida and was serving as executive vice president of the Christian Benevolent Funeral Home.[501] She died of illness at Casey's home in Washington in 2002, but her survivors included two grandsons—Lincoln and Leo Cooper.[502]

In 2006, Casey was picked by *Washingtonian* magazine as one of its "40 Lawyers Under 40" making names for themselves in the nation's capital.[503] By then a partner in the law firm, which had become Baker Botts, he served on President-elect Barack Obama's transition team in 2008, overseeing Justice Department issues. Five years later, he was nominated by President Obama to be a federal district judge in Washington.[504]

With his nomination confirmed by the Senate, Casey's investiture was July 11, 2014. Mikva echoed others in describing Cooper's disposition: "I don't think I ever heard Casey lose his temper or raise his voice."[505]

In the ceremonial courtroom on the sixth floor of the U.S. Courthouse on Constitution Avenue, Casey took the oath with his wife and sons at his side—a joyous Cooper family event with Billy's siblings among three generations on hand.

"HE LOVED SERVING THE PEOPLE"

It was not five months after the investiture that the family's joy turned to grief with the sudden death of Jay's son and namesake, Algernon Johnson "Jay" Cooper III. Just 34, an energetic young community organizer and activist with hopes for a political future, he collapsed and died December 3, 2014, at his mother's home in D.C. after experiencing chest pain and dizziness.[506]

He had much of the Cooper family's trademark drive and dynamism—even in high school and college he gained notice as host of Black Entertainment Television's *Teen Summit* program. After serving in the Marines and graduating from the University of Maryland, he worked as policy director for the D.C. Campaign to Prevent Teen Pregnancy. At the time of his death, he was seeking to provide healthy food and employment for low-income D.C. residents through an urban farming program, Freedom Farms.[507]

Just weeks before his death he announced plans to seek a seat on the D.C. Council, and family members said he had recently become engaged to be married to a high school sweetheart, Ryan Palmer. She was described on social media as his best friend and "co-pilot."[508]

A website carrying on his mission noted his commitment to "voter registration drives, coat drives, community clean-ups" along with a project he launched the year before on his birthday, August 17.

"My only birthday wish," he had written, "is that you do something kind for someone today. It can be a small thing or a big thing as long as it spreads joy. Let's make the world a better place one act of kindness at a time."[509]

"He loved the city, and he loved serving the people in the city, from the elderly to the young," his aunt, Peggy Cooper Cafritz, told the *Post*. "Jay was just on the verge of bursting forth."[510]

22

Looking Ahead

During his years at the Alabama Statehouse, Cooper spoke out in support of black women gaining political clout in government at all levels. In his later years, he expressed similar sentiments in the world of Marine officers.

When we talk about the racial challenge in the Marine Corps, we have an area that is disappointing, and that's in bringing black women into the officer ranks.

I have two young men that I took to Washington with me in 2009. These were young teenagers—these are boys who don't have dads—and I took them to Washington to see the Marine Corps parade. After that, we went to the Marine Corps Museum, which is right down the road, and I didn't know it, but the Corps was commissioning new officers. I look over and I see this black woman, with maybe her sister and her daddy, and I notice she's got the Marine uniform on but no bars on her shoulder.

I went over and asked, "Are you a new lieutenant?"'

"Yes, sir."

"Where are your bars?"

"Sir, I don't have anyone senior to pin my bars on."

Whoever was in charge had not made sure that this young officer had someone assigned to her. I said, "Ma'am, I'm a major general. May I have the honor of putting on your bars?"

"Yes, sir!"

Gary was distressed that this black woman—*a management trainee for*

Walmart, smart as she could be—had been treated poorly after entering the Marine Corps officers school.

They gave this little lady hell. They put her in a platoon with thirty-two men—thirty-two men and her. It didn't appear to me and all the folks I talked to, and that included active-duty generals, that her superiors had any interest in seeing this girl through. They didn't treat her the right way.

My daughter Shawn had a good experience. Luckily there were more women in her group—like four or five—and what's really important is to have someone to study with at night. You've got to take these written exams. But it didn't happen with this young lady.

The continuing racial struggle was also evident when Gary and Beverly attended the fortieth anniversary conference of the National Naval Officers Association in New Orleans, in 2011. The NNOA supports the recruiting and retention of minority officers in the Sea Services, and for Cooper the gathering of some 350 mostly African American Marine and Navy officers began as a moving tribute to the struggle he joined more than a half-century earlier.

It also marked the twentieth anniversary of General Carl Mundy Jr.'s address to the NNOA, the first appearance before that organization by any Marine Corps commandant, a break-through address that Cooper had recommended Mundy make.

Cooper's letter to Mundy on steps to take for the advancement of more minorities in USMC officer ranks was also quoted by generals at the New Orleans conference.[511]

Beverly had to poke me a couple of times, I was tearing up. What we've got to remember is that crying comes easy for me because when I became a young Marine lieutenant there were only about six of us.

But the conference also demonstrated that many of the things mentioned in that letter I sent to General Mundy are still not being done. In the entire Marine Corps today, can you believe there's only one black woman colonel? And the number of minority officers is still low in infantry, where they normally go on to become colonels and generals. In infantry, you lead men and have a career path.

The one hundred-plus officers at the conference were proud, good-looking youngsters. But they're in computer science. They're in data-this and data-that. Not infantry.

NEW COMMANDANT

While Gary was left gloomy by what he saw at the 2011 NNOA convention, the prospect for change was on the way.

Four-star General James F. Amos became commandant of the Marine Corps in October 2010, and in less than a year he asked Cooper and other generals to join him for a briefing in Washington. Amos was bringing the Corps' senior leadership up to speed on plans and developments, and Cooper took a seat at a table with a couple of his old friends.

General Petersen was there and General Walls was there. Normally we make it a point not to sit together. We sit around. But this time we got a table and we sat together. The commandant came over and said hello. And I said, "General, you better hope a bomb doesn't blow up over here because it's going to kill all your diversity."

He laughed like hell.

Telling the story later, Cooper laughed as well. Yet he knew it was uncomfortably close to the truth.

Amos, however, was determined to change the pattern. Under his leadership, the Marine Corps sought to preserve and showcase the history of African Americans who served with pride despite racial animosities and obstacles. In a variety of media, the USMC began celebrating the Montford Point Marines—the Corps' counterpart to the famed Tuskegee Airmen. The Corps also published an oral history, *Pathbreakers*, which provides the riveting recollections of Petersen, Cooper, Walls, and other pioneering African American Marine officers.[512]

There was a lot of concern about Amos becoming commandant because he was the first aviator. Every other commandant had been a ground fighter. But, boy, when we see the emphasis he has put on equal opportunity, both males and females, it is remarkable.

He has done a huge amount helping highlight the Montford Point

Marines. In fact, he has been an unusual commandant. Never before has there been such enthusiasm.

Southern historian Melton A. McLaurin also deserves acclaim for his vital role in telling the story of Montford Point Marines to a wide audience through his 2007 book, *The Marines of Montford Point: America's First Black Marines*, and a later documentary film with the same title, narrated by Louis Gossett Jr.[513]

The book and film are based on interviews with sixty Montford Pointers. In a Q-and-A with the University of North Carolina Press, which published the book, McLaurin said it was suggested by Dr. Clarence Willie, a retired Marine lieutenant colonel. Willie was an assistant superintendent in the Brunswick County, North Carolina, public school system who had been inspired by meetings with Montford Pointers in the 1960s. A grant from the University of North Carolina-Wilmington helped launch the project.[514]

McLaurin said the Montford Point Marines were not as famous for several reasons:

> Buffalo Soldiers were combat troops on the frontier, fighting in the Indian Wars, and were in the "glamour" unit of the Army, the cavalry—the dashing military hero imagery. The Tuskegee Airmen were flyboys, always glamorous, and officers to boot. The Montford Point Marines served as enlisted personnel, assigned primarily to service duty with ammunition or depot (supply) companies. A few were in two defense battalions, which were combat units, but never assigned to combat. In addition, they were always commanded by white officers and were never allowed to achieve officer status. But perhaps the most significant reason that they are unknown is the way in which racism is imbedded in the national narrative of World War II. Essentially blacks are not a part of the mythic narrative of that war, although they were very much involved in it. Iwo Jima and the mythology that surrounds it demonstrates this perfectly. While black units from Montford Point hit the beaches of Iwo Jima on the first day of the invasion, they are not a part of the mythology—not in John Wayne's *Sands of Iwo Jima*,

made in 1949, and, except for a five-second tip of the hat, not in Clint Eastwood's *Flags of Our Fathers*, made in 2006.[515]

Under Commandant Amos, a plan emerged to increase USMC diversity.

In 2010, a young officer wrote a letter to the Marine Corps Gazette, *the officers' magazine, in which he cited the same concerns that I had cited for Mundy. This commandant, General Amos, expressed interest, so I sent him that letter I had written in 1991. As a result of that letter, the new commandant sent correspondence to all the generals in the Marine Corps expressing his concern. He said that we should be bringing in ten percent but we have only been doing five. And he wants us to really start working to increase the numbers. He asked us as generals to give him ideas.*

Under Amos, the Corps also took a second look at Petersen's 1998 autobiography, *Into the Tiger's Jaw*. Cooper felt that for more than a decade the USMC hierarchy had failed to give an official Corps reception to this account of how a young black man out of Kansas made history as a Marine aviator and flag officer.[516]

In the book, Petersen describes in elegant detail his upbringing in a racially segregated country and his pioneering rise as a black Marine pilot who saw combat in Korea and Vietnam and fought for minority advancement as he became the Corps' first black aviator and first black Marine general. It is a story that could serve as an eye-opener to white Marine brass as well as an inspiration to young black Marine officers or would-be officers. But year after year, Gary said, it was not placed on the commandant's list of recommended reading.

Over the years, General Walls and I have written to every commandant saying, "General, please put General Petersen's book on the required reading list for officers." None of them would do it. They wouldn't even carry it in the book stores on Marine bases.

But we continued and in 2012 for the first time the new commandant, General James Amos, included General Petersen's book on the required reading list.

A review of the newly reissued book ran in the *Marine Corps Gazette* magazine under the title, "An Important History of a Changed Corps." Written by a military history professor at the Marine Corps Command and Staff College, the review described the Petersen book as "a thought-provoking and compelling autobiography, as well as a personal history of the modern U.S. Marine Corps. As such, *Into the Tiger's Jaw* is a welcome addition to the literature, and one that should find a home in all Marines' libraries."[517]

In the book, Petersen mentions the subtle slights and overt racism he experienced day-to-day as a young Marine, on and off base. Fifty years after the integration of the Corps, Cooper felt discrimination remained a problem.

> *I've got to believe some of that still exists and that might be the underlying challenge still. I listen to Rush Limbaugh saying, "I hope he fails," at the very beginning of Obama's presidency. So I tell these young officers that if you think you work hard and that you're being judged just like everybody else, you're pissing in the wind. You better get up earlier, you better run faster, and you better work harder."*

For Cooper, the Marine Corps paid tribute to his own hard work and service in many ways, particularly when he received a special invitation to 8th and I for the Marine Corps Birthday Ball—8th and I being the posting he had coveted as a young lieutenant but was denied, apparently because of his race.

> *The commanding officer there knew the story, and I was invited to be the guest speaker. The invitation said, "Major General Jerome G. Cooper, we have been told that at one time you could not receive orders to Marine Barracks. Today I have ordered you to report here—and you also have the privilege to leave whenever you desire!"*

Thanks to the aggressive campaign launched by Amos, on a summer day in 2012 the Marine Barracks was the site where the nation finally paid official tribute to those legendary Montford Point Marines. More than four hundred were presented with the Congressional Gold Medal—some posthumously and some in their eighties who had served in World War II and were able to attend only with the aid of walkers.[518]

The next year, at the Montford Point Association Building at Camp Lejeune, thirty-seven of the Congressional Gold Medals were presented, thirty-two to surviving family members—including the family of Sergeant Major Edgar Huff, one of Gary's personal heroes.[519]

In a message read at the ceremony, President Barack Obama said:

> Despite being denied many basic rights, the Montford Point Marines committed to serve our country with selfless patriotism, choosing to put their lives on the line. These men helped advance civil rights, and helped influence the decision to desegregate the armed forces in 1948.[520]

In Gary's office in Mobile is a picture of six Montford Point Marines that remains an inspiration.

The people in this picture, these Montford Point Marines, are of course the first six black men ever to become DI's. They took pride in the young black Marine officers, and what interests me is that in my first three assignments—when I was in Hawaii, when I went to Barstow, and when I went aboard ship—in each place we had a Montford Point Marine. They had trained at Montford Point, they were regular Marines, except they were a little older and more experienced.

As I said, we sort of walked on their shoulders.

FULL CIRCLE

Over the years I have returned to Notre Dame often to attend black alumni programs and other university events. I was at my fifty-fifth class reunion in 2013—about two hundred were on hand, many barely making it—and visited the grotto. That's where I would go pray as a student: "Lord, please let me pass this test or my daddy will kill me!"

At this reunion, there were familiar faces, but I was the only African American in the class still alive. My roommate, Corky Parker, had died, as had Aubrey Lewis, the football and track star.

At a reunion in 2011, Joli made sure I heard the stories of recent black graduates who would not have been able to attend Notre Dame without financial help. Joli's friend, Ramona Payne, was in the Development

Office, so I am sure they all had this planned. But these incredible young people moved me with their stories and accomplishments. They inspired me to donate $100,000 and, with my wife Beverly, to endow the J. Gary Cooper Family Scholarship Fund.

I also visited Father Hesburgh and took a photograph of him with my daughter Joli and grandson Ashley. While in his office, I noticed that he had a crystal bowl among the furnishings. For me, this was not just any crystal bowl—it was a gift he had received from a great friend of Notre Dame, Archbishop Fulton Sheen—I smiled as I felt my Notre Dame journey had come full circle.

For Hesburgh, the Cooper family scholarship fund was a milestone as well.

"It's a very important fund," Hesburgh said. "We spend so much time spending money to get black students here, to have a black student become very successful and set up his own fund—that was coming home free."

For Gary, the scholarship fund was just the latest of many, many times he has provided financial assistance for young people to attend college—helping them get to the next level "home free."

"He really gives a lot back to the community," said Shawn. "I don't think people realize how many kids' tuition he's paying."

Gary's view of this is simple: *"You know, when you help a kid go to college, one thing is for certain—you can't lose."*

For the Cooper family, generation after generation has arrived to take up the torch, excelling in American venues as divergent as the military, law, politics, arts, public health, education, finance, and community service.

"There's always been an emphasis placed on educational achievement," said Patrick. "It was always expected that you get your college degree, and always expected you get a graduate or professional degree. It's kind of a weird situation. My father went to college. His father, A. J., went to college, and A. J.'s father, Osceola Osceola, and his mother, Alice Johnson, they went to college. Here you have four generations of college-educated parents. They're kind of rare in the black community, but one of the benefits of it is there are certain expectations created for folks educationally. My older daughter, Sophie, she went to Yale and she had her master's degrees, one from Michigan and one from Columbia. She's now getting her law degree in Berkeley. She'll make it five generations."

PATH BREAKERS

On a sweltering hot summer day—July 13, 2012—Major General Gary Cooper joined top officials of the Navy and Marine Corps in the courtyard of the Pentagon. This was not just an ordinary gathering of the brass. It was to honor pioneering men and women of color in a "Tribute to African-American Leadership," including those, like Cooper, who came after the Montford Pointers. The ceremony, highlighted by the unveiling of a new Pentagon exhibit, designated twelve Marines and the Navy's "Golden 13" for this historic tribute.[521]

Cooper and Petersen, with front-row seats, were among those exemplary Marines honored as "Path Breakers."

The invitation had arrived in Mobile out of the blue. After Cooper got it, he checked to see who had RSVP'd. Missing from the list was the eighty-year-old Petersen, who lives on the shore of Chesapeake Bay.

So I called the general and said, "General, listen—"

"Aw, Gary," he replied, "I don't like that stuff. The traffic and all."

"But general, this will not be a ceremony without you. You're our senior and our first general. This is about YOU."

Nothing doing. Cooper had a couple of other people call him, but Petersen was still saying "No." So Cooper called again.

I think what broke him was, I said, "General, I will hire a limousine to come and pick you up." It's a pain driving from Baltimore in that traffic. Anyway, he was too proud for that. He came.

Cooper was accompanied by his daughter, Marine Captain Shawn Cooper.

I couldn't see all the people there because they ushered us in. We sat on the front row, to the left of the center of the stage. General Petersen was next to me. Next to him was Cliff Stanley, a retired two-star, a PhD, and now the assistant Secretary of Defense for Manpower. Very senior position. Next to Cliff was Charlie Bolden, the head of NASA. He went to the Naval Academy, a retired Marine two-star—he flew the spaceship that put the Hubble telescope down. He tells us we are HIS mentors.

We had there almost every black Marine general who has ever lived, except maybe one or two. General Walls was there, our third general— my friend who I met on a trail in Vietnam.

General Petersen and I were so pleased—these youngsters looked so sharp.

Cooper and Petersen looked fit as well, Marines to the core, with big smiles for the occasion, and much to admire about the history they helped set in motion.

We got to see one young man, Ron Bailey, who only the week before became the commanding general of the First Marine Division—that's a historic division located at Camp Pendleton. General Petersen hugged him and said, "We can't believe this—general of the First Marine Division!"

Back in 1991, Bailey had been one of the young black Marine officers invited by Cooper to hear from the three original path-breakers—Davis, Gravely and Petersen.

The "Golden 13" honored in the ceremony were the first African Americans commissioned as Navy officers in 1944. Twelve were commissioned as ensigns and one as a warrant officer boatswain. The twelve Marine "Path Breakers" were those who were "firsts" in various ways, such as Captain Frederick C. Branch, the first African American to receive a commission in the Marine Corps. He pinned on his second lieutenant's bars in November 1945.[522]

Many of those honored, like Branch, were deceased.

As the event ended, honorees and well-wishers gathered for pictures. The Pentagon courtyard was steaming hot on this summer day in D.C.

Those of us who had on suits were just soaking wet. Most of us didn't stay around to socialize. We were just happy to still be standing.

For Cooper, the work ethic that brought him to this moment was not solely driven by the color of his skin or a determination to make Marine Corps history, to be honored as a Path Breaker.

When I was a young officer and I served aboard the ship and I wanted to go to Vietnam and I wanted to do these things, the one thing I think we've got to understand is that I really wanted these jobs because I was a Marine. The fact that I was going to be the first black Marine seldom entered my mind.

When I went to Da Nang and they told me I couldn't get a rifle company, I had no concern at all with me being black and not getting a company. What I had concern about was every Marine officer's dream is to command a rifle company. That was my main concern. That's why I had to request mast."

Similarly, when Cooper time and again urged Marine Corps brass to understand the need for diversity, he was not raising the issue out of concern for his own career. He might be seen as nothing more than a tall kid from Down the Bay, but he was the one whose Mobile family took on Jim Crow at every turn, and he could take care of his own future, thank you very much.

When I would raise concerns about diversity, I didn't raise it for myself, but I would look behind me and say, "Who's coming up?"

Acknowledgments

I AM GRATEFUL FIRST and foremost to Gary Cooper for the generous time, personal documents, thoughtful recollections and enthusiasm he gave to this book, which he made an all-around pleasure for me to pursue.

It was Gary's younger daughter, Shawn Cooper of Atlanta, who set the project on its course with an email seeking an author to write a biography of her father. The email actually was not sent to me. It was sent to Julia Cass of New Orleans, the co-author of *Black In Selma: The Uncommon Life of J. L. Chestnut, Jr.* As it happened, Julia is a friend, and she had received Shawn's email not long before arriving as a houseguest of my wife, Penny, and me. Out of the blue, I mentioned my interest in a Gary Cooper book; Julia produced Shawn's email. A sense of destiny ensued.

Gary's wife, Beverly, and his other children—Patrick Cooper of Albuquerque and Joli Cooper-Nelson of Tampa—joined Shawn in helping the book come together, as did Gary's first cousin, Judi Stephenson of Pasadena, California, who provided crucial, first-person background on the Mouton family in Lafayette, Louisiana, along with family photographs dating back a century. Judi's sister, Marilyn Funderburk of Washington, D.C., and many others among Gary's family and wide range of friends— from childhood, Notre Dame, the military, politics and business—were also vital to my telling the Cooper story. Their voices and recollections resonate in the text across decades.

Among them, I am particularly grateful to the Marines of Mike Company and Hill 55 who served with Gary in Vietnam and shared with me recollections of a time when their enormous personal courage became an indelible part of American history.

This book would not have been possible without the many people who made my career with the Associated Press both long and gratifying: Atlanta Chief of Bureau Ron Autry, Birmingham Correspondent Hoyt Harwell, and Montgomery Correspondent Rex Thomas were there for me at the start, and Washington news editor David Pace, Birmingham Correspondent Jay Reeves, Statehouse Reporter Phillip Rawls, and Montgomery Photographer Dave Martin were among scores of great AP talents who provided long-term support.

I'm grateful to Howell Raines, of Fairhope, Alabama, and Paradise Township, Pennsylvania, who was an inspiration from our early years in Birmingham and wrote a perfectly worded recommendation to help launch my AP career. And in my post-AP life, my thanks to Jeb Schrenk of Mobile and Tom Gordon of Birmingham, who made the transition a writer's joy.

Garry Mitchell, who succeeded me as AP correspondent in Mobile, was unfailingly helpful on my port city visits during work on this book, as were Donald and Holle Briskman, whose friendship has long made Mobile a highlight of our travels.

I am grateful to Suzanne La Rosa and Randall Williams, a friend of more than forty years, whose interest in publishing the book with NewSouth and advice in its editing were essential in bringing it to completion.

I am thankful also for others who have given me an important boost along the way: Jim Carrier and Trish O'Kane of Burlington, Vermont, Pam Horowitz and Julian Bond of Washington, D.C. and Destin, Florida, Marcia DeSonier of Tunnel Springs, Alabama, Winifred Green of New Orleans, Larry Weaver and Gabrielle Thompson of Manhattan, Kansas, Skip Tucker and Ken Hare of Montgomery, Rose Battle of Huntsville and her brother, Bill Battle, of Atlanta, and Bill Dawson, the rare liberal conscience from the West Side of Birmingham where I grew up.

This book was inspired in many ways by Wayne Greenhaw, a Montgomery friend whose enjoyment of the writer's life and dedication to the craft influenced countless writers young and old. We miss Wayne and his great friend, Tom Cork, whose own keen eye for good writing served as a guide for me; and I'm grateful for the encouragement I received on this book from their wives, Sally Greenhaw of Birmingham and Betty Cork of Water Sound, Florida, gifted talents in their own right.

This book could not have been written without the love and support of family all along the way—Penelope Jenkins and her daughter, Ruby Harriford, in New Orleans; Savannah and David Ferster in Alexandria, Virginia, with their children Ellis, Teddy, and Julia, the baby girl who will always be in our hearts; and in Montgomery, Penny, my wife, best friend, and best editor.

Notes

NOTES TO PROLOGUE

1. Gary Cooper interview with author.
2. Gidget Fuentes, "Is Requesting Mast career suicide?" *Marine Corps Times* website, Sept. 21, 2008.
3. Gary Cooper interview with author.
4. Gary Cooper interview with author.
5. Gary Cooper papers, personal documents, news clips, and letters—*The Spirit of Notre Dame*, Fall 2009, a University of Notre Dame publication.
6. "Giants of Black Capitalism," *Ebony*, May 1969, pp. 164–172.
7. Author conversation with Pam Horowitz.
8. Gary Cooper interview with author.

NOTES TO CHAPTER 1

9. Gary Cooper interview with author; Shawn A. Bivens, *Mobile, Alabama's People of Color: A Tricentennial History, 1702–2002*, Volume One. (Victoria, Canada, Trafford Publishing, 2004) p. 203, 232.
10. Gary Cooper interview with author; Gary Cooper papers, personal documents, news clips, and letters—a circa-1976 profile of Peggy Cooper, including her family's ancestors, in an unidentified publication. The piece had been photocopied, with the names and dates of birth and death for several Moutons handwritten to one side of the text. The unidentified family member who wrote the information apparently was living in Lafayette, Louisiana, and corrected some of the details in the published text. The photocopy includes a full-page portrait of Louisiana Governor Alexandre Mouton, who is identified in the handwriting as the father of Paul Joseph Julien Mouton, a great-grandfather of Gary Cooper.
11. Gary Cooper papers, personal documents, news clips, and letters—a circa 1976 profile of Peggy Cooper; Judi Stephenson correspondence and interview with author; National Governors Association website. Note: "Alexandre" is at times spelled "Alexander" in historical documents, and the NGA listing of him as the eleventh governor differs numerically from some other histories.
12. Alexandre Mouton information at http://files/usgwarchives.net/la/lafayette/bios/moutona.txt, a profile submitted by Mike Miller to the Internet Genealogy Project; la-cemeteries.com/Governors/Mouton, Alexander; http://genealogy.com/ftm/l/a/t/Harrison-L-LA-tour/WEBSITE-0001/UHP-1948.html.
13. Alfred Mouton information at la-cemeteries.com/Notables/Civil War/Mouton, Alfred.shtm; http://thesouthsdefender.blogspot.com/2010/03/

alfred-mouton-hero-of-acadian-people.html; http://www.scvtaylorcamp.com/ lmfiles/LA-CC-1%20-%20Lafayette,%20Lafayette%20Parish.JPG.
14. Judi Stephenson correspondence and interview with author.
15. Gary Cooper papers, personal documents, news clips, and letters—a circa 1976 profile of Peggy Cooper.
16. Judi Stephenson correspondence and interview with author; Gary Cooper papers, personal documents, news clips, and letters—a circa-1976 profile of Peggy Cooper.
17. Judi Stephenson correspondence and interview with author; Gary Cooper papers, personal documents, news clips, and letters—a circa-1976 profile of Peggy Cooper
18. Gary Cooper interview with author.
19. Judi Stephenson correspondence and interview with author.
20. Hampton University history at http://www.hamptonu.edu/about/history.cfm.
21. Gary Cooper interview with author.
22. Patricia Riles Wickman, *Osceola's Legacy* (Tuscaloosa: University of Alabama Press, 1991), p. 58.
23. Owen Edwards, "A Seminole Warrior Cloaked in Defiance," *Smithsonian*, October 2010.
24. Wickman, *Osceola's Legacy*, p. 58.
25. Gary Cooper papers, personal documents, news clips, and letters—a circa-1976 profile of Peggy Cooper; Shawn Cooper Papers—1900 Census records for Adelade Cooper.
26. Gary Cooper interview with author.
27. Bivens, *Mobile, Alabama's People of Color*, p. 82.
28. Edward O. Wilson and Alex Harris, *Why We Are Here: Mobile and the Spirit of a Southern City* (New York, London: Liveright Publishing, 2012), p. 161.
29. Bivens, *Mobile, Alabama's People of Color*, p. 82.
30. "Cooper Named To Fund Post," *Mobile Press-Register*, Sept. 26, 1956.
31. Gary Cooper interview with author.
32. Gary Cooper papers, personal documents, news clips, and letters—"The Christian Benevolent Insurance Company, 1922–1982," corporate history dated March 1984.
33. Ibid.
34. Gary Cooper interview with author.
35. Suzanne E. Smith, *To Serve the Living: Funeral Directors and the African American Way of Death* (Cambridge: The Belknap Press of Harvard University Press, 2010), pp. 41–43.
36. Merah S. Stuart, *An Economic Detour: A History of Insurance in the Live of African Americans*, (College Park, Md.: McGrath Publishing Co., 1940), p. 36.
37. Hortense Powderbaker, *After Freedom: A Cultural Study in the Deep South*, (New York: Atheneum, 1969), p. 122.
38. Smith, *To Serve the Living*, pp. 42–43.
39. Carol Jenkins and Elizabeth Gardner Hines, *Black Titan: A.G. Gaston and the Making of a Black American Millionaire*, (One World/Ballentine, 2003).
40. Gary Cooper interview with author; Paulette Davis-Horton, *Avenue: The Davis Avenue Story: The Place, The People, The Memories* (Mobile, Horton Inc., 1991), p. 202.
41. Davis-Horton, *Avenue*.
42. Gary Cooper interview with author.
43. Gary Cooper papers, personal documents, news clips, and letters—Gary Cooper in a videotaped interview for a Tricentennial project focusing on African Americans in Mobile. The videocassette is dated 12–02–99, but the interviewer's name is not on the videocassette nor mentioned in the preserved copy of the tape.
44. Gary Cooper interview with author.
45. Cathleen Medwick, "Art House: Supporting Talented Young Artists of Color," *O, The*

Oprah Magazine, August 2009.
46. Gary Cooper papers, personal documents, news clips, and letters—"The Christian Benevolent Insurance Company, 1922–1982."
47. "Giants of Black Capitalism," *Ebony* magazine, May 1969, pp. 164–172.
48. Ibid.

NOTES TO CHAPTER 2
49. Gary Cooper speech at Spring Hill College, July 28, 2013.
50. Bivens, *Mobile, Alabama's People of Color*, p. 168.
51. Leah Rawls Atkins, *Alabama: History of a Deep South State* (Tuscaloosa: University of Alabama Press, 1994), p. 104.
52. *Mobile: The New History of Alabama's First City* (University of Alabama Press, 2001), Allen Cronenberg, pp. 223–225.
53. Ibid., p. 219.
54. Gary Cooper papers, personal documents, news clips, and letters—Cooper video-taped interview for Tricentennial project.
55. Gary Cooper speech at Spring Hill College, July 28, 2013.
56. Eric Reynolds, "The Interview: A. J. Cooper," FOX 10 TV, March 22, 2012.
57. Bivens, *Mobile, Alabama's People of Color*, p. 219.
58. Ibid.
59. Gary Cooper interview with author; Bivens, *Mobile, Alabama's People of Color*, p. 243.
60. Harold Jackson interview with author.
61. Ibid.
62. Gary Cooper interview with author.
63. Ibid.
64. Ibid.
65. Bivens, *Mobile, Alabama's People of Color*, p. 203.
66. Ibid.
67. Ibid.
68. Gary Cooper papers, personal documents, news clips, and letters—Archbishop Sheen letter to Cooper, Oct. 5, 1953.
69. Gary Cooper interview with author.
70. Gary Cooper papers, personal documents, news clips, and letters—O. O. Cooper letter to A. J. Cooper, July 9, 1953.
71. Isabel Wilkerson, *The Warmth of Other Suns* (New York: Random House, 2010), p. 197.
72. "Cooper Named to Fund Post," *Mobile Press-Register*, Sept. 26, 1956.
73. Ibid.
74. Reynolds, "The Interview," FOX 10 TV.

NOTES TO CHAPTER 3
75. Father Theodore Hesburgh interview with author.
76. Father Theodore Hesburgh, with Jerry Reedy, *God, Country, Notre Dame: The Autobiography of Theodore Hesburgh* (South Bend: University of Notre Dame Press, 1999), pp. 181–182; Jack Bass, *Taming the Storm* (New York: Doubleday, 1993), Federal Judge Frank M. Johnson Jr. family photograph.
77. Father Theodore Hesburgh interview with author.
78. Gary Cooper interview with author.
79. Gary Cooper interview with author.
80. History of Spring Hill, from SHC website at http://www.shc.edu/page/history-spring-hill-college.
81. Gary Cooper papers, personal documents, news clips, and letters—Notre Dame

class credit records.

82. Charlesetta Ferrill Cooper interview with author.
83. Nathan Thompson, *Kings: The True Story of Chicago's Policy Kings and Numbers Racketeers* (Chicago: The Bronzeville Press, 1994).
84. Ibid., p. 76.
85. Ibid., p. 146.
86. Illinois landmarks at http://www.cityprofile.com.
87. Thompson, *Kings*, p. 25.
88. Charlesetta Ferrill Cooper interview.
89. Ibid.
90. Gary Cooper interview with author; Gary Cooper papers, personal documents, news clips, and letters—family photos.
91. Waluhaje hotel history at http://www.atlantatimemachine.com/misc/waluhaje.htm.

NOTES TO CHAPTER 4

92. Bernard C. Nalty, "The Right to Fight: African-Americans in World War II," a pamphlet in a series published by the History and Museums Division of the U.S. Marine Corps, 1995, pp. 1–3.
93. Ibid.; Lauren Armstrong, "The Story of the Montford Point Marines," *FRAtoday* magazine of the Fleet Reserve Association, December 2010.
94. Gary Cooper interview with author.
95. "The Story of the Montford Point Marines," *FRAtoday*, December 2010; Gary Cooper interview with author.
96. "The Story of the Montford Point Marines," *FRAtoday*, December 2010.
97. Ibid.
98. *Path Breakers: U.S. Marine African American Officers in Their Own Words*, compiled and edited by Fred H. Allison and Col. Kurtis P. Wheeler, USMCR, (Washington, D.C., History Division, United States Marine Corps, 2013), p. 225.
99. Executive order information at http://www.trumanlibrary.org.9981.htm.
100. Lt. Gen. Frank E. Petersen interview with author.
101. *Path Breakers*, p. 42.
102. Gary Cooper interview with author.
103. Gary Cooper papers, personal documents, news clips, and letters-USMC personnel records.
104. *Into the Tiger's Jaw: America's First Black Marine Aviator, the Autobiography of Lt. Gen. Frank E. Petersen*, with J. Alfred Phelps. (Novato, Calif., Presidio Press, 1998), p. 112.
105. Lt. Gen. Frank E. Petersen interview with author.
106. Ibid.
107. *Into the Tiger's Jaw*, p. 114.
108. *Path Breakers*, p. 43.
109. Lt. Gen. Frank E. Petersen interview with author.
110. Gary Cooper interview with author.
111. Thompson, *Kings*, pp. 40–46.
112. Robert D. D'avila, "Obituary: Maj. Kurt Chew-Een Lee, 88, was Korean War Hero," *The Sacramento Bee*, March 4, 2014.
113. Gary Cooper papers, personal documents, news clips, and letters—copy of Wieseman endorsement.
114. Matt Schudel, "Vicente T. 'Ben' Blaz, Marine general and Guam delegate, dies at 85," *The Washington Post*, Jan. 23, 2014.
115. Gravely biographical material in arlingtoncemetery.net/samuelgravely.htm.
116. Gary Cooper interview with author.

117. Gary Cooper interview with author; Gary Cooper papers, personal documents, news clips, and letters—Daniel Freeman, email, Feb. 12, 2015.
118. Gary Cooper papers, personal documents, news clips, and letters—Wieseman letter to Cooper, Jan. 27, 1966.

Notes to Chapter 5

119. Gary Cooper interview with author.
120. Gidget Fuentes, "Is Requesting Mast career suicide?" *Marine Corps Times* website, Sept. 21, 2008.
121. Gary Cooper interview with author.
122. From USMC website for *The 3rd Marine Division and Its Regiments*, list of commanding officers for the 3rd, 9th, p. 35.
123. Gary Cooper interview with author.
124. Jack Shulimson and Maj. Charles M. Johnson, USMC, "U.S. Marines In Vietnam: The Landing and the Buildup, 1965," *History and Museums Division, USMC Headquarters*, 1978, website http://www.marines.mil.
125. Gary Cooper papers, personal documents, news clips, and letters—Declassified USMC filing of staff strength levels during 1–31 May 1966 for the 3rd Battalion, 9th Marines.
126. Capt. Francis J. West Jr., "Small Unit Action in Vietnam—Summer 1966," *History and Museums Division, USMC Headquarters*, 1967, p. 3.
127. USMC Command Chronology, 3rd Battalion, 9th Marines, May 1966, at http://www.vietnam.ttu.edu/virtualarchive/, website of Virtual Vietnam Archive, Texas Tech University.
128. Gary Cooper papers, personal documents, news clips, and letters—GySgt. Jack Baird, "Marines Kill 25 VC at An Hoa," *Stars & Stripes*, undated clip.
129. Gary Cooper papers, personal documents, news clips, and letters—Letter to Dan Freeman, Aug. 4, 1966.
130. James Webb, "Heroes of the Vietnam Generation," *American Enterprise Institute*, July/August 2000, at website http://www.jameswebb.com/articles.
131. Gary Cooper interview with author; Charlie Tutt interview.
132. Brig. Gen. George Walls interview with author.
133. *Path Breakers*, p. 63.
134. Gary Cooper papers, personal documents, news clips, and letters—Letter to Dan Freeman, Aug. 4, 1966.
135. Gary Cooper papers, personal documents, news clips, and letters—"Heroic Marine's Last Letter," story in a saved clip from an unidentified newspaper, clearly a Chicago paper, without the author or date of publication.
136. VietnamWarCasualties.org, website at http://www.vietnamwarcasualties.org/, lists Lance Cpl. Daniel Eugene Morris of North Arlington, N.J., and Pfc. William John Schulz of Stone Park, Ill., as members of Mike Company in the 3rd, 9th, who were killed Aug. 20, 1966, and lists Pfc. Thomas Robert Kyle Jr. of Park Ridge, N.J., as being a rifleman with the 3rd, 9th, who was killed Aug. 20, 1966, but the company, presumably Co. M, is not named.
137. Gary Cooper papers, personal documents, news clips, and letters—Letter to mother, Sept. 5, 1966.
138. Ibid.

Notes to Chapter 6

139. Gary Cooper papers, personal documents, news clips, and letters—Letter from Father Co.

140. Gary Cooper papers, personal documents, news clips, and letters—Letter to his mother, Nov. 19, 1966.
141. Gary Cooper papers, personal documents, news clips, and letters—Letter to his mother, Sept. 5, 1966.
142. Gary Cooper papers, personal documents, news clips, and letters—Letter to his mother Nov 19, 1966.
143. Ibid.
144. Gary Cooper papers, personal documents, news clips, and letters—Letter to Dan Freeman, April 24, 1967.
145. Gary Cooper papers, personal documents, news clips, and letters—Letter to his mother, Nov. 19, 1966.
146. Dr. Barry Booth interview with author.
147. Gary Cooper papers, personal documents, news clips, and letters—Letter to Dan Freeman, April 24, 1967.
148. Material throughout this section, "Officers' Mess," is drawn from the delightfully phrased recollections of John Nichols in a letter to the author, dated March 19, 2011.
149. Gary Cooper papers, personal documents, news clips, and letters—USMC citation with Cooper's Bronze Star.
150. Gary Cooper papers, personal documents, news clips, and letters—Letter to Cooper from Gov. Lurleen Wallace, May 23, 1967.

NOTES TO CHAPTER 7

151. Gary Cooper interview with author.
152. Charlesetta Ferrill Cooper interview.
153. *Path Breakers*, pp. 83–84.
154. http://www.history.com/this-day-in-history/100000-people-march-on-the-pentagon
155. Steven Morris, "How Blacks Upset the Marine Corps," *Ebony* magazine, December 1969, pp. 55–62.
156. Lt. Gen. Frank E. Petersen interview with author.
157. Ibid.
158. James Webb, *Heroes of the Vietnam Generation*, American Enterprise Institute, July/August 2000, website http://www.jameswebb.com/articles.
159. Gary Cooper papers, personal documents, news clips, and letters—Cathy Aldridge, "Montford Pointers Convene At Hilton," *New York Amsterdam News*, Sept. 2, 1967.
160. http://www.marinemedals.com/andersonjames.htm.
161. Gary Cooper interview with author.
162. E. Madison Cockrell, "Local Insurance Executive Dead in Home Here," *Mobile Beacon and Alabama Citizen*, Nov. 16, 1968, p. 1.
163. Matt Metcalfe interview.
164. The Metropolitan Club history at http://www.metropolitanclubnyc.org/
165. Matt Metcalfe interview.
166. Gary Cooper papers, personal documents, news clips, and letters—"The Christian Benevolent Insurance Company, 1922–1982."
167. Gary Cooper interview with author.
168. Gary Cooper papers, personal documents, news clips, and letters—"Wanted Man Shot By Bondsman," *Mobile Press-Register*, undated clip of brief story.

NOTES TO CHAPTER 8

169. Gary Cooper papers, personal documents, news clips, and letters—"Major Gen. Cooper: Sharp, on the go, anything but retired," National Naval Officers Association

magazine, 2005.

170. Gary Cooper papers, personal documents, news clips, and letters—Gordon Tatum Jr., "Scholarship: A fitting tribute," *Mobile Press-Register*, written for his column, "Backstage and Studio," April 1989, an otherwise undated clip from the newspaper.
171. Bivens, *Mobile, Alabama's People of Color*, p. 154.
172. Wilson and Harris, *Why We Are Here*, p. 161.
173. Ibid., pp. 161–162.
174. Bivens, *Mobile, Alabama's People of Color*, p. 154.
175. Gary Cooper papers, personal documents, news clips, and letters—Tatum, "Scholarship," *Mobile Press-Register*.
176. Ibid.
177. Ibid.
178. Mobile: The New History of Alabama's First City, (Tuscaloosa and London, University of Alabama Press, 2001), Billy Hinson, pp. 205–206, Keith Nicholls, p. 247.

Notes to Chapter 9

179. Eric D. Duke, "A Life in the Struggle: John L. LeFlore and the Civil Rights Movement in Mobile, Alabama (1925–1975)," M.A. thesis, Florida State University, 1998, p. 12.
180. MTNH, Keith Nicholls, pp. 256–257. Scotty E. Kirkland, "Freedom on Trial: *NAACP v. Alabama*," *Alabama Heritage*, Summer 2016, pp. 38-47. The state's initial argument was that the New York-based NAACP had failed to register in Alabama as a "foreign corporation" and should be barred from conducting "illegal" operations. When the state asked for the names and addresses of its thousands of Alabama members, the NAACP sought to protect them from white racist reprisals, refusing to comply, only to be slapped with a $100,000 fine. Even though the U.S. Supreme Court in 1958 ruled for the NAACP and upheld for the first time the right of freedom of association in America, the state's attorneys and the Alabama Supreme Court continued to balk. It was only after the U.S. Supreme Court ruled again in June 1964 that the Alabama ban ended.
181. Mobile: The New History of Alabama's First City, (Tuscaloosa and London, University of Alabama Press, 2001), Harvey H. Jackson III, p. 289.
182. Ibid.
183. Jeff Amy, "The Plot to Kill John LeFlore," *Mobile Press-Register*, June 28, 2007, p. 1.
184. Ibid.
185. Mobile: The New History of Alabama's First City, (Tuscaloosa and London, University of Alabama Press, 2001), Keith Nicholls, p. 261, p. 268.
186. Gary Cooper interview with author; Gary Cooper papers, personal documents, news clips, and letters—Cooper photo.

Notes to Interlude (Jay, Peggy, and Mario)

187. Jay Cooper remarks videotaped at the 40th anniversary and national convention of the National Black Law Students Association, in Detroit, March 26–30, 2008, https://www.youtube.com/user/NBLSA.
188. Ibid.
189. Eric Reynolds, "The Interview: A. J. Cooper," FOX10tv.com, March 22, 2012.
190. Ibid.
191. Steve McConnell, "Meet the Candidate: A. J. Cooper," smcconnell@gulfcoastnewspapers.com, Oct. 3, 2007, Updated Jan. 17, 2012.
192. Ibid.
193. Eric Reynolds, "The Interview," FOX10tv.com.
194. Alex Poinsett, "Homeboy's Dixie Return Pays Off," *Ebony* magazine, December

1972, pp. 163–168.
195. Ibid.; U.S. Census by decade.
196. Reynolds, "The Interview," FOX10tv.com.
197. Ibid.
198. "Homeboy's Dixie Return," *Ebony*, pp. 163–168.
199. Ibid.
200. Ibid.
201. "Alabama Black Mayor Faces More Than Racial Unrest," the *Washington Post*, as published in the *Geneva (Ala.) Times*, Nov. 29, 1972.
202. Jay Cooper profile for Alabama Lawyers Association, http://www.ala-lawyers.org/algernon-cooper-jr/.
203. "Alabama Black Mayor," *Post*, as published in the *Geneva (Ala.) Times*, Nov. 29, 1972.
204. "Homeboy's Dixie Return," *Ebony*.
205. McConnell, "Meet the Candidate," smcconnell@gulfcoastnewspapers.com.
206. Ibid.
207. "Mayor Cleared in Kickback Case," Associated Press, as published in the *Tuscaloosa (Ala.) News*, Sept. 16, 1978.
208. Fred Barbash, "Prichard's black mayor has had share of problems," the *Washington Post*, as published in the *Tuscaloosa (Ala.) News*, Aug. 8, 1978.
209. Jette Skadhauge, interview for Blacktie, a Denver-based company that advises on philanthropic projects, 2012.
210. Peggy Cooper Cafritz remarks at George Washington University's commencement May 15, 2011.
211. Burt Solomon, the *Washington Century: Three Families and the Shaping of the Nation's Capital*, (Harper Perennial, 2005), p. 260.
212. Peggy Cooper Cafritz remarks at GW commencement, May 15, 2011.
213. Cathleen Medwick, "Art House: Supporting Talented Young Artists of Color." *O, The Oprah Magazine*, August 2009, (On the web at http://www.oprah.com/home/Home-Decorating-Inside-the-Home-of-Art-Patron-Peggy-Cooper-Cafritz.)
214. Richette L. Haywood, "Washington D.C., public school saves lives and creates stars," *Ebony* magazine, January 1996, pp. 37–42.
215. Peggy Cooper Cafritz remarks at GW commencement, May 15, 2011.
216. Solomon, the *Washington Century*," p. 257.
217. Peggy Cooper Cafritz resume materials; The GW and Foggy Bottom Historical Encyclopedia/Cafritz, Peggy Cooper. (Website at http://encyclopedia.gwu.edu/index.php?title=Main_Page).
218. Solomon, the *Washington Century*, p. 257.
219. Ibid., p. 257.
220. Peggy Cooper Cafritz biographical materials.
221. Solomon, the *Washington Century*, p. 255.
222. The GW and Foggy Bottom Historical Encyclopedia/Cafritz, Peggy Cooper. (Website at http://encyclopedia.gwu.edu/index.php?title=Main_Page.)
223. Mario Cooper interview.
224. Ibid.
225. Jacob Levenson, *The Secret Epidemic: The Story of AIDS and Black America*, (New York, Pantheon Books, 2004), p. 209.
226. Mario Cooper interview.
227. Ibid.
228. Ibid.
229. Ibid.
230. Ibid.

NOTES TO CHAPTER 10

231. Gary Cooper interview with author.
232. Ibid.
233. Ibid.
234. *Mobile: The New History of Alabama's First City*, (Tuscaloosa and London, University of Alabama Press, 2001), Keith Nicholls, pp. 264-265; Gary Cooper papers, personal documents, news clips, and letters—Mildred Thompson, OP, PhD, "The Most Pure Heart of Mary Parish Over 100 Years," (November 1999), p. 8.
235. Gary Cooper papers, personal documents, news clips, and letters—*Mobile Press-Register*, "Cooper Voices Concern Over Board Appointment."
236. Gary Cooper papers, personal documents, news clips, and letters—Cooper letter to editor of *Mobile Press Register*, Jan 8, 1972.
237. Paul Kirkland interview.
238. Jack Bass, excerpt from "Oral Histories of the South," Bert Nettles interview, July 13, 1974, in collection of the University of North Carolina at Chapel Hill.
239. Jim Atchison interview.
240. Ibid.
241. Ibid.
242. Gary Cooper papers, personal documents, news clips, and letters—Bill Sellers, "Election Analysis Notes End of Bloc Voting," *Mobile Press-Register*, 1973, otherwise undated news story clip.
243. Jim Atchison interview.
244. Gary Cooper papers, personal documents, news clips, and letters—"Election Analysis," *Mobile Press-Register*.
245. Gary Cooper interview with author.
246. Ibid.
247. Ben Knight, *Florence TimesDaily*, Aug. 19, 1973, p. 7.
248. "Legislator loses eye to gunshot," Associated Press, in the *Tuscaloosa News*, July 23, 1975; Dana Beyerle, *TimesDaily*, Jan. 17, 1993, p. 1C.
249. "Rep. Ray Burgess of Anniston dies," Associated Press, in the *Gadsden Times*, Sept. 20, 1975.
250. George Altman, "Former State Senator Pierre Pelham Dies," *al.com*, Dec. 4, 2009.
251. Gary Cooper interview with author.
252. Ibid.
253. Roy Hoffman, "Dig reveals story of America's last slave ship—and its survivors," *al.com*, Aug. 9, 2010.
254. Gary Cooper interview with author.
255. Mobile County Probate Court website, "History of the Court." Moore information at http://probate.mobilecountyal.gov/judge-profiles-john_L_Moore.asp.
256. Gary Cooper interview with author.
257. James Harrell interview.
258. Janie Nobles, "Cooper Gearing Up for ABC Assault," *Mobile Press-Register*, Jan. 7, 1977.
259. Ibid.; Gary Cooper interview with author; "Job skills act gets OK," Associated Press, in *Mobile Press-Register*, April 27, 1977.
260. "Cooper Gearing Up," *Mobile Press-Register*.
261. Gary Cooper interview with author.

NOTES TO CHAPTER 11

262. Gary Cooper papers, personal documents, news clips, and letters—"Gary Cooper Seeking 2nd Term in House," *Mobile Press-Register*, June 13, 1978.

263. James Harrell interview.
264. Rex Thomas, Associated Press, in *Mobile Register*, Jan. 10, 1975, p. 7A.
265. Gary Cooper papers, personal documents, news clips, and letters—Copy of speech.
266. Will Campbell interview.
267. Gary Cooper papers, personal documents, news clips, and letters-Copy of speech.
268. Gary Cooper papers, personal documents, news clips, and letters—Letter from Phillip L. Browning, Feb. 24, 2011.
269. Gary Cooper interview with author.
270. Ibid.
271. Gary Cooper papers, personal documents, news clips, and letters—Mike Sherman, "Governor ousts top-ranking blacks," the *Anniston Star*, March 31, 1981.
272. Ibid.
273. Gary Cooper interview with author.
274. Gary Cooper papers, personal documents, news clips, and letters—newspaper clippings.
275. Gary Cooper papers, personal documents, news clips, and letters—Ted Bryant, "Blacks fare poorly in Montgomery this year," *Birmingham Post-Herald*, April 6, 1981.
276. Gary Cooper papers, personal documents, news clips, and letters—"The Drastic Fix," *Montgomery Advertiser*, June 9, 1981.
277. Gary Cooper papers, personal documents, news clips, and letters—Bob Ingram, "The Alabama Scene," *Alabama Magazine*, April, 1981.
278. Gary Cooper interview with author.
279. Gary Cooper papers, personal documents, news clips, and letters—"The Alabama Scene," *Alabama Magazine*.
280. Gary Cooper papers, personal documents, news clips, and letters—Darryl Gates, "400 protest at Capitol against James," *Montgomery Advertiser*, April 2, 1981.
281. Gary Cooper papers, personal documents, news clips, and letters—Cynthia Smith, "Social workers laud Cooper," *Montgomery Advertiser*, April 2, 1981.
282. Gary Cooper interview with author.
283. Gary Cooper papers, personal documents, news clips, and letters—Scott Shepard, Associated Press, "Board Votes To Fire Cooper," news story clipping, April 3, 1981.

NOTES TO CHAPTER 12

284. Gary Cooper interview with author; Gary Cooper papers, personal documents, news clips, and letters—USMC historical calendar for 1971
285. Gary Cooper papers, personal documents, news clips, and letters—"Cooper named chief of Marine battalion," *Mobile Press-Register*, May 3, 1977.
286. Brig. Gen. Joe Wilson interview.

NOTES TO INTERLUDE (PATRICK)

287. Patrick Cooper interview.

NOTES TO CHAPTER 13

288. Gary Cooper interview with author.
289. Ibid.
290. Ibid.
291. Talladega College historical materials at http://www.amistadresearchcenter.org.
292. Gary Cooper interview with author.
293. "Beirut Marine Barracks Bombing: October 23, 1983," http://www.navalhistory.org.
294. Gary Cooper interview with author.
295. Gary Cooper papers, personal documents, news clips, and letters—Copy of USMC

fitness report of Nov. 10, 1983.
296. *Into The Tiger's Jaw*, p. 264.

NOTES TO CHAPTER 14

297. Dan Weikel, "Black general salutes King, cites racial gains," the *San Diego Union*, Jan. 16, 1985.
298. Ibid.
299. Gary Cooper papers, personal documents, news clips, and letters—"Mobilian to head top unit," *Mobile Press-Register*, July 15, 1985.
300. Brig. Gen. Joe Wilson interview.
301. Ibid.

NOTES TO INTERLUDE (SHAWN)

302. Shawn Cooper interview.
303. Gary Cooper interview with author.
304. Shawn Cooper interview.

NOTES TO CHAPTER 15

305. Gary Cooper papers, personal documents, news clips, and letters—Marine assignments; "Cooper named major general," *Mobile Press-Register*, Feb. 7, 1988; Gary Cooper interview with author.
306. *Path Breakers*, pp. 214–215.
307. Ibid., p. 88.
308. Gary Cooper papers, personal documents, news clips, and letters—funeral program.
309. Dominic Cooper interview.
310. Gary Cooper papers, personal documents, news clips, and letters—"Cooper gets NAACP award," *Mobile Press-Register*, July 15, 1989.
311. Gary Cooper papers, personal documents, news clips, and letters—Copy of Jimmy Faulkner letter to Montgomery Mayor Emory Folmar, Dec. 2, 1988.
312. Gary Cooper papers, personal documents, news clips, and letters—Copy of letter from Montgomery Mayor Emory Folmar, who was Alabama Republican Party chairman, to Jimmy Faulkner, Dec. 5, 1988.
313. Gary Cooper papers, personal documents, news clips, and letters—Copy of letter from U.S. Sen. Howell Heflin, D-Ala., to Frederick McClure, assistant to the president for legislative affairs, April 10, 1989.
314. Gary Cooper interview with author.
315. Brad Clemenson, "Cooper approved for Air Force post," *Mobile Press-Register*, Nov. 22, 1989.

NOTES TO INTERLUDE (BEVERLY)

316. Beverly Cooper interview.
317. Bivens, *Mobile, Alabama's People of Color*, p. 372.
318. Sonny Callahan interview.
319. Sam Roberts, "Harry Briggs Jr., Relegated to Footnote In Landmark Rights Case, Dies at 75," *New York Times*, Aug. 20, 2016, p. B8; a lengthy summary of the case may also be found at Dr. Robert E. Botsch, University of South Carolina Aiken, at http://polisci.usca.edu/aasc/briggsvelliott.htm
320. Bruce Smith, "SC judge who first wrote 'separate is not equal' lauded," Associated Press, in the *State*, April 5, 2014.
321. Beverly Cooper interview.
322. Ibid.

Notes to Chapter 16

323. Gary Cooper interview with author.
324. Gary Cooper papers, personal documents, news clips, and letters—USMC news release.
325. Lt. Gen. Frank E. Petersen interview with author.
326. Ibid.
327. Brig. Gen. George Walls interview with author.
328. Gary Cooper papers, personal documents, news clips, and letters—List of attendees.
329. Lt. Gen. Willie J. Williams interview.
330. Gary Cooper interview with author.
331. Gary Cooper interview with author; Gary Cooper papers, personal documents, news clips, and letters—Note from Ruth Thornton, Sept. 26, 2006.
332. Gary Cooper papers, personal documents, news clips, and letters—Note from Ruth Thornton, Sept. 26, 2006.
333. Gary Cooper papers, personal documents, news clips, and letters—Copy of letter to Gen. Merrill A. McPeak, July 24, 1991.
334. Gary Cooper papers, personal documents, news clips, and letters—Copy of letter from Gen. Lloyd "Fig" Newton, Jan. 15, 1993.
335. Gary Cooper interview with author.
336. Beverly Cooper interview.
337. Gary Cooper interview with author.
338. Harold Jackson interview.
339. Gary Cooper papers, personal documents, news clips, and letters—Copy of email from Kevin Jackson, June 16, 2011.
340. Gary Cooper interview with author.
341. Gary Cooper papers, personal documents, news clips, and letters—Copy of letter from Navy Secretary Garrett.
342. Gary Cooper papers, personal documents, news clips, and letters—Copy of the *Mentor*, April 30, 1993.
343. Gary Cooper papers, personal documents, news clips, and letters—Maj. David Fax, "Secretary Cooper—A Legacy To Remember," the *Mentor*, April 30, 1993.
344. Gary Cooper papers, personal documents, news clips, and letters—Maj. David Fax, "The Honorable J. Gary Cooper Steps Aside," the *Mentor*, April 30, 1993.
345. Ibid.
346. Daniel L. Haulman, PhD., email to author, June 15, 2015. Haulman, as chief of the Organizational History Division, Air Force Historical Research Agency, at Maxwell AFB, is author of the definitive chronology of the Tuskegee Airmen, included in *The Tuskegee Airmen, An Illustrated History: 1939–1949* by Joseph Caver, Jerome Ennels, and Daniel Haulman (Montgomery: NewSouth Books, 2011).
347. Gary Cooper papers, personal documents, news clips, and letters—"The Honorable," the *Mentor*.

Notes to Chapter 17

348. Gary Cooper interview with author.
349. Gary Cooper papers, personal documents, news clips, and letters—Cooper correspondence to Gen. Carl E. Mundy Jr. on Nov. 13, 1991 referencing Mundy's letter of July 1, 1991.
350. Ibid.
351. Gary Cooper interview with author.
352. Gary Cooper papers, personal documents, news clips, and letters—Cooper correspondence to Gen. Carl E. Mundy Jr. on Nov. 13, 1991 referencing Mundy's letter

of July 1, 1991.
353. Ibid.
354. Gary Cooper papers, personal documents, news clips, and letters—Gen. Carl E. Mundy Jr.'s correspondence to Cooper on July 10, 1992.
355. Gary Cooper papers, personal documents, news clips, and letters—Gen. Carl E. Mundy Jr.'s prepared remarks in July 10, 1992 correspondence to Cooper.
356. Art Pine, "Apology Given For Marine Chief's Remarks," the *Los Angeles Times*, Nov. 3, 1993.
357. William Yardley, "Gen. Carl E. Mundy Jr., Outspoken Marine Corps Leader, Dies at 78," *New York Times*, April 9, 2014.
358. *Path Breakers*, p. 184.
359. *Path Breakers*, p. 179, p. 189.
360. Mark Thompson, "Commandant of Marine Corps Doesn't Mince Words," the *Seattle Times*, Nov. 28, 1993.
361. Gary Cooper papers, personal documents, news clips, and letters—copy of transcribed remarks by Cooper in an interview July 9, 1993, for a World War II commemoration. The interview became a draft of an uncompleted Cooper memoir in 2006.
362. Gary Cooper interview with author.
363. CGP—Cooper remarks prepared for Alden Lawson service.
364. Gary Cooper interview with author.
365. Nettie Stewart interview.
366. Ibid.
367. Ibid.
368. Gary Cooper interview with author.
369. Nettie Stewart interview.
370. Ibid.
371. Gary Cooper interview with author.
372. Gary Cooper papers, personal documents, news clips, and letters—Copy of report from the USDE to Talladega College President Dr. Joseph B. Johnson, Sept. 15, 1994.
373. Gary Cooper papers, personal documents, news clips, and letters—Copy of lawsuit filed; Julie L. Nicklin, "Talladega College Board Accused of Allowing Misuse of Funds," the *Chronicle of Higher Education*, Vol. XLII, No. 13, Nov. 24, 1995.
374. Gary Cooper papers, personal documents, news clips, and letters—Letter to Cooper from Talladega College President Joseph B. Johnson, Feb. 7, 1993.
375. Gary Cooper papers, personal documents, news clips, and letters—Copy of lawsuit filed.
376. Jenny Cromie, "Who forged loan application remains $1 million question," the *Anniston Star*, October 25, 1994.
377. Gary Cooper interview with author.

Notes to Chapter 18
378. Gary Cooper interview with author.
379. Ibid.
380. Laura B. Randolph, "A Black-and-White Alabama Homecoming," *Ebony* magazine, November 1997, pp. 124–132.
381. Gary Cooper interview with author.
382. Ibid.
383. Gary Cooper papers, personal documents, news clips, and letters—Jeff Hardy, "Mobilian Cooper new envoy to Jamaica," *Mobile Press-Register*, October 22, 1994.
384. Gary Cooper papers, personal documents, news clips, and letters—Letter from Brig. Gen. E.H. Simmons to Cooper, October 18, 1994.

385. Gary Cooper papers, personal documents, news clips, and letters—Nicole Lewis, "A Lady Who Gets Things Done," the *Gleaner*, July 12, 1995.

386. Gary Cooper papers, personal documents, news clips, and letters—Copy of speech given to Jamaican Council of Churches' dinner, Nov. 9, 1995.

387. Gary Cooper papers, personal documents, news clips, and letters—"US Ambassador, church firm on gambling," the *Daily Observer*, Nov. 18, 1995.

388. Gary Cooper papers, personal documents, news clips, and letters—Rev. Ralston B. Nembhard, "A Breach of Protocol," *Jamaica Observer*, Nov. 21, 1995

389. Gary Cooper papers, personal documents, news clips, and letters—Dr. Leachim Semaj, "Hypocrisy and Gambling," *Sunday Herald*, Nov. 19, 1995.

390. Suzette A. Haughton, *Drugged Out: Globilization and Jamaica's Resilience to Drug Trafficking*, (Lanham, Maryland: University Press of America, 2011), pp. 193–194.

391. Gary Cooper papers, personal documents, news clips, and letters—"Interception of Fishing Vessel," *USIA Foreign Media Report*, July 31, 1997.

392. Haugton, *Drugged Out*, p. 186.

393. Gary Cooper papers, personal documents, news clips, and letters—"Interception of Fishing Vessel," *USIA Foreign Media Report*, July 31, 1997.

394. Gary Cooper papers, personal documents, news clips, and letters—U.S. Embassy statement, July 8, 1997.

395. "The 'Silver Dollar' Incident: U.S.-Jamaican Relations at New Low," *Council on Hemispheric Affairs*, Memorandum to the Press 97.15, July 18, 1997.

396. Sonny Callahan interview.

397. Ibid.

398. Ibid.

399. Larry Rohter, "Michael Manley, ex-Premier of Jamaica, is Dead at 72," *New York Times*, March 8, 1997.

400. Gary Cooper interview with author.

401. The *Gleaner*, March 29, 2015.

402. The *Gleaner*, July 12, 2012.

403. Gary Cooper papers, personal documents, news clips, and letters—Jamaica news story clipping of Associated Press report on *Mobile Press-Register* interview with Gary Cooper.

404. Gary Cooper papers, personal documents, news clips, and letters—Jamaican newspaper story clips.

405. Gary Cooper papers, personal documents, news clips, and letters—"I was misquoted—US ambassador," the *Observer*, Aug. 7, 1997; Jeff Hardy, "Jamaica boos," *Mobile Press-Register*.

NOTES TO CHAPTER 19

406. Patrick Cooper interview.

407. Chip Drago, "Native son eyes Magic City Hall," *Mobile Bay Times*, Feb. 28, 2997.

408. Ibid.

409. Joseph D. Bryant, "Cooper decided to do something about city," *Birmingham News*, Sept. 20, 2007.

410. Ibid.

411. Patrick Cooper interview.

412. Eric Velasco, *Birmingham News*, Nov. 14, 2007.

413. Russell Hubbard, *Birmingham News*, Dec. 8, 2009.

414. *Birmingham News*, Jan. 19, 2010.

415. Joli Cooper-Nelson personal documents, resume and biographical material.

416. Ibid.

417. Ibid.
418. "Black Alumni Legacy Family Supports the Campaign," the *Spirit of Notre Dame*, (University of Notre Dame, Department of Development) Fall 2009.
419. Shawn Cooper interview.
420. Ibid.; James Harrell interview.

NOTES TO CHAPTER 20

421. Meredith Heagney, "John W. Rogers Jr. Honors his Trailblazing Parents," University of Chicago Law School, http://www.law.uchicago.edu, October 26, 2012.
422. Gary Cooper interview with author.
423. Ibid.
424. Gary Cooper papers, personal documents, news clips, and letters—Copy of email to Cooper from Neil Armstrong.
425. Ibid.
426. Gary Cooper interview with author.
427. Gary Cooper papers, personal documents, news clips, and letters—Clip of Associated Press pickup of story by *Mobile Press-Register*.
428. Gary Cooper interview with author.
429. Gary Cooper papers, personal documents, news clips, and letters—Montford Point Association newsletter item for Nov. 4, 2006.
430. George Werneth, "Black or White, Marines are One," the *Leatherneck* magazine, Nov. 12, 2007.
431. Robyn Dixon, "The not-so diplomatic ambassador," *Los Angeles Times*, May 23, 2008; "British, U.S. Diplomats Detained in Zimbabwe," The Sydney Morning Herald, June 6, 2008.
432. Gary Cooper papers, personal documents, news clips, and letters—Copy of email to Cooper from U.S. Ambassador to Zimbabwe James D. McGee, July 22, 2008.
433. Gary Cooper papers, personal documents, news clips, and letters—"Major Gen. Cooper: Sharp, on the go, anything but retired," *National Naval Officers Association* magazine, 2005.
434. Ibid.
435. Gary Cooper interview with author.
436. Gary Cooper papers, personal documents, news clips, and letters—Clip of news story by George R. Altman, "Cooper leaves USA group, rips school's race record," *Mobile Press-Register*, July 2007.
437. Ibid.
438. Ibid.
439. Gary Cooper interview with author.
440. "USA, Cooper should resolve differences," *Mobile Press-Register*, July 15, 2007.
441. Gary Cooper papers, personal documents, news clips, and letters—Cooper videotaped interview for Tricentennial project.
442. Gary Cooper papers, personal documents, news clips, and letters—Copy of Birmingham city news release announcing Cooper's selection for 2001, list of past recipients; Gary Cooper papers, personal documents, news clips, and letters—Copy of Cooper remarks at Birmingham event.
443. Gary Cooper papers, personal documents, news clips, and letters—Copy of Copper letter to Birmingham Mayor Bernard Kincade, Dec. 4, 2001.
444. Gary Cooper papers, personal documents, news clips, and letters—Copy of speech titled "Miracle of America."

NOTES TO CHAPTER 21

445. Dominic Cooper interview.
446. Jay Cooper profile for Alabama Lawyers Association, http://www.ala-lawyers.org/algernon-cooper-jr/
447. Ibid.; Gary Cooper interview with author.
448. Steve McConnell, "Meet the Candidate: A. J. Cooper," filed online at gulfcoastnewspapers site, October 3, 2007, Updated Jan. 17, 2012.
449. History and mission of National Black Law Students Association from website, http://www.nblsa.org.
450. Jay Cooper remarks videotaped at national convention of NBLSA, in Detroit, March 26–30, 2008, its 40th anniversary meeting, on https://www.youtube.com website.
451. Peggy Cooper Cafritz profile in the *GW and Foggy Bottom Historical Encyclopedia*, on the web at encyclopedia.gwu.edu.
452. Peggy Cooper Cafritz professional resume.
453. Ibid.
454. Burt Solomon, the *Washington Century: Three Families and the Shaping of the Nation's Capital*, (Harper Perennial, 2005), pp. 114–115, pp. 156–157, p. 258.
455. David Montgomery and DeNeen L. Brown, "Fire at Home of Peggy Cooper Cafritz Scorches Washington's Cultural Landscape," the *Washington Post*, July 31, 2009.
456. Rachel L. Swarns, "In Collection's Ashes, a Heritage's Seeds," *New York Times*, Aug. 8, 2009.
457. Cathleen Medwick, "Art House: Supporting Talented Young Artists of Color." *O, The Oprah Magazine*, August 2009. (On the web at http://www.oprah.com/home/Home-Decorating-Inside-the-Home-of-Art-Patron-Peggy-Cooper-Cafritz.)Stephanie Cash, "An African-American Legacy Lost to Flames," *Art in America*, Oct. 22, 2009.
458. Pam Horowitz in conversation.
459. Peggy Cooper Cafritz profile in the *GW and Foggy Bottom Historical Encyclopedia*, on the web at encyclopedia.gwu.edu; "In Collection's Ashes," *New York Times*, Aug. 8, 2009.
460. Peggy Cooper Cafritz profile in the *GW and Foggy Bottom Historical Encyclopedia*.
461. Candidate statement, Nov. 1, 2000.
462. Jacqueline Trescott, "A Man for All Stages," the *Washington Post*, Dec. 6, 2006.
463. "Art House," *O, The Oprah Magazine*, August 2009.
464. "Fire at Home of Peggy Cooper Cafritz." *Post*, July 31, 2009.
465. Ibid.
466. Ibid.
467. Amy Argetsinger and Roxanne Roberts, "Peggy Cooper Cafritz suffers second fire," the *Washington Post*, Reliable Source website, Nov. 23, 2009.
468. Patrick Cooper interview.
469. "Peggy Cooper Cafritz suffers second fire," *Post*, Nov. 23, 2009.
470. "Art House," *O, The Oprah Magazine*, August 2009.
471. Penelope Green, "Everything In a Big Way," *New York Times*, Jan. 15, 2015.
472. Ibid.
473. Mario Cooper interview.
474. Jacob Levenson, *The Secret Epidemic: The Story of AIDS and Black America*," (New York, Pantheon Books, 2004) p. 127.
475. Mario Cooper interview.
476. Ibid.
477. Levenson, *The Secret Epidemic*, p. 127.
478. Michelle Willens, "The Other Mario," *New York* magazine, Dec. 9, 1991.
479. Levenson, *The Secret Epidemic*, p. 126

480. Mario Cooper interview.
481. Levenson, *The Secret Epidemic*, pp. 133–134,
482. Mario Cooper, "Get Your Black Up!" *Body* magazine online, thebody.com, February 2006.
483. Levenson, *The Secret Epidemic*, pp. 135–136.
484. Ibid., p. 141.
485. Sean Strub, "Don't Speak," *POZ* magazine, February/March 1996, online https://www.poz.com/magazine/poz-februarymarch-1996.
486. Levenson, *The Secret Epidemic*, pp. 144–145.
487. "Get Your Black Up!" the *Body*, February 2006.
488. Levenson, *The Secret Epidemic*, pp. 214–216, pp. 218–220, p233.
489. David. W. Dunlap, "From AIDS Conference, Talk of Life, Not Death," *New York Times*, July 15, 1996.
490. Levenson, *The Secret Epidemic*, pp. 236–237.
491. "Get Your Black Up!" the *Body*, February 2006.
492. Mario Cooper interview.
493. Sean Strub, executive director of SERO Project, in a remembrance shared with Mario's friends May 31, 2015.
494. Gary Cooper interview with author.
495. Ibid.
496. "Weddings: Amy Jeffress, Casey Cooper," *New York Times*, May 2, 1999.
497. "Christopher Cooper elected president of Stanford Law Review," Stanford University News Service, April 20, 1992.
498. Zoe Tillman, "Covington's Casey Cooper Chosen for D.C. District Court," the *BLT: The Blog of Legal Times*, Aug. 2, 2013.
499. "Weddings," *New York Times*, May 2, 1999.
500. Kim Eisler, "40 Lawyers under 40," *Washingtonian*, July 1, 2006.
501. "Weddings," *New York Times*, May 2, 1999.
502. "Obituaries," the *Selma Times-Journal*, May 28, 2002.
503. "40 Lawyers under 40," *Washingtonian*, July 1, 2006.
504. "Covington's Casey Cooper," the *BLT*, Aug. 2, 2013.
505. Zoe Tillman, "D.C. Federal District Judge Casey Cooper Takes Oath," *Legal Times*, July 11, 2014.
506. Mike DeBonis, "A. J. Cooper, D.C. Council candidate, Dies at 34," the *Washington Post*, Dec. 3, 2014.
507. Ibid.
508. Ibid; website with information about A. J. Cooper III and his mission at http://www.ajcooperdc.org/#!about-ajciii/ceu8.
509. Website with information about A. J. Cooper III and his mission at http://www.ajcooperdc.org/#!about-ajciii/ceu8.
510. "A. J. Cooper," *Post*, Dec. 3, 2014.

Notes to Chapter 22
511. Gary Cooper interview with author.
512. Ibid.
513. Melton A. McLaurin, *The Marines of Montford Point: America's First Black Marines*, (University of North Carolina Press, Chapel Hill, 2007).
514. "A Conversation with Melton A. McLaurin, The University of North Carolina Press, Jan. 9, 2007, online at http://www.ibiblio.org/uncp/media/mclaurin/conversation_mclaurin.pdf.
515. Ibid.

516. Gary Cooper interview with author; Frank E. Petersen and J. Alfred Phelps, *Into The Tiger's Jaw*, p. .

517. Paul D. Gelpi, "An Important History of a Changed Corps," *Marine Corps Gazette* magazine, June 2012.

518. Jim Michaels, "Montford Point Marines take home Congressional Gold Medal," *USA Today*, June 28, 2012.

519. Matthew Adkins, "Montford Point Marines, families receive Congressional Gold Medals," the *Daily News*, Jacksonville, N.C., posted on March 23, 2013, at http://www.jdnews.com.

520. Ibid.

521. Gary Cooper interview with author; Gary Cooper papers, personal documents, news clips, and letters—Path Breaker ceremony program and materials.

522. Gary Cooper papers, personal documents, news clips, and letters—Path Breaker ceremony program and materials.

Index